Also by Stephen Spignesi

Stephen King, American Master: A Creepy Corpus of Facts About Stephen King & His Work

Dr. Bizarro's Eclectic Collection of Strange and Obscure Facts

Also by Michael Lewis

Random Commuter Observations (RCOs): Living the Dream on the Way to Work

ELTON JOHN
FIFTY YEARS ON

The COMPLETE GUIDE to
the MUSICAL GENIUS of
ELTON JOHN and BERNIE TAUPIN

STEPHEN SPIGNESI and MICHAEL LEWIS

Post Hill
PRESS

A POST HILL PRESS BOOK
ISBN: 978-1-64293-327-7
ISBN (eBook): 978-1-64293-328-4

Elton John: Fifty Years On:
The Complete Guide to the Musical Genius of Elton John and Bernie Taupin

Cover art by Cody Corcoran
Cover photo by Kevin Mazur

Post Hill Press
New York • Nashville
posthillpress.com

Published in the United States of America

I dedicate *Elton John: Fifty Years On* to my dear friends and fellow musicians **Nick Fradiani Sr.** and **Tom D'Agostino**, who know why…

—Stephen

This book is dedicated to all classic rock bands and their fans. New music still gets released, but nothing new can match the tunes from the '60s and '70s. May this music live on for generations to come....

Samantha Lewis and **Sydney Lewis**:
do what you can to pass this music on.

—Michael

"My career is gonna be very short. One and a half years, that's all. I want to quit while I'm at the top and then I'll fade into obscurity."

—Elton John
The Record Mirror, February 20, 1971

TABLE OF CONTENTS

Part II: ESSAYS AND INTERVIEWS

INTRODUCTION

TEACHER, I NEED YOU

ELTON JOHN TAUGHT me how to play the piano.

I have been playing Elton John's songs since I was in my teens. I don't mean playing them on vinyl, cassette, 8-track, MP3, or CD (although there certainly was, and still is, plenty of that), but rather playing them on the piano. I learned, played, and sang as many of Elton's songs as I could handle as a self-taught piano player.

And I did, in fact, get good.

In the seventies, I had a piano/vocal act in the New Haven, Connecticut, area. This was back in the day when clubs had grand pianos instead of DJs.

My stage name was Stephen John. Many people laughed and said, "Oh, you're trying to copycat Elton John with your name, right?" I laughed along with them but then explained that, no, I wasn't trying to be Connecticut's Elton with my name; my middle name is actually John, so all I did was drop my last name as a performer. It was musical kismet.

And even though I described myself as "self-taught," again, the truth is Elton John taught me how to play the piano. Learning his fingering and riffs for songs like "Amoreena," "Tiny Dancer," "Don't Let the Sun Go Down On Me," "Levon," "Sorry Seems To Be The Hardest Word," "Your Song," and hundreds more was a master class in rock piano. And I quickly learned to adapt his fingering and riffing techniques and apply them to everything I played (unless I was learning something very specific, like the Beatles's "Martha My Dear," a song which took me weeks to learn and which does not suffer improvisation gladly).

Elton is a classically-trained and blues-inspired pianist. This makes for some truly magnificent songs and instrumental compositions. And his voice—both iterations (more on that later)—was made for rock and roll.

Considering the magnitude of his song discography—around five hundred songs, give or take—we can still state with certainty that, just as there is such a thing as a "Stephen King novel," there is also such a thing as an "Elton John song." Certain riffs, chord progressions, melodic phrases, and lyrical reveries are instantly recognizable as "Elton-esque," for lack of a better term.

Whether it's a rocker off 2016's *Wonderful Crazy Night* or a ballad from *Elton John* or *Madman Across the Water*, it will sound like an Elton John song. This is an indication of a lifelong devotion to craft and creativity and the development of a personal, identifiable style.

Elton John, after fifty years of making music, is revered—and not just by fans. To wit:

- There are three albums of Elton John covers done by the biggest music stars in the world: *Two Rooms* (1991), *Revamp* (2018), and *Restoration* (2018).

- The background vocals for the song "White Lady White Powder" on the *21 at 33* album are sung by The Eagles.

- The background vocals for the song "Cage the Songbird" on the *Blue Moves* album are sung by Graham Nash and David Crosby. (Stephen Stills must have been busy?)

- "Candle in the Wind 1997," Elton and Bernie's revision of "Candle in the Wind" ("Goodbye England's rose...") as a tribute to Princess Diana after her untimely death, is the biggest-selling single in the UK and the second-biggest selling single in music history (after Bing Crosby's "White Christmas").

- The biggest music stars in the world routinely show up at Elton John concerts to sing duets with the Rocket Man, including Lady Gaga, Miley Cyrus, George Michael, Bruce Hornsby, Lionel Richie, Mary J. Blige, Bryan Adams, Demi Lovato, Shawn Mendes, and many more. (See the sidebar on Elton John and Billy Joel's "Face to Face" concert tours in this volume.)

- Stars line up to collaborate with Elton. He's the piano player on Wham!'s 1986 hit "The Edge of Heaven." He played piano on tracks by The Hollies. He has collaborated with Bob Dylan, Luciano Pavarotti, Jackson Browne, John Lennon, Neil Sedaka, Dionne Warwick, Kate Bush, Fall Out Boy, Engelbert Humperdinck, Red Hot Chili Peppers, Guns N' Roses, Jack White, A Tribe Called Quest, Leon Russell, Sara Bareilles, and Queen, to name a few.

Elton himself has admitted he doesn't usually write lyrics (although he did contribute the "There's a man over there" lyric to "Border Song."). Thus, it's quite fortunate that he met Bernie Taupin, isn't it? Bernie is a chap who most certainly *can* write lyrics. Reportedly, Elton also wrote "What have I got to do to make you love me?," the first line of "Sorry Seems to Be the Hardest Word."

Bernie wrote the lyrics to "Your Song" when he was, as he described himself, "a seventeen-year-old virgin." He gave the lyrics to Elton and it took the piano man fifteen minutes to write the song, which many polls say is the fans' favorite. In a recent documentary, Elton agreed with the interviewer that it was fifteen minutes "well-spent."

This book is a song-by-song look at Elton's body of work, focusing primarily on the thirty studio albums released to date.

Why such detailed study? Because Elton and Bernie's work is *just that important. And just that wonderful.*

— Stephen Spignesi
New Haven, Connecticut
2019

PART I:

THE MUSIC

This section looks at the music of Elton John, album by album, and song by song. Our intention is for these entries to serve as a companion of sorts as you listen to the albums, providing insight, background, trivia, and other stuff about each of the 323 songs on Elton John's thirty canonical studio albums.

What kind of "stuff"?

For instance, did you know that "Rocket Man" was inspired by a Ray Bradbury short story? And is "Tiny Dancer" really about Maxine Feibelman, and if it is, who is Maxine Feibelman? And did you know Neil Young sang backing vocals on Elton's album with Leon Russell, The Union? And that Elton did a duet with Andrea Bocelli?

That kind of stuff.

Elton John has achieved fifty-seven Top 40 hits in his career—out of 128 official singles. That leaves plenty of deep cuts to discuss and perhaps call attention to. Not every song on every album gets airplay, so we hope this song-by-song review will introduce you to Elton songs with which you may not be familiar, and encourage you to have a listen.

(And by the way, if there is just one somewhat lesser-known song that we'd especially call your attention to, it's "American Triangle." It might be Elton and Bernie's most important.)

Steve and Mike

LEGEND
B = Ballad
R = Rocker
I = Instrumental

NOTE: Please remember that the opinions and assessments offered within are those of your authors and in no way do we claim them to be definitive or the last word on Elton and Bernie's music. We tried to be primarily objective, but we're Elton and Bernie fans as well as writers studying their work, so some personal views may pop up here and there.

1

THE ALBUMS AND THE SONGS

1. *Empty Sky* (1969)

Empty Sky was Elton John's first official album. It was released on June 6, 1969, in the UK, but not until January 13, 1975, in the US. Elton was twenty-one when he began recording *Empty Sky.* He was living at the Salvation Army at the time. Several songs that Elton would later play and re-record on the piano were played on harpsichord for this album. There are some interesting tracks on this record, but it mostly serves as a harbinger of what Elton was capable of and the leaps and bounds his talent would make over the years. Well, actually over one year. His next album, *Elton John*, is more highly regarded than *Empty Sky*. In 2015, *Rolling Stone* had this to say about *Empty Sky* (and style points to writer Andy Greene for "twee"): "Elton John seemed to arrive out of nowhere when 'Your Song' exploded on American radio in 1970 and his self-titled LP flew up the charts. Many presumed it was his first album, but the previous summer he had released *Empty Sky* in England. The eight-minute title track is a strong rocker and the beautiful ballad 'Skyline Pigeon' remained a part of John's live repertoire for decades, but the majority of the album is simply too twee and slight. The production is thin and simply can't compare to the work that John crafted in the 1970s with the brilliant Gus Dudgeon. 'Making the *Empty Sky* album still holds the nicest memories for me,' John said years later. 'I suppose it's difficult to explain the enthusiasm we felt as the album began to take shape.' The rest of the world wouldn't share John's enthusiasm until his timeless second record hit shelves the following year."

1. **"Empty Sky"** (8:28, R) This is Elton's first song on his first album and it was immediately obvious that this new songwriting team of John and Taupin was heads above what was common at the time. The bongo beginning, the chord changes, the lyrics, the incredible chorus, the super-long ending and the fade and return.... Who were these guys?

2. **"Val-Hala"** (4:12, B) If we didn't know better, this song, with its weird spelling, could easily be heard as a lost Bob Dylan song. Elton goes out of his way to sound like Dylan with his singing. It also sounds like something The Band would have written and recorded. It's got great chord changes and a very rustic sound that foreshadows Elton and Bernie's musical visits to the American West. (Even though Valhalla is a hall in Norse mythology in Asgard that is ruled over by Odin, nowhere near Wyoming. But that's nitpicking.).

3. **"Western Ford Gateway"** (3:16, B) We've always felt that this song vividly illustrates the influence of the Beatles on Elton's songwriting. The beginning of this song (when the singing starts) is suggestive of "A Day in the Life," isn't it? Go ahead, sing along. You'll see. Many fans (including your humble writers) feel this is one of the best songs on *Empty Sky*.

4. **"Hymn 2000"** (4:29, B) This is a weird song, and not a favorite of your authors. The lyrics are bizarre and pretentious, and the chord changes seem random and pedestrian, particularly the chorus. The lyrics bring to mind songs that must have incredible, deep-seated meaning to the songwriter, but result in complete confusion on the part of the listener. Certain songs by Tori Amos, for example, often have arcane, Byzantine lyrics that we just *know* must mean a lot to Tori, but confuse the hell out of anyone trying to make sense of them. "Cornflake Girl" (which will be referred to again in this book), for example: "She's

putting on her string bean love." Exsqueeze me? "Hymn 2000" is like that. Apparently Elton has never performed this song live. Maybe he doesn't like it much either.

5. **"Lady What's Tomorrow"** (3:10, B) This is a by-the-numbers ballad that isn't all that memorable. Don't get us wrong—it's still heads above lots of similarly-constructed and-themed ballads written then (and now, truth be told), but there's probably a reason Elton has never performed it live, except once on the radio.

6. **"Sails"** (3:45, R) Lucy and the narrator are sailing on a merchant vessel "in search of the living or the spices of China." It's not clear who Lucy is, but the sense is she's the sailor's daughter, based on her gleeful announcement that she had guessed the number of bales in the back room and her covering the sailor's eyes with her fingers—things an adolescent girl would do. Musically, the song rocks with compelling chord changes and a blistering guitar break by Caleb Quaye. It's a lesser-known deep cut that would probably be a successful single if a contemporary band did a remake.

7. **"The Scaffold"** (3:18, B) Bernie Taupin must have been reading about the "Orient" while working on songs because "The Scaffold" makes two Far Eastern-themed songs in a row on *Empty Sky*. The opening line is "In Orient where wise I was to please the way I live." Elton uses his best Dylan-esque voice, and it's a pleasant-enough-sounding, but rather lame, folky song… and the lyrics are super weird.

8. **"Skyline Pigeon"** (3:37, B) This song is so good, it's the only one Elton continued to play from the *Empty Sky* album in concerts throughout his career. It's a gorgeous piano ballad that is as moving today as it was when it was first released. On *Empty Sky*, Elton plays harpsichord on the song, but moved to piano for later releases. Bernie Taupin has described his lyric for this song as "fairly naïve."

Eighteen-year-old Ryan White died of AIDS in 1990 contracted from a blood transfusion he received in his early teens. Ryan was a hemophiliac and was given contaminated blood. He was diagnosed in December 1984 and given six months to live. He lived six years, however, and died on April 8, 1990. Elton John and Ryan White had become friends during Ryan's teen years and Elton John not only served as a pallbearer at his funeral on April 11, 1990, but performed "Skyline Pigeon" in Ryan's memory. Elton formed his AIDS Foundation in part because of his friendship with Ryan White.

9. "Gulliver/Hay Chewed/Reprise" (6:59, I, B) "Hay Chewed" is a jazz instrumental. "Gulliver" is about the death of a dog and, if you're an animal lover (as both your authors are), is a very upsetting song. 'Nuff said.

BEST SONG: "Skyline Pigeon"

2. *Elton John* (1970)

Elton has acknowledged this album as his breakout record, and he's right. It was released on April 10, 1970, and in 2012 it was inducted into the Grammy Hall of Fame as an important historical record. It's a good album, but not of the caliber of what was to come. *Rolling Stone* wrote, "As hesitant as one might be to own up to it in the light of all the superlative-drooling and hive-breaking-out that's been going on since his first American visit, Elton John really is a gas. The sad part is that those assigned to give him a hand in the recording studio during these sessions were apparently something less than positive about his being a gas and consequently gave him all manner of over-production as well as a hand, the result being that his first American album is something less than the gas it might have been. The major problem with *Elton John* is that one has to wade through so damn much fluff to get to Elton John."

1. **"Your Song"** (4:02, B) This was the song that made Elton John "Elton John." It's a beautiful ballad that Bernie Taupin himself has described as a song written by a seventeen-year-old who had obviously never had sex (Bernie was seventeen when he wrote the lyrics). Elton has described it as a "perfect song," and he plays it at every concert. The Hollies wanted to record this song, but Elton beat them to it. Bernie is quoted as saying, "This one is the one I recall like it was yesterday.... I see this song as a bookend and its counterpart would be a song like 'Sacrifice.' 'Your Song' [is] a song about absolute naiveté in love while 'Sacrifice' is the complete opposite, the story of someone who's seen and done it all, as far as love's concerned, and come out the other end scarred but realistic about certain aspects of the real world." Bernie is on record as having written the lyrics sitting at Elton's mom's kitchen table. He was not on a roof, nor, it is assumed, was there moss on the table. No less a musical luminary than John Lennon heard "Your Song" and said, "[Elton John is] the first new thing that's happened since [the Beatles]."

Kevin Winter via Getty Images

2. **"I Need You to Turn To"** (2:35, B) This is a pretty love song which is performed only with strings and a harpsichord. The lyrics are direct and sweet and express the heartfelt love the singer has for his beloved. Notable lines include, "You're my guardian angel who keeps out the cold," and "You're pure and you're gentle with the grace of a dove." It's essentially a somewhat forgotten track, but still a lovely example of Elton and Bernie's ability to write a love song.

3. **"Take Me to the Pilot"** (3:47, R) Even Bernie Taupin has admitted he doesn't know what this song means. Is it about a trans person or cross-dresser ("For he may be she…"), and why is the singer/narrator "bent with high treason"? And who the hell is the pilot

anyway, and where is he? Regardless of its ultimate meaning, or lack thereof, it is a kickass rocker that has long been a staple at Elton's concerts.

4. **"No Shoe Strings on Louise"** (3:31, R) This is Elton doing a Jagger-esque forgettable, pastiche, country-western song, and it's not a pretty sight (sound). Apparently, Louise is a venal hooker ("She milked the male population clean" and she "goes to church to pray for Lucifer") and there are no shoe strings on her. Like we said, forgettable.

5. **"First Episode at Hienton"** (4:48, B) This is a song about a first love, written as a stately, piano-driven ballad that is pleasant enough on the surface, but ultimately a bit saccharine and plodding. Her name was Valerie, and the song chronicles the narrator's initial flirtations with her when she was a schoolgirl (and he made fun of her clothes) and her transformation into a woman, signaled by the line, "Now Valerie's a woman."

6. **"Sixty Years On"** (4:35, B) This melodic song's opening line and other lyrics are a vivid example of what young people (twenty-year-old Bernie Taupin, in this case) think "old" means. It thematically resonates (albeit more gloomily) with the Beatles's "When I'm Sixty-Four." Elton sings, "Who'll walk me down to church when I'm sixty years of age?" Just as Paul sang about likely needing help to eat when he was sixty-four. The funny thing is, when Paul was sixty-four, he was performing in three-hour live concerts (and still is, at seventy-plus). It's unlikely he was asking "Will you still feed me?" y'know? Bernie and Elton thought they'd need help walking to church when they were sixty. Once again, the narrator is a veteran who has "laid down" his gun. It's a lament, perhaps about his wartime past, perhaps about losing his faith. All in all, it's a significant song in the Elton/Bernie oeuvre.

7. **"Border Song"** (3:22, B) This is one of Elton's greatest ballads, and it begins with the elements of traditional piano/vocal ballads, but then veers into a lane that makes incredible use of

a gospel choir and strong assertive strings. It's a pro-tolerance anthem, too, which includes the (written by Elton) in-your-face lyric, "There's a man over there. What's his color? I don't care." This song was covered by Aretha Franklin, which says a lot about its gospel underpinnings.

8. **"The Greatest Discovery"** (4:12, B) A little kid is introduced to his "brand new brother." The kid is told by the singer "They have made for you a friend." Siblings everywhere relate to this song. Musically, it's a classic chord progression Elton has used previously, especially the opening "G-Bm/F#" chords to start off the verses (see "The Canon" sidebar at the end of the song reviews).

9. **"The Cage"** (3:28, R) The "ah-roo" chorus alone in this rocker makes it a fun song. The lyrics are somewhat vague and talk about the cellar being the "room in your lives." There's a vague reference to an abusive father, and the narrator's assertion that he's never lived in a cage. Like we said, a tad vague. But still a toe-tapping rocker. And again, there's that "ah-roo."

10. **"The King Must Die"** (5:23, B) This is a standard Elton John song, in that Elton received the words from Bernie and then he came up with chords and melody. So musically, it's average, if a wee bit forced and overlong. Lyrically, though, it comes closer to narrative poetry in its depiction of the plot to kill a king.

BEST SONG: "Your Song"

3. *Tumbleweed Connection* (1970)

This is an amazing concept album, even though Elton is on record as saying that was not their intention when putting the album together. It was released on October 30, 1970. Elton and Bernie had never set foot in America when they wrote and recorded this album of American West-influenced songs. Bernie, certainly, had done a lot of reading about the American Old West and American history in general in order to come up with lyrics that are undeniably on point regarding the American West experience. It was, and still is, a fascinating historical period for not only Americans. See: *Deadwood*. *AllMusic.com* wrote, "A loose concept album about the American West, *Tumbleweed Connection* emphasized the pretensions that always lay beneath their songcraft. Half of the songs don't follow conventional pop song structures; instead, they flow between verses and vague choruses. These experiments are remarkably successful, primarily because Taupin's lyrics are evocative and John's melodic sense is at its best."

1. **"Ballad of a Well-Known Gun"** (4:59, R) A rock song by two young Brits about being robbed by the Pinkertons in the Old West? Now *that's* unique. The poor bastard, who is the "well-known gun" of the title, gets robbed and the thieves ask him for his name. He spends the rest of his life terrified they're going to come after him, and he laments, "Now they've found me." Good song.

2. **"Come Down in Time"** (3:25, B) This is one of Elton and Bernie's loveliest ballads and there's an ongoing discussion as to whether the narrator actually unites with his beloved or just ends up "counting the stars in the night." The last lines suggest that even though she told him to "come down in time," she hasn't shown up. This was supported by the line in a previous verse when he says, "I'm getting to thinking if she's coming at all." As sad as it might be, this is a beautiful song in C/A minor.

3. **"Country Comfort"** (5:06, R) It seems that Grandma, at eighty-four, needs help running the farm, Deacon Lee is writing a new sermon for Sunday, and down at the well, they got a new

machine. For two young British lads, Elton and Bernie pretty much nail what American country life is like, and, using their narrators' voices, rave about how much they love it. This song is a lot of fun and, with an irresistible sing-along chorus, captures a lifestyle England never experienced. See what reading can do? (The first official release of this song was not on this album. Rod Stewart covered it on his album *Gasoline Alley* four months earlier.)

4. **"Son of Your Father"** (3:48, R) This is a rather ordinary rocker in which Elton uses a standard (and overused in rock) 1-4-5 chord pattern (for the most part) with a few change-ups for the chorus. Lyrically the song tells a story that could be a movie if it was adapted into a screenplay. Two guys get into an argument on a farm. One is blind and one has a hook for a hand. Mayhem and death ensue. Reportedly, Elton has never performed this song live anywhere.

Cadejacksoncampbell

5. **"My Father's Gun"** (6:20, B) This song is an example of a perfect Elton/Bernie collaboration. There have been certain sets of lyrics by Bernie that Elton immediately connected with and was able to write a song that seemed like it was "meant to be," if that makes any sense. (The songs we refer to have usually been his biggest hits, too, e.g., "Tiny Dancer," "Daniel," "Your Song," "Rocket Man," "Levon," "Candle in the Wind," etc.) "My Father's Gun" is one of those songs. It feels like Elton and Bernie sat together and Bernie created lyrics for Elton's melody and vice versa. But that's not how it came into being, of course (See: *Two Rooms*). The song tells the story of a Confederate soldier whose father has died and the son inherits his father's gun. He takes it up and continues to fight for the cause of the South.

6. **"Where to Now St. Peter?"** (4:11, R) This is yet another song on this record from the point of view of a Civil War soldier, only this time, the guy's dead. The lyrics are first person, and the soldier directly addresses St. Peter, the saint who, in Christian mythology, guards the gates of heaven. There are some compelling lines in this song, including "I may not be a Christian, but I've done all one man can" and "I understand I'm on the road where all that was is gone." This is one of Elton and Bernie's more contemplative songs, seeing as it's about what happens after we die. (Also, some fans believe the "blue canoe" phrase refers to a canoe-shaped pill and that the whole song is a hallucinatory experience.) It's in the unusual-for-Elton key of B major.

7. **"Love Song"** (3:41, B) This song, which is a duet sung with the late Lesley Duncan, was solely written by Duncan. It's a pretty love song with some Beatles-esque guitar finger-picking. It's in B flat/G-minor and is pleasant enough for a few listens.

8. **"Amoreena"** (5:00, R) This is a rocking love song sung to and about, of course, Amoreena, who apparently can brighten the daybreak in the cornfield. The song was played during the opening credits of Al Pacino's 1975 hit movie *Dog Day Afternoon*. Musically, this is classic Elton: piano riffs, and the piano as the driving instrument

> Only someone with that wild, uninhibited view of his music would dare ask the audience to sing along—something that is almost never done anymore—or drop to his knees, like Jerry Lee Lewis used to do, in a rousing piano finale on "Burn Down the Mission." It worked wonderfully well.
>
> By the end of the evening, there was no question about John's talent and potential. Tuesday night at The Troubadour was just the beginning. He's going to be one of rock's biggest and most important stars. Beyond his vocals, melodies and arrangements, there is a certain sense of the absurd about John as a performer that is reminiscent of the American rock stars of the mid-1950s.
>
> *From Robert Hilburn's original August 27, 1970, review of Elton John's historical performance at The Troubadour.*

throughout. It's in the key of G, and Elton revels in the opportunity to use the piano for funk.

9. "Talking Old Soldiers" (4:06, B) This is one sad song, that's for sure. The soldier, old Joe, who has "a graveyard as a friend," sits at the bar and drinks every day. The song is presented as a conversation between a bar patron and Joe. The bar patron offers Joe another glass of beer and listens to him talk about his past. But the generous guy isn't really listening to Joe. After Joe has told him about growing old and losing his friends—and we realize he may also be suffering from PTSD—the visitor wraps up the conversation by telling him to ignore what other people say because "you've got your memories."

10. "Burn Down the Mission" (6:22, R) This is one of Elton and Bernie's greatest achievements. Four key changes, an epic story about a hapless soul doomed to die for his attempts to help his loved ones, multiple rhythmic changes, and a great vocal performance by Elton make for an Elton classic. Elton played this song in concert well over six hundred times from 1977 through 2012, but seemed to then retire it from live performances.

BEST SONG: TIE: "My Father's Gun" and "Burn Down the Mission"

4. *Madman Across the Water* (1971)

This is an undeniably great album. Is it Elton's magnum opus? Many fans who consider *Goodbye Yellow Brick Road* the greatest album Elton John ever released would consider that question blasphemous, yet *Madman* is so good, it's a valid question. This record came out on November 5, 1971, and is as fresh-sounding today as the day it was released. *Rolling Stone* wasn't crazy about the album: "*Madman* won't really crush any John fans, for he sings with the same power and brilliance he's shown since he broke. But, it probably won't draw any either. *Madman* is a difficult, sometimes impossibly dense record. America is worthy of a better story than this record and Elton John needs a better story than this to sing."

1. **"Tiny Dancer"** (6:15, B) This is one of the greatest piano rock songs ever written. Yeah, we said it. So, is it about Bernie Taupin's girlfriend and later wife Maxine Feibelman? In a 1973 interview with *Rolling Stone*, Paul Gambaccini says to Bernie, "Elton says 'Tiny Dancer' *is* about Maxine. Is that true?" to which Bernie replies, "That's true, yes." The credits to *Madman Across the Water* end with "With love to Maxine," and Maxine herself has stated that she was, in fact, a "seamstress for the band." But Bernie later told *Rolling Stone* it was about all California girls: "I guess I was trying to capture the spirit of that time, encapsulated by the women we met, especially at the clothes stores and restaurants and bars all up and down the Sunset Strip. They were these free spirits, sexy, all hip-huggers and lacy blouses, very ethereal the way they moved.... They had this thing about embroidering your clothes. They wanted to sew patches on your jeans." So is it about Maxine or not? Yes and no. We take Bernie at his word. It was about the entire California experience, but there are also specific lines that seem to be about Maxine. Plus—and this is probably the most relevant fact—Bernie himself said, "Yes, that's true," when asked if the song was about Maxine. Regardless, it's an awesome, classic song. Even before *Almost Famous*.

2. **"Levon"** (5:22, R) There is often a temptation when discussing the Elton John discography to make bold, sweeping statements

like "If Elton had written only (fill in the blank), his legacy would be cemented in musical history for all time." "Levon" would be one of those songs if someone were nonsensical enough to make that statement. So, what is "Levon" about? Bernie Taupin said of the lyrics, "It was a free-form writing. It was just lines that came out that were interesting." Elton says, "It's about a guy who just gets bored doing the same thing. It's just somebody who gets bored with blowing up balloons and he just wants to get away from it but he can't because it's the family ritual." Also, "Alvin Tostig" is apparently completely fictional, and the fact that his son is named "Jesus" seems to have no religious meaning. Maybe it is just free-form writing? Regardless, "Levon" is a classic. And it has one of the greatest piano beginnings of all time (co-author Stephen says, "It was fun learning it.").

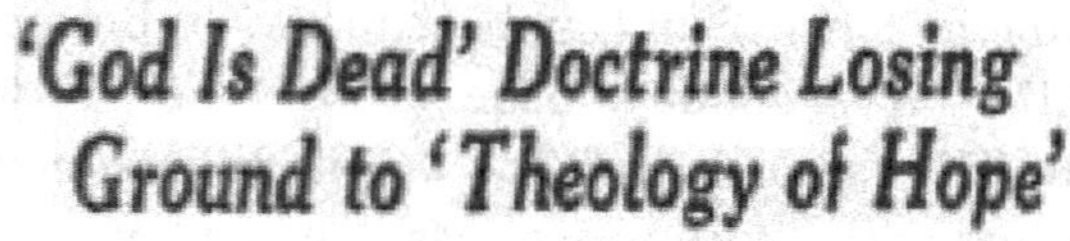
'God Is Dead' Doctrine Losing Ground to 'Theology of Hope'

> The phrase "God Is Dead" (cited in "Levon") actually did appear in *The New York Times*. It was on the front page of the March 24, 1968, issue of the newspaper.

3. "Razor Face" (4:44, R) A young man sings to a man known as "Razor Face," likely a homeless alcoholic returning to the place he once called home. He's ailing ("Needs a man who's young to walk him round"—which some have interpreted as a reference to Razor Face being gay, but we don't see it), and the narrator calls him "his old friend" and offers him a "bottle of booze." This song has been called by some critics one of Elton's most underrated songs, but frankly, we've always rated it quite highly and it is, after all, off *Madman Across the Water*. How can any song from that record be underrated?

Bert Verhoeff / Anefo

4. **"Madman Across the Water"** (5:56, R/B) Who is this "madman across the water" anyway? Is it Elton? Bernie? Richard Nixon? This title track is extraordinary, both musically and lyrically. The story is told in two voices: the visitors to the insane asylum and the guy institutionalized (the madman) they are there to see. (This is according to Bernie Taupin.) "Madman" is an odd song that has immediate appeal. There is an undercurrent of edginess throughout the song that the stabbing strings and Elton's vocal reinforce. And the song seems to want to go on forever. At one 1973 live performance, Elton and company played the song for twenty minutes. Interestingly, a much more bizarre version of

Davey Johnstone, *Rolling Stone*, 2019: "We've been trying to do this song 'Madman Across the Water,' but we can't get the guitar part right for it. Would you be interested in coming down and trying?" I said, "Of course," and came in. When you're that age, [Davey was about twenty-nine at the time], you don't turn down anything, period. I showed up and there was this quiet, shy little guy behind the piano. Gus said to me, "Davey, this is Reg. Reg, this is Davey." They played me the song and he played me the riff he wanted the guitar be prominent on. I went, "Well, what about this?" and played a riff and he went, "That's it!"

"Madman" (with sound effects) was recorded for the *Tumbleweed Connection* album but discarded.

5. **"Indian Sunset"** (6:45, B) *Rolling Stone* magazine has called this "the greatest song that Neil Young never wrote." We find that apt. The song is a narration by a Native American (we defer here to the current term for America's first residents) mourning the death of his Iroquois "warlord." (The song also uses another term—"squaw"—that is very politically incorrect these days. It used to mean Native American woman or wife; now, apparently, it's considered an ethnic slur and some sources claim the word means "vagina.")

6. **"Holiday Inn"** (4:17, R) This is "a day in the life of a touring band" song and it can be summed up as: band gets to town, band stays in a Holiday Inn, band does the gig, and band moves on. It's got a country-rock feel to it with some terrific bass lines by Brian Odgers. Plus, there's a wonderful frisson of energy when the strings come in. Nice song.

7. **"Rotten Peaches"** (4:56, R) This song is about a prisoner lamenting his life and his days now spent picking rotten peaches. The opening chord progression moves up the scale from A to Bm to A/C# and it almost sounds optimistic, so to speak. But then there's a D minor chord that tells us, "Uh, oh…this guy's story is not a pleasant one." And it isn't. We learn he's had his

fill of cocaine and pills and that there ain't no green grass in a US State Prison. The chorus feels like a fun sing-along with a lyric that is the poetically structured "rotten peaches rotting in the sun...." In the chorus he admits, "Mercy, I'm a criminal...." Maybe we can listen to this as a cautionary tale? Perhaps, but musically, it's a lot happier than the words indicate.

8. **"All the Nasties"** (5:08, B) This song is an all-time-classic Elton John ballad and a real highlight of the album. Elton's trademark piano work is extraordinary. Elton introduces this song in concert as a "song about criticism." It's about the maturing of "a full-blooded city boy into a full-blooded city man." It's got a great, repeated "Oh my soul" fadeout, too.

9. **"Goodbye"** (1:48, B) My (Stephen's) lifelong friend Tom (one of those to whom this book is dedicated) reminded me recently of the two of us sitting in my room listening to *Madman* the year it came out (I was eighteen, Tom was seventeen) and being awestruck by this particular track. We had long endeavored to write a minor key piano ballad that only needed the right words and the right chords to move the listener. Elton and Bernie went and beat us to it—and did it in under two minutes. And the final "I'll waste away..." refrain is sad beyond description.

BEST SONG: "Tiny Dancer"

5. *Honky Château* (1972)

This is a highly acclaimed Elton John album, and it appears on many fans' and music critics' "Top 10 Elton Albums" list. Just the appearances of "Rocket Man" and "Mona Lisas and Mad Hatters" makes this record far superior to many works by other artists that may not even boast one major song. The album was recorded in the French mansion Château d'Hérouville and reached Number 1 on the US charts. "Honky Cat" and "Rocket Man" were the singles released from *Honky Château.* The album itself was released on May 19, 1972. *Rolling Stone* wrote, "Elton John's *Honky Château* is a rich, warm, satisfying album that stands head and shoulders above the morass of current releases and has now succeeded in toppling the Stones from the top spot on the charts in only three weeks. Musically more varied, emotionally less contrived, lyrically more lucid than *Tumbleweed Connection*, *Château* rivals Elton John as his best work to date and evidences growth at every possible level."

1. **"Honky Cat"** (5:13, R) This was the second single from the album and is a fun, kind of funky tune lamenting childhood idylls on the farm. The narrator talks about how naïve he was back on the farm, and how, after reading some books and magazines and learning about the ladies in New Orleans, his eyes were open. The song is in the key of G with Elton playing both a Fender Rhodes electric piano and a grand piano. This was—and is—a popular Elton song and it peaked at Number 8 on the US Billboard Hot 100 chart. He's performed it almost six hundred times in concert, as recently as 2013.

2. **"Mellow"** (5:32, B) This is a lovely ballad using one of Elton's favorite chord progressions. It's a love song in which a lover extolls the beauty and wonder of his paramour. Lyrically, this could have been pretty saccharine if Bernie had turned up the cringy descriptions of the scenes in bed, but he's pretty reserved. He does talk about "Wrecking the sheets real fine," and how his lover curls her toes, but overall, it's not something your grandmother would find offensive. It's got a great chorus and is in the key of F. Elton has rarely performed this live, and never after 1972.

3. **"I Think I'm Going to Kill Myself"** (3:35, R) This is a tongue-in-cheek (we hope) depressive's theme song. When the song begins, the narrator hates mankind and the world, and is bored and thinking about buying a .44. He's clearly not the happiest of dudes. We later find out he's obviously a teenager going through typical "I hate my parents" teenage angst. He's got a ten o'clock curfew, he can't use the car ("who do they think they are?"), and he assures the listener that they could save his life if Brigitte Bardot visited him every night. All righty, then. Elton did this one live close to one hundred times between 1972 and 2012.

4. **"Susie (Dramas)"** (3:25, R) This funky, countrified rocker is about the narrator, an "old hayseed harp player," and his love for his "pretty little black-eyed girl" Susie. It's fun, but somewhat forgettable. It's in the key of D and is the type of rocker we've heard Elton do repeatedly. He performed this live about a dozen times in the year the album came out.

5. **"Rocket Man"** (4:45, B) This was the first single released from *Honky Château*, and the song is always in the Top 10 Elton John songs, no matter who compiles the list. Bernie Taupin wrote the lyrics after re-reading Ray Bradbury's classic short story "The Rocket Man" (from *The Illustrated Man* anthology). The song has been weighted with multiple interpretations—depending on who's doing the interpreting—but its longevity is timeless. Elton performs this song at every concert, totaling close to two thousand performances of the song through May 2019. (In fact, as I write this on May 23, 2019, we know that Elton did "Rocket Man" last night—May 22, 2019—in Hanover, Germany.)

6. **"Salvation"** (3:58, R) The word "salvation" means deliverance from harm and/or sin. Lyrically, this song is about precisely that. Musically, it's incredibly accomplished, with elegant guitar licks and fills and a stunning bass line. The theme of the song is expressed in the first verse: "I have to say my friends, this road goes a long, long way, and if we're gonna find the end, we're gonna need a helping hand...." It's an entreaty to everyone for

unity, compassion, and generosity of spirit. Why hasn't this been commandeered for use as an anthem of sorts for people and groups espousing the same principles? Or has it? Elton only performed this song live a couple of times the year the album came out.

7. **"Slave"** (4:22, R) This country rocker is sung by a slave who gets whipped, watches his woman cry, and swears to one day burn down the whorehouse. It's a plea for freedom, with graphic descriptions of the horror that slaves endured in the antebellum American South. The song is in G, with a swinging verse and melody. The chorus shifts to E minor and is a perfect complement to the rest of the song. This is one more example of Elton and Bernie's attempt to capture the reality of Americana, in all its manifestations. There is precisely one account of Elton performing this song in concert, and it took place on September 29, 1972, in the New Haven Arena in author Steve's hometown of New Haven, Connecticut. (**Note from Steve**: I might actually have been at that concert, but I'm not 100 percent certain.)

8. **"Amy"** (4:03, R) The singer is in love with an older, more experienced girl named Amy in this funky rocker named after one of your authors' wife. (Hint: It's Mike.) (Note from Mike: Not really, but if Steve can claim an Elton song was inspired by his cat, "Chloe," we can bestow the same faux honor on Amy Lewis.) It's a fairly standard Elton rocker with an organ solo and some seriously rocking piano voicings from Elton. James Dean gets a shout-out from the not-even nineteen narrator. "Amy" is teenage angst (and lust) at its finest. Elton played this live once, in England, the year the album came out.

Author Mike Lewis and Amy Lewis

9. **"Mona Lisas and Mad Hatters"** (5:00, B) This is one of Elton and Bernie's greatest ballads and one of our personal favorites. It's beautiful, and the perfect marriage of Bernie's poignant lyrics and a sensational Elton melody. This is one of Elton's personal favorite songs as well, and the lyrics reportedly came about after Bernie Taupin heard a gunshot while staying in a New York hotel (see *Reg Strikes Back* for details about the 1988 sequel to this song, "Mona Lisas and Mad Hatters, Part Two.") Elton has played this live almost seven hundred times through 2017 (when he did it at almost every show during his residency at Caesars Palace in Las Vegas, Nevada).

10. **"Hercules"** (5:20, R) This is a basic rocker known more for its novelty value—"Hercules" is Elton John's chosen and legally codified middle name—than its musicality. The lyrics are playful, and since they're from the pre-"Elton is out" era, have Elton's doppelganger, Hercules, talking about "I like women," and "I've always liked it that way," etc. Supposedly, this was going to be the third single released from the *Honky Château* album, but it never happened. Elton had fun performing this live over one hundred times through 2011.

BEST SONG: TIE: "Rocket Man" and "Mona Lisas and Mad Hatters"

6. *Don't Shoot Me I'm Only the Piano Player* (1973)

This was Elton's sixth studio album and it was released on January 26, 1973, and produced two singles. This is a pop album that revels in that hybrid of silver screen fantasy and fifties American rock 'n' roll. *Rolling Stone* liked this album: "Visually, musically, and in every other way, *Don't Shoot Me I'm Only the Piano Player* is an engaging entertainment and a nice step forward in phase two of Elton John's career, the phase that began with *Honky Château*. The essence of Elton's personality, on record and in performance, has always been innocent exuberance, a quality intrinsic in most of the best rock 'n' roll of the Fifties and early Sixties." The title, according to David Buckley in *Elton: The Biography*, came after an evening Elton spent with Groucho Marx. Apparently, Groucho—to put it bluntly—broke Elton's balls all night long until Elton threw up his hands and proclaimed, "Don't shoot me! I'm only the piano player!" Elton said in an interview that he made *Don't Shoot Me I'm Only the Piano Player* on the verge of a nervous breakdown. He was sick and didn't think he could do it, but forced himself to finish it before he went on vacation the following July. Elton has said that he can't listen to *Don't Shoot Me* now, but can and does perform songs from it in concert.

1. **"Daniel"** (3:54, B) This was the second single released from *Don't Shoot Me* and it reached Number 1 on the Billboard Adult Contemporary chart. It's a lovely ballad in the key of C, and it apparently meant more than the final released lyrics led fans to believe. Bernie Taupin said this about "Daniel": "The original lyric of 'Daniel' had another verse, which basically explained what the song was about. But because it was too long, we left it out and, of course, to this day people are still wondering what that song is about. It's basically about a young boy whose older brother is a Vietnam vet who comes home to the farm, and he can't find any peace, so he flies off to Spain where he can hopefully find some. It's written from the boy's point of view as he watches him fly away." Elton has performed this song, a huge fan favorite, close to 1,600 times in concert. It's a timeless classic.

2. **"Teacher I Need You"** (4:10, R) This is a fun and funny song about a young boy's crush on his teacher. She was long and

lean, a "middle-aged dream," and the kid sits in class "trying to look intelligent." He tells us he's got "John Wayne stances" and "Errol Flynn glances," but ultimately, "it doesn't mean a doggone thing." Musically, it begins with the great rolling piano arpeggio that Elton is so good at, and the song has one of Elton's better choruses, specifically the "Oh teacher, I need you" sequence. Elton performed this song a few times in 1973 when the album was released and then brought it back in concert in 1982 and 1984. This song got a lot of FM airplay even though it was never released as a single.

3. **"Elderberry Wine"** (3:34, R) This is a great rocker about an ex-wife. Apparently, her good qualities included aiming to please him, making him black-eyed peas, picking crops, making elderberry wine, getting him hot, and keeping him drunk all the time. Elton released this as the B-side of "Crocodile Rock" making for one of his more interesting (and rocking) singles releases. It got FM radio play, and Elton performed it in concert a couple of dozen times in 1973 and 1974.

4. **"Blues for My Baby and Me"** (5:42, B) This song is about a couple leaving for the West and the girl's father being angry and dead set against his daughter going. The father hates the young man: He said, "...honey, get wise to his game, he'll get you in trouble I know it, those bums are all the same." Musically, it starts off with an almost spoken-word recitation of the conflict between the couple and the father before moving into a very traditional Elton-esque chorus. Dee Murray's bass throughout this song—but especially in the beginning sequence—is excellent, with some lines matching the vocal. This makes for a very "Beatles" feel to the song. Plus, the strings during the chorus add a lot. Elton does not seem to have ever performed this in concert. This is one of the prettier songs on the album.

5. **"Midnight Creeper"** (3:55, R) This song is about a creep—we all know the type. It's a standard rocker with some disturbing and misogynistic lyrics. Apparently the singer keeps "long-haired

ladies who look so fine" locked in his cellar. Hmm. He doesn't think they mind, though. Right. The song has a great forward momentum and a cool horns arrangement by Gus Dudgeon. Elton does not seem to have ever performed this one live in concert either.

6. **"Have Mercy on the Criminal"** (5:57, B) This song starts with a blistering guitar riff reminiscent of 1970s "Layla" by Eric Clapton and Derek and the Dominos, then immediately slows down to become a sad and ultimately tragic ballad about an escaped criminal. Bernie's lyrics are *vivid*, to say the least: "Have you ever seen the white teeth gleam while you lie on a cold damp ground, you're taking in the face of a rifle butt while the wardens hold you down." This song would have fit on *Madman Across the Water*, and Elton has performed it in concert over two hundred times, as recently as 2017. It has a Paul Buckmaster string arrangement and a sizzling Davey Johnstone guitar solo. This is one of the more notable songs from *Don't Shoot Me*.

7. **"I'm Gonna Be a Teenage Idol"** (3:55, R) This is a funky rocker about a young guy aspiring to be, well, Elton John. "I pray to the teenage God of Rock, if I make it big let me stay on top." Is this song about the mindset Elton and Bernie inhabited while starting out? Probably. It's a great pop song, with a cool chorus, and Elton played it in concert in 1998 and 2012, resurrecting it after twenty-five years.

8. **"Texan Love Song"** (3:33, R) This song is about interlopers and intolerance and bigotry. The narrator hates outsiders, specifically long-haired fairies who like "drug-crazy songs," and them "Negro blues," and their "communistic politics." The pissed-off guy may kill these folks from out of town because they drink his beer and fool around with the local ladies. At the very least, he wants to run them off. Musically, it's a countrified folk song perfectly in synch with a million songs like it that we've all heard. Lyrically, however, it is obviously a satirical tirade against people who Bernie and Elton probably came across from time to time.

He paints a picture of Texan guys who are proud of their necks being "good and red" and leaves it to the listener to pass much-needed judgment on these types of people. To Elton's credit, he actually performed this song live—*in Texas*—on August 7, 1998. We cannot help but wonder how it went over, y'know?

9. **"Crocodile Rock"** (3:58, R) This was the first single from *Don't Shoot Me*, and it reached Number 11 on the Billboard Adult Contemporary chart. As corny, cheesy, clichéd, and just plain dumb as this song is, it is a beloved fan favorite. "I remember when rock was young...." Elton has performed this song consistently in concert from 1972 through 2019. In the lyrics, Bernie invents a dance called the "Crocodile Rock," which he tells us competed with "Rocking Round the Clock." And let's face it: the "la la la la" refrain is tailor-made for sing-alongs.

10. **"High Flying Bird"** (4:12, B) This is a gorgeous ballad that harkens back to "Skyline Pigeon," but might actually be a better song than that early track. In the ages to come, when travelers in the realm of music ask why Elton and Bernie were such great songwriters, they can listen to this song and understand. The lyrics themselves are fairly dark, however, its beautiful chorus notwithstanding. The "High Flying Bird" of the title is a druggy girl who ends up killing herself. "The white walls of your dressing room are stained in scarlet red." Considering that she killed herself in a "dressing room," she may have been an actress or, more likely, a musician. Elton did perform this song in concert a couple of dozen times, but not for over a decade. It's one of those "sway and hold up a lighter" songs, but it is a depressing song. It's in A flat, a key mostly skilled composers and pianists work in.

BEST SONG: "High Flying Bird"

7. *Goodbye Yellow Brick Road* (1973)

> Yellow Brick Road *is like the ultimate Elton John album. It's got all my influences from the word go—it encompasses everything I ever wrote, everything I've ever sounded like.*
>
> —Elton John

This album was released on October 5, 1973—Elton's second album of 1973—and is undoubtedly a great record, but upon repeated re-listenings, we can't help but feel some songs could have been left off without harming the excellence of the record one whit, specifically "Dirty Little Girl," "Your Sister Can't Twist," "The Ballad of Danny Bailey," and one or two others. This is not us saying these songs are bad. Quite the contrary: they are perfectly fine Elton John/Bernie Taupin songs. The term "ordinary" comes to mind. But on a record with just about every other song being an instant and enduring classic, ordinary just doesn't cut it. *Rolling Stone* wrote, "*Goodbye Yellow Brick Road* is a massive double-record exposition of unabashed fantasy, myth, wet dreams, and cornball acts, an overproduced array of musical portraits and hard rock 'n' roll that always threatens to founder, too fat to float, artistically doomed by pretension but redeemed commercially by the presence of a couple of brilliant tracks out of a possible 18.... The format of *Goodbye Yellow Brick Road* is straight ultramodern British music hall revue, numerous and largely unconnected musical tableaux accompanied by plenty of rock synthesized flash, and the inspection of the inner feelings of several different versions of the Elton John persona."

1. **"Funeral for a Friend/Love Lies Bleeding"** (11:09, I, R) This is one of Elton and Bernie's greatest compositions, and at least one of your authors wants "Funeral for a Friend" played at his funeral. (~~Hint:~~ Confession: It's Steve, who saw Elton perform this live at Madison Square Garden back in the day. Elton laid on top of the piano in a pitch-dark MSG for the opening synth

part. Very powerful.) (Hey, this is Mike. I love the song and coincidentally I'm listening to it as I write this. But I don't think I want it playing at my funeral.) According to Elton, this duo was not written as a duo, nor intended to be a single seamless work. In a documentary about *Goodbye Yellow Brick Road*, Elton revealed that the only real reason he kept them together and followed "Funeral for a Friend" with "Love Lies Bleeding" was because they were both in the key of A and he felt they fit together nicely (damn, the man was right as rain). The instrumental section uses an ARP synthesizer, along with Elton's piano and then the full band. It segues perfectly into "Love Lies Bleeding," a "rage against a breakup" rocker that uses the metaphor of "lost love" equals "dying flowers." Everything about this eleven-minute, nine-second epic works, and it's one of Elton and Bernie's most memorable musical achievements.

2. **"Candle in the Wind"** (3:50, B) This may be Elton's most famous song. Whether it's his best or not is sometimes debated. It's not, but its iconic status gives it a status and appeal that is only surpassed by certain other Elton classics, i.e., "Tiny Dancer," "Rocket Man," and "Bennie and the Jets," of course. And the whole Princess Diana/England's Rose thing catapulted it to stratospheric levels of popularity and an enormous global presence. Originally written about Marilyn Monroe, the lyrics speak poignantly of young love from afar. The singer admits "I would have liked to have known you but I was just a kid…" which speaks to the universal adoration of Marilyn, only amplified by her tragic, too-young death. On the TV series *Classic Albums*, Bernie said of the song…

I always loved the phrase. Solzhenitsyn wrote a book called Candle in the Wind. *Clive Davis I remember used it as a term to describe Janis Joplin. For some reason, I kept hearing this term. I thought what a great, great way to describe somebody's life.… To be quite honest, I was not enamored with Marilyn Monroe. What I was enamored with was the idea of fame or youth or somebody being cut short in the prime of their life. Basically the song could have been about James Dean, it could have been about Montgomery*

Clift, it could have been about Jim Morrison. Anyone whose life was cut short at the prime of their career, and how we glamourize death. How we immortalize people, and that's really what that song is about.... Nobody is allowed to die a quiet or an honorable death. We cannot leave it alone. We have to always find something to keep it alive, and all those elements are encompassed in that song.

The song has been widely covered, including versions by Kate Bush, Billy Joel, Ed Sheeran, Wham!, and others. In 2003, Elton recorded an acoustic version of the song using the original vocal from the *Goodbye Yellow Brick Road* 1973 track. After Princess Diana's death on August 31, 1997, Bernie Taupin rewrote the lyrics to memorialize the late Princess ("Goodbye, England's rose...") and Elton performed it at her funeral. Elton performs this song at just about every concert to this day.

3. **"Bennie and the Jets"** (5:23, R) One Gmaj7 chord—the opening chord of this classic—is all Elton has to play in concert to drive the crowd completely nuts. Elton originally did not want to release "Bennie" as a single. He is quoted as saying, "To this day, I can't see 'Bennie and the Jets' being a hit. I fought tooth and nail against it coming out from the *Yellow Brick Road* album.... Never in a million years...did I ever think I was gonna have a black record on the charts, and then that was the first time I topped the R&B charts." He ultimately agreed, however, and it became a huge hit, even on the R&B stations (which scored him an appearance on *Soul Train* in 1975). Gus Dudgeon talked about the song on the *Classic Albums* TV series: "We put on some sound effects which are basically from an Elton concert.... You've got Jimi Hendrix applause from the Isle of Wight, which is running on a loop, which is faded in whenever we wanted to... dubbed in some whistles and handclaps doing the wrong beat because English audiences always do the wrong beat, they're always on the 'on' instead of the 'off,' which drives me crazy, but that's what they do." The song is about a band, and Elton has said it's a parody of the vagaries and excesses of the music industry. His 1984 live performance of "Bennie" at Wembley Stadium

ran just under eleven minutes and included solos incorporating Glen Miller's "In the Mood," blues improvisations, classical riffs, the theme from *Close Encounters of the Third Kind*, and more. It's a classic. Elton opens his concerts with "Bennie" these days and has performed it almost two thousand times.

4. **"Goodbye Yellow Brick Road"** (3:13, B) This song is a classic that some fans, critics, and musicologists have rated as Elton and Bernie's best song ever. There is no denying it is brilliant. Elton's music, with its walking bass and frequent chord changes, is irresistible. Bernie's lyrics speak to both the specific (I feel used and I'm not going to take it any more) and the universal (life is short, stop singing the blues and get on with it). The song is almost fifty years old and still sounds as fresh as the first time we heard it. One of the greatest live performances of this song took place at Madison Square Garden in 2000 when Elton brought Billy Joel onstage as a guest and they did it together. (Also, the best cover ever of this song might just be Sara Bareilles's version in Atlanta in 2013. Elton is known to have said no one needs to cover the song ever again after Sara's version.) Elton does this song at almost every concert.

5. **"This Song Has No Title"** (2:23, B) The title of this song tells us the song has no title. So what's the title? The title is "This Song Has No Title" (paging Mr. Schrödinger…paging…) Seriously, though, we've always felt that the song is actually a contemplation on the timelessness of the artistic experience. In the final verse, the narrator posits being an artist and "turning the wheel." The wheel of life, i.e., the wheel of the universe, turns…and art shows us truth. It's got a pretty melody and a tonal shift for the chorus. This is somewhat underrated, but shouldn't be. Elton only performed this live a handful of times in 1973 and 1974.

6. **"Grey Seal"** (4:00, R) This is a pumped-up, more elaborately produced version of a 1969 single that was much more minimalist in its execution. The early version is appealing; likewise is this version, but it's perhaps an unnecessary remake (we like the

original). The song itself boasts somewhat inscrutable lyrics, and the occasional veering-towards-clichéd chord sequence, but it's fun and one of those tunes you can sing along with after hearing it a single time. Elton has performed this song more than 250 times in concert, but it is never consistently on the playlist. He's done it in 1974, 1998, and then in 2012 through 2017.

7. **"Jamaica Jerk-Off"** (3:39, R) Elton does reggae. The lyrics refer to the debacle Elton and his team experienced when attempting to record *Goodbye Yellow Brick Road* at a Jamaica recording studio. The island was not at all hospitable due to several factors, the political climate being one of them. So, Team Elton went back to the Château d'Hérouville in France to record the album. Its sexual meaning notwithstanding, the common interpretation of the title is that the whole Jamaican experience was nothing but a big jerk-off. Musically, the song is a rather ordinary reggae tune, but it's still fun to hear Elton and the band doing a Marley-esque tune. Elton does not perform this in concert.

8. **"I've Seen That Movie Too"** (5:59, B) This is a terrific ballad with an equally terrific lyric by Bernie Taupin. The song expresses plainly the lament of a lover who knows with certainty his paramour is lying to him. He spells out his betrayal using the metaphor of the movie: "where the players are acting surprised, saying love's just a four letter word...." It's in the truly sad key of F minor, and the accompanying strings contribute to the gloomy, melancholy feel of the song. Fair warning: don't listen to this if you're suspicious of your boyfriend, girlfriend, husband, or wife, or after a breakup. Elton doesn't perform this song in concert.

9. **"Sweet Painted Lady"** (3:54, B) We can easily imagine Frank Sinatra or even Frank Ocean crooning this bluesy torch song about a lady of the night "with no name" and the narrator's evening spent with her. The lyrics are perhaps a bit too on the nose (she is "getting paid for being laid") but it's a mellow, almost nostalgic ballad that was never released as a single, for obvious reasons. Elton has performed it a few times in concert over the years, with the last performance occurring in 1999.

10. **"The Ballad of Danny Bailey (1909–34)"** (4:23, R) This is another Western-themed story song that could have fit on *Tumbleweed Connection.* It's about a bootlegger shot dead at the age of twenty-five. It's an okay, somewhat by-the-book rocker. Kind of forgettable, frankly. Bernie had this to say about the song: "Danny Bailey is John Dillinger or Pretty Boy Floyd or Clyde Barrow. He's my composite gangster, I just love creating characters." It doesn't seem that Elton has performed this in concert.

11. **"Dirty Little Girl"** (5:00, R) This is the most repulsive and misogynistic song on *Goodbye Yellow Brick Road.* Our view—and all we'll say about it—is essentially, "what were they thinking?"

12. **"All the Girls Love Alice"** (5:09, R) This is a rocker about a sixteen-year-old lesbian hooker. It's kind of gross and unpleasant...but it does rock. Elton likes this song and has performed it more than five hundred times in concert.

13. **"Your Sister Can't Twist (But She Can Rock 'n Roll)"** (2:42, R) This is a pedestrian 1-4-5 rocker that Elton did better with "Saturday Night's Alright (for Fighting)." This is the kind of song that a cover band will hammer out at a club or dance and the people will go nuts, and frantically do the twist. A somewhat forgettable track that would not have been missed if was omitted from the final track listing. Elton performed it live once in 1974 but then resurrected it for concerts in 2013 through 2017.

14. **"Saturday Night's Alright (for Fighting)"** (4:57, R) How long did it take you, fellow guitarists, to want to figure out the opening G/D riff to this song? As soon as you heard it? We know many for whom that is the correct answer. "Saturday Night's Alright (for Fighting)" has got one of the greatest opening riffs in rock—it's akin in popularity to the opening of Led Zeppelin's "Whole Lotta Love" (which may or may not be the most famous opening riff of all time. "Revolution" is up there, as is "Smoke on the Water" "Layla," "Smells Like Teen Spirit," "Back in Black," "Satisfaction,"

and "Purple Haze."). Who knew Elton and company could rock this hard? Sure, "Crocodile Rock" rocked, but there is a much harder edge to "Saturday Night" (the singer tells his parents, "Don't give me none of your aggravation, we had it with your discipline…"). This classic—it's been covered by The Who, Kid Rock, and Nickelback—is one of the best and most irresistible tracks on *Goodbye Yellow Brick Road*. Bernie Taupin had this to say about the song: "So much of my imagery at that time came from my childhood. 'Saturday Night's Alright (for Fighting)' totally recalls when I was fourteen or fifteen going to all these places in the North of England like the Meccas, Ballrooms, Boston Gliderdromes, and that's what happened. Too much beer and, bang, somebody would start a fight. It was all over the place. It's steeped in the days of the Mods and Rockers and all the confrontations. It was just a straight forward Saturday night's alright for drinking, fighting and getting screwed up." Bernie also noted on the *Classic Albums* TV series, "A lot of the power of that song comes from the chords…. It has one of the great, strident, blistering guitar chords ever created. And you don't even have to wait for the lyrics to come in."

15. **"Roy Rogers"** (4:07, B) This is a lovely, nostalgic ballad about lost youth that has some really wonderful lyrics, including "Comic book characters never grow old…" and "You just seem older than yesterday, and you're waiting for tomorrow to call." Bernie Taupin said, "'Roy Rogers' is really one of those songs, I think, that's a perfect marriage of lyric and melody, too. And it really, really is indigenous of my childhood. All I watched was Westerns…that was really a total homage. He was up there. He was my hero. He was my savior." The song sounds like an Old West ballad, and the added touch of Davey Johnstone's slide guitar really makes it work as a country song. The tune ends with the narrator watching Roy and Trigger hitting the hilltop "while the wife and kids are in bed." Nice. Elton has performed this a few dozen times in concert over the years, with the last reported performance taking place in 2014.

16. **"Social Disease"** (3:42, R) The singer's an alcoholic, unwashed lowlife living in an apartment he pays for by supplying the landlady with booze and sleeping with her on demand. Musically, the song comes off as something of a novelty, and we can't help but be reminded of the Beatles's "Ob-La-Di Ob-La-Da" or "Maxwell's Silver Hammer"—with a banjo. This is not a song Elton performs in concert.

17. **"Harmony"** (2:46, B) Years before Adele and Lionel Ritchie, Elton himself started a song with a memorable "Hello." "Harmony" is a beautiful song, and the production is great—especially the harmonies and orchestral arrangement. What's it about? Reuniting with an old girlfriend with an eye toward possibly rekindling the romance? Maybe. Probably. Regardless of the interpretations of Bernie's lyrics, it's one of their all-time greats. Elton has performed this song many times in concert over the years.

BEST SONG: TIE: "Bennie and the Jets" and "Goodbye Yellow Brick Road"

8. *Caribou* (1974)

This was Elton's eighth studio album and it was released on June 28, 1974, and produced two singles. *Rolling Stone* wasn't crazy about this album: "Nearly every song on *Caribou* suffers from a blithe lack of focus, an almost arrogant disregard of the need to establish context or purpose. It's as if Elton and his band are so convinced of their own inherent inspiration they no longer feel the need to establish coherent moods. Shifting from sentimental to heavy to mocking, they not only fail to touch all bases but undercut what credence they might possibly have achieved." That view notwithstanding, this album has "The Bitch Is Back," "Don't Let the Sun Go Down on Me," and several lesser known deep cuts (like "Pinky") that are great additions to the Elton John songbook.

1. **"The Bitch Is Back"** (3:44, R) This was the second single from *Caribou* and it peaked at Number 4 on the Billboard Hot 100 chart. The title reportedly refers to Elton himself when he was in diva mode. In *His Song*, Elton biographer Elizabeth Rosenthal reveals the title's genesis: "[Taupin] later revealed that his then-wife Maxine coined the song's recurring phrase in response to one of Elton's notoriously bad moods. 'Oh God, the bitch is back!' she exclaimed. The song, in essence, was born. All Bernie had to do was flesh it out." Like "Saturday Night's Alright (for Fighting)," the opening guitar riff for "The Bitch Is Back" kicks ass. Elton was a good sport about the song and was known to introduce it in concert with "This is a song not referring to anyone in the audience, but mainly to me." He has played the song live more than 1,500 times. Lyrically, the star of the song is an outright rebel and, perhaps, a lapsed Catholic? "Eat meat on Friday, that's all right," he sings. Also, he gets high at night "sniffing pots of glue." However, he later asserts that he's "stone cold sober as a matter of fact." Are the lyrics all pretense? The "bitch" playing up his rep? Whatever. The song rocks and is a fun look at Elton and Bernie not taking "Elton John" too seriously. And it's the first Elton song we hear in *Rocketman*.

2. **"Pinky"** (3:54, B) This is a pretty love song about a girl named Pinky who apparently is as "perfect as the Fourth of July." It's a

classic Elton ballad, with poignant chord changes and a change-up chorus that works nicely to set off the more traditional musical construction of the verses. Great harmonies, too. Elton doesn't do this song in concert.

3. **"Grimsby"** (3:47, R) This song is an ode to an English coastal seaport called Grimsby. Apparently, Bernie and/or Elton had some good times in Grimsby, and talked about moving from "boyhood to man" there. Or so you would think. In *His Song*, Elton biographer Elizabeth Rosenthal reports that Elton teased Bernie to write the song because Randy Newman had written a song about Cleveland (and Baltimore, for that matter. And later, LA!). Musically, the song is a very Elton-esque rocker with some interesting harmonies and a restrained vocal by Elton. It's highly likely the song is an inside joke amongst Elton and Bernie. The lyrics talk about growing up in Grimsby, a coastal town, but Bernie actually grew up on a farm. Elton performed this song in concert around twenty times in 1974.

4. **"Dixie Lily"** (2:54, R) This song is in the vein of "Honky Cat" and has a honky-tonk piano and a soprano sax solo by Lenny Pickett. It's a foot-stomper (it has a mandolin but could easily accommodate a banjo) about a guy sitting in a little rowboat watching the *Dixie Lily* showboat heading from Louisiana to Vicksburg, Mississippi. Not much else to call attention to this song, although Elton liked it enough to perform it several dozen times in concert, including almost forty times in 1995, and again in 2003.

5. **"Solar Prestige a Gammon"** (2:52, R) Musically, this is an okay song, reminiscent of "Maxwell's Silver Hammer" or "Ob-La-Di Ob-La-Da." It's a puzzle why Elton would choose to include an obvious novelty song on the album. For fun? Or as filler? Some fans skip this one when it pops up on a play of the album or on random rotation. It's just dumb. 'Tis one, not surprisingly, that has never been on Elton's concert playlist.

6. **"You're So Static"** (4:52, R) This song is something of a rant against what Elton called "groovy, trendy American ladies." It's

about a guy who gets his watch taken by a hooker in lieu of payment and it's got the Tower of Power horn section. Elton does not seem to have performed this one live. Musically, it's one of Elton's less original songs. We've heard a lot of this before.

7. **"I've Seen the Saucers"** (4:48, B) This is a ballad about a UFO abductee. Bernie is a big science fiction fan. "Rocket Man" was inspired by a Ray Bradbury short story. The narrator tells us he's seen the saucers, and at the end of the song, it seems they come for him and take him away, but he is hopeful that if he doesn't say anything, they'll get him back "by the morning light." Musically, it's a standard Elton ballad with echoes of "Someone Saved My Life Tonight." And we're treated at the beginning of the track to what we are supposed to interpret as the sound of a spacecraft taking off or landing. Elton has not performed this one in concert.

8. **"Stinke**r" (5:20, R) This is a bluesy number about a creepy guy—the "stinker" of the title—with dirt "in his toes" and dirt "up his nose." Chester Thompson of the Tower of Power plays organ, and there's a pounding bass line and gritty guitar. It uses the traditional 1-4 chord progression for the verses, but switches to more melodic chord changes for the chorus. It's okay—if you like when Elton and his band play the blues. He has not performed this in concert to date.

9. **"Don't Let the Sun Go Down on Me"** (5:36, B) This was the first single from *Caribou* and it reached Number 2 on the Billboard Hot 100 chart and Number 3 on the Billboard Adult Contemporary chart. It reached Number 1 on the UK chart. Is this one of Elton's greatest ballads? Yes. It's about a failed relationship that the singer does not want to give up. I'll let a "fragment" of you wander free (what a guy), he tells her, but losing her completely would be like the sun going down on him. That's all well and good, and understandable, but then we get to the darkness of the song: "Don't discard me just because you think I mean you harm." Does this mean she's afraid to

stay with him? Well, that shines a whole different light on this guy's seeming desperation to not lose her, doesn't it? The album version is an incredibly powerful production, complete with a horn section and background vocals sung by Carl Wilson and Bruce Johnston of the Beach Boys, and Toni Tennille of Captain and Tennille. It's easy to understand why this song became an immediate hit, why it has been performed by Elton in concert more than 1,800 times, and why it has been widely covered. One of the most memorable performances of this song (available on YouTube) is Elton's duet with George Michael, first at Live Aid in 1985, and later in 1991. It's a classic.

10. **"Ticking"** (7:33, B) This is definitely one of the darker songs in Elton and Bernie's discography. Why? Because it's a sympathetic song about a mass murderer. Musically, it's Elton at the piano with a synthesizer thrown in for flavoring. This song is forty-five years old and is as timely as when it was first written. In 2003 in England, Elton introduced the song like this: "We're going to do a slightly more serious song now. This song was written for an album in the early '70s called *Caribou*. It's a song that deals with violence in America in about the year 1973. When Bernie wrote the song, we thought things would get better—not worse. Well, here we are thirty years on, down the line, and things have gotten worse. And so, the song is more relevant than when it was written and it's called 'Ticking.'" The lyrics read like a news article from right now. There was a bit of controversy about this song for being, as mentioned, seemingly sympathetic to the mass killer. This line rankled people: "Promising to hurt no one, providing they were still, a young man tried to make a break, with tear-filled eyes you killed." The song may have been inspired by the 1966 Charles Whitman "Texas Tower" mass shooting in Austin, Texas, although school shootings were always in the news and Bernie may have just been writing about them in general. Elton did this song live more than 150 times, with his last live performance of the song occurring in 2009.

BEST SONG: "Solar Prestige a Gammon" (Just kidding.) "Don't Let the Sun Go Down on Me"

9. *Captain Fantastic and the Brown Dirt Cowboy* (1975)

This was Elton's ninth studio album and it was released on May 19, 1975, debuted at Number 1, and produced one single. *Rolling Stone* loved this concept album: "This is one of Elton John's best albums. He hasn't tried to top past successes, only to continue the good work he's been doing. And he's succeeded, even taking a few chances in the process. The record is devoid of the gimmicky rock numbers from the *Don't Shoot Me, I'm Only the Piano Player* phase. It isn't weighted down with the overarranging and overproduction that marred so much of *Goodbye Yellow Brick Road*. It sounds freer and more relaxed than *Caribou*. His voice sounds rough, hoarse, almost weary. But that only helps make him sound more personal and intimate than in the past." In a 2006 interview with Cameron Crowe, Elton said, "I've always thought that *Captain Fantastic* was probably my finest album because it wasn't commercial in any way.... [It] was written from start to finish in running order, as a kind of story about coming to terms with failure—or trying desperately not to be one."

1. **"Captain Fantastic and the Brown Dirt Cowboy"** (5:46, R) This great opening track starts off quietly, shuffling along with an acoustic guitar and simple instrumentation—including Elton on the Fender Rhodes electric piano—then builds to a full-blown rocker. It's an autobiographical song chronicling the early days of Elton and Bernie's partnership. Elton is Captain Fantastic, who, as we know, was "hardly a hero" as Reg, before taking on the Elton John mantle. Bernie is the Brown Dirt Cowboy, wondering if he should make his way out of his home in the woods. Enduring "cheap easy meals," their collaboration soon flourished; "hand in hand went music and the rhyme." Like any great superhero duo, they're coming to save your neighborhood, one song at a time. Elton has performed this song dozens of times in concert, and it is the first chapter chronicling the odyssey of Elton and Bernie.

2. **"Tower of Babel"** (4:28, B) This rock ballad is a look at the decadence that was part and parcel of Elton and Bernie's experience in the years when Elton was as big as big can get in the music business. The picture the song paints is bleak, its

pop sound notwithstanding: Drugs, booze, hookers, dealers, adulation, and ultimately ennui and spiritual degradation. *Rolling Stone* did not like the lyrics to this song. They wrote, "Taupin has been dabbling in this sort of allegorical, pseudo-religious crap for a while—but it is definitely out of control here." That speaks to a possible misreading of the lyrics' intent, i.e., simply describing a scene of debauchery doesn't mean the writer is either praising or condemning what was going on. It could simply be observational—journalistic, if you will. Regardless, though, the song works as a snapshot of that era in their lives and careers and, frankly, the lyrics do not teach us anything we didn't already know. As Elton told Cameron Crowe, "We lived that story." It seems Elton has rarely performed this in concert, with only one performance—at Wembley Stadium in 1975—on the record.

3. **"Bitter Fingers"** (4:35, R) This is a great song, one that is arguably as good as any Beatles song (not that such a comparison is necessary—we're just speaking to the excellence across the board of this song: lyrics, instrumentation, songwriting, performance, etc.). The song is about Elton and Bernie's early days trying to make it in the music business and having to write songs for other singers. The song begins with some singer telling Elton and Bernie, "I'm going on the circuit, I'm doing all the clubs, and I really need a song, boys, to stir those workers up." The chorus speaks to our heroes' frustration: "It's hard to write a song with bitter fingers…." Musically, as mentioned, this, in our opinion, is as good as a Beatles song. The song gets a little dark as the joylessness rears its ugly head: "I like the warm blue flame, the hazy heat it brings, it loosens up the muscles and forces you to sing…." They're so frustrated by having to turn out hits on demand that smoking dope seems a reasonable panacea. This would have made a great second single from the album. Elton did this song a dozen or so times in concert in 1975, and then not again until thirty years later, in 2005, when he performed it in Atlanta.

4. **"Tell Me When the Whistle Blows"** (4:20, R) The essence of this bluesy rocker is the line, "Has this country kid still got his soul?" because that line speaks to Bernie Taupin's life story: growing up on a farm and then becoming a world-famous lyricist for one of the most successful rock performers of all time. Musically, it's got an eclectic arrangement, with Elton's classic band sound (and Fender Rhodes electric piano) dominating, plus a funky horn section and guitar riffs that have a Steely Dan feel to them. This is another great track from a great Elton album. Elton performed this song in concert a dozen or so times in 1975 and 1976, and then brought it back a dozen or so times in 2004 and 2005. It seems the last time he did it live was at Madison Square Garden in New York in 2005.

5. **"Someone Saved My Life Tonight"** (6:45, B) This song is about Elton's suicide attempt and, as incongruous as it sounds to say, it is one of the most beautiful songs he and Bernie have ever written. Elton wrote the song while on a cruise; Bernie wrote the lyrics to describe a time in their lives as accurately as possible and to attempt to communicate the depth of Elton's confusion about his identity. Elton was planning on marrying Linda Woodrow, but Long John Baldry (the "Sugar Bear" of the lyrics) talked him out of it. In a 2010 interview with the *Philadelphia Daily News*, Woodrow (now Hannon) said that after Elton broke up with her she "was devastated." The song is long (it's Elton's longest single), and in the key of A flat, not an easy key to write in. It is one of Elton's more musically accomplished songs. The song reached Number 4 on the US Billboard Hot 100. As for the lyrics, many fans wondered what Elton was singing about when he told his soon-to-be ex-fiancée he didn't want to "pay your H.P. demands forever." Some have guessed "H.P." stood for "High Pressure" or even "Hot Pants." The letters actually stand for "Hire Purchase" packets, which is like an American installment payment plan, but which is deducted automatically from your wages every week.

6. **"(Gotta Get a) Meal Ticket"** (4:01, R) This song rocks. Its message is blatant: it's about Elton and Bernie trying to make it in the music business when the company takes half of what you earn: "Don't leave us stranded in the jungle with fifty percent, that's hard to handle." And "When the line's been signed, you're someone else." Musically, it's as heavy as "Saturday Night's Alright (for Fighting)" and Elton's songwriting is better here. Elton performed this live in concert intermittently from 1975 through 2005.

7. **"Better Off Dead"** (2:37, R) This is a sophisticated, complex song that would fit nicely in a Broadway musical. Elton's songwriting here is some of his best. Lyrically, we learn that people are getting arrested at the end of a night full of drunks and whores. The message of the song is probably best expressed in the last line, "You're better off dead if you haven't yet died." In a 1990 radio interview on the *Classic Album Series* show, Elton

Linda Woodrow Hannon talked to the media prior to the release of *Rocketman*. Linda was the woman Elton had been planning on marrying in the early seventies. He ultimately broke up with her and the song "Someone Saved My Life Tonight" is about that whole sequence of events. Here's a look at some of what she said:

"We decided to get married. We went and we found a flat in Mill Hill. We bought furniture for it.... I went off to the antiques store and bought myself an engagement ring, because neither him or Bernie had any money, so I was kind of having to support them.... His mother had ordered the wedding cake and it's true what the song says. He did come back at four o'clock in the morning and tell me that it was over.... I hope he hasn't forgotten about me, but I'm disappointed I'm not in the movie."

and Bernie said the song was about hitting the pubs after recording the *Empty Sky* album and watching through the windows as the "drunks and whores" got arrested. This is undoubtedly one of the duo's most musically and lyrically interesting songs. Elton clearly likes, and is proud of, this song. He has performed it around four hundred times in concert, the most recently being in May 2018 at Caesars Palace in Las Vegas.

8. **"Writing"** (3:40, R) Writing about the writing process can be a dicey proposition: unless you're a writer, most people don't care about how their beloved books, songs, movies, and TV shows come into being. A writer friend of ours was talking to a world-renowned fantasy writer (you'd know his name) about doing an authorized biography of him, and the writer said something along the lines of, "Why on earth would anyone care about a writer's life? It consists of nothing but sitting at a keyboard, for the most part. Writers are pretty boring people." That's probably mostly true, but there are occasions where a writer discussing how they write can be fascinating. Stephen King's seminal book *On Writing* is one example. This song is another. This is a jaunty, acoustic rocker about Bernie and Elton writing their songs. "Will the things we wrote today sound as good tomorrow?" the lyrics ask. In a 1989 interview with *Music Connection*, Bernie said, "There's a song on the *Captain Fantastic and the Brown Dirt Cowboy* album called 'Writing' which I think does a very good job summing up that [early] period of time. It's about honing your craft, about discovering each other's working patterns."

9. **"We All Fall in Love Sometimes"** (4:15, B) This is a beautiful ballad in the vein of "Talking Old Soldiers," "Goodbye," "Sorry Seems to Be the Hardest Word," and others. It's about Elton and Bernie's relationship as a songwriting team, but also as a "couple," in the sense of being each other's creative and spiritual soul mates. In a 2013 interview with *Rolling Stone,* Elton talked about this song, and his relationship with Bernie: "I cry when I sing this song, because I was in love with Bernie, not in a sexual way, but because he was the person I was looking for my entire

life, my little soul mate. We'd come so far, and we were still very naïve. I was gay by that time and he was married, but he was a person that, more than anything, I loved, and the relationship we had was so odd, because it was not tied at the hip. Thank God it wasn't tied at the hip, because we wouldn't have lasted. That relationship is the most important relationship of my entire life." This is another classic from *Captain Fantastic* with an absolutely epic ending. Elton has played this a few dozen times in concert over the years, and it's been covered by Chris Martin of Coldplay, Jeff Buckley, and others.

10. **"Curtains"** (6:15, B) This stately ballad closes *Captain Fantastic* and foreshadows 1982's "Empty Garden (Hey Hey Johnny)." It's a song of farewell that is restrained and contemplative. Elton has done this song a few dozen times in concert and it has also been covered by Alice in Chains, Jeff Buckley, and others. It's got a hypnotic, repeating ending that reminds us of a "Hey Jude" fadeout. This song is a beautiful way to wrap things up for *Captain Fantastic and the Brown Dirt Cowboy*.

BEST SONG: "Someone Saved My Life Tonight"

Single Release

"Philadelphia Freedom" (5:38, R) This song is named for the Philadelphia Freedoms professional tennis team. Elton and Bernie wrote it as a tribute to Elton's friend tennis pro Billie Jean King. It is an homage to the Philadelphia soul sound and the lyrics have been widely interpreted as patriotic ("From the day that I was born I've waved the flag"). Musically, it's got a catchy chorus and is a fan favorite. Elton has performed it close to 1,800 times in concert.

10. *Rock of the Westies* (1975)

This was Elton's tenth studio album and it was released on October 24, 1975, and produced two singles. *Rolling Stone* was rather tepid in its review of this record: "*Rock of the Westies* is mostly high-energy rock 'n' roll produced by Gus Dudgeon with characteristic gloss. Though the personnel in John's band have changed somewhat, Dudgeon and John have altered only superficially the basic Elton John sound, which is seamlessly mechanistic. Rock merely steps up the pace and accentuates the gaudy textures of electric keyboards and synthesizers at the expense of orchestration." When was the last time you read that a musician's music was "seamlessly mechanistic"? The album ended up at Number 37 on *Billboard's* Year-End chart

1. **"Medley (Yell Help/Wednesday Night/Ugly)"** (co-written with Davey Johnstone) (6:13, R) This is not a great medley; i.e., the songs don't seem to go together and the result is a disjointed six-minute aural jumble with background vocals by Patti LaBelle. The opening song is repetitive, and we found ourselves wondering how many times Elton would repeat "Yell Help" before moving on to something hopefully more interesting. The middle song, "Wednesday Night," is disposable, and the final song, "Ugly," is Bernie at his most misogynistic. ("I'll even pay sometimes for a woman that's ugly." Yikes.) We can't help but wonder how many fans listened to this substandard opening track and then moved on to another album. Granted, assuming the album doesn't work because of one song is shortsighted, but you know how people are.

2. **"Dan Dare (Pilot of the Future)"** (3:30, R) "Dan Dare" was a hero character who made his debut in the British comic book *Eagle* in 1950. This is more or less a song about growing up and giving up childish things, in this case, Bernie's fascination with Dan Dare, the Pilot of the Future. Davey Johnstone uses a talk box on the track and it's a reasonably listenable funk track that fits on an album with more rock songs than ballads.

3. **"Island Girl"** (3:42, R) This was the first single released from *Rock of the Westies*, and it was a huge hit that reached Number 1 on the Billboard Hot 100 chart. The song is about a Jamaican prostitute in New York City who apparently works for the "racket boss." A black dude wants to take her away from a life of sex work: "He want to save you but the cause is lost." She's six-foot-three, and she scratches her john's back "just like a rake." Musically, this song is the very definition of "catchy." And it's got a marimba and Kiki Dee singing backup. Lyrically, though, there's some ambiguity, particularly regarding the last line, which is "He one more gone, he one more John who make the mistake." So, what's the mistake? Some have interpreted that to mean that Island Girl kills her johns after they're finished. However, the more common interpretation is that Island Girl is either a transsexual or a cross-dresser and that the johns make the mistake of having sex with a man. Elton performed this song in concert consistently from 1975 through 1990.

4. **"Grow Some Funk of Your Own"** (co-written with Davey Johnstone) (4:43, R) This was the second single from *Rock of the Westies* and it reached Number 14 on the US Billboard Hot 100 chart. Kiki Dee sings backing vocals. This is a guitar-riff-driven rocker that owes its funk in a large part to Davey Johnstone (although Elton's percussive piano certainly holds its own). There's a reason Davey is given a co-writer credit for this song. The song tells the story of an Americano getting busted for seemingly making a move on a Mexican señorita, something her boyfriend is unhappy about. It's a raging rocker along the lines of "Saturday Night's Alright (for Fighting)" and "The Bitch Is Back." Elton performed this a couple of dozen times in concert in 1976, but interestingly, it did not chart in the UK.

5. **"I Feel Like a Bullet (In the Gun of Robert Ford)"** (5:28, B) This is a beautiful piano ballad (one of Elton's best) that served as the "B-side" on a double-A-side single with "Grow Some Funk of Your Own." It reached Number 14 on the US Billboard Hot 100 chart. Once again, we get a history lesson from Bernie. The singer

feels guilty for breaking up with girls and admits as much in the line, "Breaking up's sometimes like breaking the law." He feels he does it in a less than honorable way—acting just like Robert Ford when he shot Jesse James in the back. Musically, it has echoes of "Someone Saved My Life Tonight." This is a fantastic song that we believe should have been the official A-side of the single. It probably would have scored higher than Number 14. We all know that Elton fans are suckers for his ballads.

6. **"Street Kids"** (6:23, R) How can you not love a song that has the line "I'm a juvenile delinquent in an East End gang"? This tune is about a street gang, and the musical construct of the song suggests the cacophony and unremitting stress of living life under the pressure of knowing that without even a moment's notice you could be in a fight, where you might get "gasoline burning in my eyes." There's a persistent guitar riff running through the song that contributes to the sense of edgy anxiety street kids live with every day. It seems Elton has performed this song in concert a grand total of one time in August 1975 at The Troubadour in West Hollywood.

7. **"Hard Luck Story"** (Written by Ann Orson/Carte Blanche) (5:10, R) This song fades *in* as well as out. It's about a guy who works hard and neglects his wife. She really doesn't seem to mind that he comes home tired, although, at one point, she does tell him that she sees no "future in our lives." The narrator understands how his carping about how hard he works and how tired he is comes across to her: "All you hear are hard luck stories…'cause you're still the wife of a working man." Musically, it's got a throbbing bass beneath Elton's hard-hitting piano. The song also features Ray Cooper on percussion. Kiki Dee had released a version of this song in 1974 prior to its appearance on *Rock of the Westies*, sung from the unhappy wife's perspective. She also sings backup vocals on Elton's track. "Ann Orson/Carte Blanche" is an Elton John/Bernie Taupin pseudonym. Elton never performed this in concert.

8. **"Feed Me"** (4:00, B) This song is about a junkie in a psychiatric institution or a locked ward in a hospital or prison, begging his keepers to "feed my needs and then just let me go." Musically, it's a jazzy ballad in a minor key with electric piano played by James Newton-Howard, which gives it an "airy" feel of sorts. Ray Cooper's wind chimes also contribute to the surreal atmosphere of the track, making us feel what it's like for a drug addict who wants nothing more than to get high. Bernie's lyrics are *vivid*: "I feel like a carcass, white like a marrow bone…I heard the ambulance scream, I saw the red light flashing." This is the only track on *Rock of the Westies* on which Elton does not play an instrument, and he does not seem to have performed this in concert. It's a memorable track with a haunting melody that tells a seriously dark story.

9. **"Billy Bones and the White Bird"** (4:24, R) This is a weird song with which Elton closes *Rock of the Westies*. Is it about, or inspired by, Coleridge's poem *The Rime of the Ancient Mariner*? Maybe. Is it about drug use? Maybe. Musically, it's a rather pedestrian Bo Diddley-esque rocker. The chord changes for the instrumental are interesting, but lyrically, it's a bit of a slog. For example, Elton sings the phrase "check it out" close to fifty times. Check it out! Imagine if they had ended the album with "Island Girl" instead. Just a thought.

BEST SONG: "I Feel Like a Bullet (In the Gun of Robert Ford)"

11. *Blue Moves* (1976)

> *"The trouble with making an album is that I always feel I've got to try and please everybody—an impossible task! I tried not to do that with* Blue Moves, *and as a result, it worked out quite well."*
>
> —Elton John

This was Elton's eleventh studio album and it was released on October 22, 1976. It produced three singles. *Rolling Stone* wrote, "*Blue Moves*...means to be taken seriously. It has been elaborately arranged and recorded, yet none of the arrangements have the subtlety that John's piano used to provide.... *Blue Moves* is no different than most double albums in that it contains nowhere near enough good songs to justify the extended length, but songs are no longer the focus. Instead, *Blue Moves* is preoccupied with sound, with instrumental interludes and tidy segues, to the exclusion of sense. It attempts to satisfy the ears while leaving the emotions completely unaroused. In fact, *Blue Moves* is the musical equivalent of a dumb but gorgeous one-night stand."

1. **"Your Starter for..."** (written by Caleb Quaye) (1:23, I) This is an interesting instrumental written by guitarist Caleb Quaye to start off the album. It's pleasant enough, but there's nothing all that memorable about it. It goes right into "Tonight," which the ellipsis at the end of the title suggests is the complete title of the duo: "Your Starter For Tonight." (No disrespect intended, but why do we get a vision of an index card paper-clipped to a menu listing "Tonight's Appetizers"?)

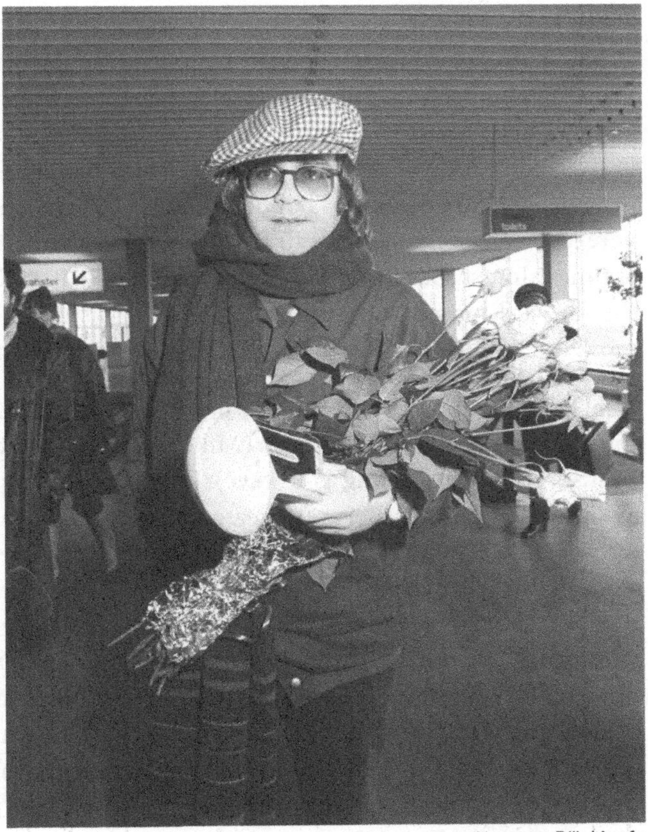

Hans van Dijk / Anefo

2. **"Tonight"** (7:52, B) The opening instrumental section of this song is kind of like "Funeral for a Friend 2.0." It's okay, but second to "Funeral" for sure. The part of the song with lyrics is about a couple having an argument and the guy just wants to go to sleep. It's ultimately a melancholy ballad in which the singer is using an argument with his lover as a metaphor for being sick and tired of life itself. Sort of. Elton has admitted *Blue Moves* is an all-time personal favorite of his, but he had previously announced he was done touring. Perhaps his sense of feeling overloaded translates to this album? Critics have used the word "excessive" to describe *Blue Move*'s overall aura. We disagree with that particular point of view.

3. **"One Horse Town"** (co-written with James Newton Howard) (5:56, R) "One Horse Town" begins with a two-minute instrumental section, co-written with James Newton Howard, before Elton jumps in, talking about seeing a Cadillac for the first time. This song seems to want to be another "Funeral for a Friend/Love Lies Bleeding" but unlike those classics, the melody here just isn't all that memorable. It's kind of weird, actually, and at times almost sounds off-key. The throbbing F# bass line drives the forward momentum, but it's a song you listen to and then move on. It's not something you need to hear again, immediately.

4. **"Chameleon"** (5:27, B) This song is in your friendly author Steve's top ten favorite Elton John songs (Mike likes it, too, but he is not as ensorcelled by the song as is Steve). It's magnificent and counts as one of Elton and Bernie's greatest ballads. Elton originally wrote "Chameleon" for the Beach Boys to record. They passed. (Oops.) It's a stunning ballad using the beautiful descending diatonic chord progression that we talk about elsewhere in this volume (the "Let It Be," "Whiter Shade of Pale," "When I Was a Boy," etc., progression. See the sidebar "The Canon" at the end of the song reviews). This is an all-time great song with superb production values, harmonies, and instrumentation. (Toni Tennille sings backing vocals on the track, and her husband, the late Captain Daryl Dragon, arranged backing vocals on the record for his friend Elton.)

5. **"Boogie Pilgrim"** (co-written with Davey Johnstone and Caleb Quaye) (6:05, R) This is a shuffling, bluesy rocker about income inequality and inequity in the justice system (we're not kidding). This song is somewhat notable for Elton's falsetto, R&B-ish, scat-like vocalizing, but there's not all that much to it. (Fantastic bass line, though. Kudos to Kenny Passarelli.)

6. **"Cage the Songbird"** (co-written with Davey Johnstone) (3:25, B) This is a memorable song because of its subject: the death of legendary French singer Edith Piaf. The lyrics, however, depict her committing suicide when she actually died of liver cancer at the young age of forty-seven (although the argument can be

made that there is validity in the old saying "drinking yourself to death"). She had been an alcoholic for years and her drinking and drug use ultimately took its toll. Her last words were, "Every damn thing you do in this life, you have to pay for." Musically, "Cage the Songbird" is a listenable ballad and is also notable for who's singing background vocals on the track: Graham Nash and David Crosby.

7. **"Crazy Water"** (5:42, R) This was the third and last single from *Blue Moves* and it is a standard rocker that has sections that sound like "Amoreena." It seems to be about "missing whalers" and those in peril on the sea.

8. **"Shoulder Holster"** (5:10, R) Here's another song that would have felt right at home on *Tumbleweed Connection*, except for its somewhat later time period. Dolly Summers, a girl with a Sears charge card and a Mustang, gets cheated on by her boyfriend, a blackjack hustler named Candyfloss. She chases after him with a "piece between her breast" and when she finally finds him, she dumped "her pistol in a ditch" and headed home. She couldn't go through with killing him, but we're left wondering if it was because she still loved him or, as the song concludes, "You can never, never tell if the Law's about." The song's a basic countrified rocker with a raspy vocal by Elton.

9. **"Sorry Seems to Be the Hardest Word"** (3:48, B) This was the first single from *Blue Moves* and it is a beautiful and almost unbearably sad ballad, and is unquestionably a classic Elton/Bernie song. Elton wrote the first line, which immediately triggered the title to Bernie. The "It's sad (so sad) it's a sad, sad situation" line is one of the best lines, both musically and lyrically, in a pop song, ever. Elton has performed "Sorry" over 1,100 times in concert and it never fails to score. He's also done the song as a duet with Billy Joel, as well as an absolutely incredible live performance with k.d. lang. Elton also recorded an awesome duet of the song with Ray Charles, and it was the last recording Ray ever made.

10. **"Out of the Blue"** (6:14, I) This is a kick-ass instrumental. It's got a driving rhythm that makes us think it could go on forever, with players taking turns at shredding. This one works.

11. **"Between Seventeen and Twenty"** (co-written with Caleb Quaye and Davey Johnstone) (5:17, R) This song seems to be about Bernie Taupin's suspicions that his wife Maxine was cheating on him. (She was). It's a slow-paced rocker with a decent melody and structure. A nice touch is describing the narrator's emotions using colors: "I'm blue tonight, I'm red when I'm mad, I'm green when I'm jealous, yellow when I'm sad…" It's also a cautionary tale about how the rock 'n' roll life can destroy relationships. (It can.)

Songs Influenced by Maxine "Tiny Dancer" Feibelman Taupin

Tiny Dancer • I Feel Like a Bullet (In the Gun of Robert Ford) • Between Seventeen and Twenty • Mellow • Lovesick • I Cry at Night

12. **"The Wide-Eyed and Laughing"** (co-written with Davey Johnstone, James Newton Howard, Caleb Quaye) (3:27, B) This is a weird one. It's got kind of a Crosby, Stills & Nash feel to it, but it's not as accessible as their stuff is; this is not "Guinnevere," the Elton John interpretation, but it seems to want to be. Listenable, but not one we put on replay.

13. **"Someone's Final Song"** (4:10, B) This is about the death of a writer, and the lyrics by Bernie Taupin imagine a songwriter writing his last line and then dying. Some commentary on this song posited that the song was about Elton John wanting to commit suicide. Bernie wrote the lyrics, though, and we think it was him trying to paint a picture of a depressed writer who can't go on. Does the narrator commit suicide? It seems so. The line, "I know it's wrong, but I can't stand to go on living…life this way." Its dark theme aside, it truly is a lovely piano ballad.

14. **"Where's the Shoorah?"** (4:09, B) First of all, what's a shoorah? In Hebrew, it means a Biblical verse. Another meaning is "council." So, in the song when the mother of the young man meets his girlfriend and asks "Where's the shoorah?", it could mean she wants to know what verse they'll read when they marry, or when is the council to allow him to marry outside his religion. Musically, it's a very pretty, classic Elton-esque ballad, with a great gospel choir singing background, and a "Someone Saved My Life Tonight" feel to it. It seems Elton has not performed this in concert.

15. **"If There's a God in Heaven (What's He Waiting For?)"** (co-written with Davey Johnstone) (4:25, R) Good question. This is an anti-capitalism/anti-income inequality/anti-war rocker that excoriates the "so many big men…out making millions," and says that if God can't hear the children, "then he must see the war." As in others of his social commentary odes, Elton contrarily goes with an upbeat tempo and a major key feel to the song that belies the depictions in the lyrics.

16. **"Idol"** (4:08, B) This song is a not-very-flattering depiction of a burned-out rock star of the fifties who "went from lamé suits right down to tennis shoes to peanuts from the lion's share." And if this song reminds you of the story of Elvis, it's probably because the song reminds everybody of the story of Elvis. It's very jazzy, and a song that foreshadows Elton's similar jazzy *A Single Man* song, "Shooting Star." Elton's superb singing on "Idol" is notable.

17. **"Theme from a Non-Existent TV Series"** (1:19, I) A brief minor key instrumental for, as Elton tells us, a TV show that doesn't exist. We can see it working as such, we suppose, although the tune could easily veer into "filler" territory if we think enough about it, y'know?

18. **"Bite Your Lip (Get Up and Dance!)"** (6:43, R) This was the second single from *Blue Moves* and it is a good, old-fashioned rock 'n' roll song to finish off the album. Basically, the song is a

In the UK 2017 *Nation's Favourite Song* documentary, Elton talked about one of the few times (perhaps the only time?) that he wrote the music for a song first and then went to Bernie to write lyrics to fit. It was for "Don't Go Breaking My Heart," the very successful 1976 duet he did with Kiki Dee (and perennial karaoke favorite). For some reason, Elton and Bernie wrote the song under the pseudonyms "Ann Orson" and "Carte Blanche." They used the same aliases for the song "Hard Luck Story."

call to dance in a club: "Strobe light on funky feet, soul children in the disco heat." It does go on forever, though. How much dancing can the soul children do before collapsing anyway?

BEST SONG: TIE: "Sorry Seems to Be the Hardest Word" and "Chameleon"

12. *A Single Man* (1978)

This is the first *non*-Bernie Taupin and Elton John album. It was released on October 16, 1978, and Bernie didn't write the lyrics for a single track. Most lyrics for *A Single Man* were begun by Elton and then finalized by English singer-songwriter Gary Osborne. *Rolling Stone* wrote, "*A Single Man* demonstrates just how thin the line really is between disposable radio pop and elevator music, and suggests that, for all of Elton John's public whining about not being taken seriously, the only thing that's ever mattered to him is that the hits keep coming.... *A Single Man* is nothing more than a collection of trivial hooks performed about as perfunctorily as possible." Ouch.

1. **"Shine on Through"** (3:45, B) A nice, somewhat by-the-numbers ballad about a couple's breakup. The production packs a punch, particularly when the drums, backing vocals, and Paul Buckmaster's orchestral arrangement kick in. Pretty, but a somewhat understated track to launch Elton's first "no Bernie" record.

2. **"Return to Paradise"** (4:15, R) This has a reggae feel to it, but in certain spots, we're reminded of melody lines from, believe it or not, *Titanic: The Musical.*

3. **"I Don't Care"** (4:23, R) The narrator has holes in his shoes, bills piling up, and a car that won't start, but he's happy and he don't care 'cause he has his love. That's pretty much the essence of this G major, two-chord (plus a B minor on the chorus) rocker.

4. **"Big Dipper"** (4:04, R) This is a song about two gay guys with big dippers. i.e., big di…well, you get the point. And the metaphor is so blatant that the song was not allowed on the Russian release of *A Single Man*. Musically, it's a basic, slow, blues-influenced rocker. Other than the lurid meaning, there's not a whole lot memorable about "Big Dipper," other than the guys' big dipp… we think we'll stop now.

5. **"It Ain't Gonna Be Easy"** (8:27, B) This is a slow-moving, bluesy ballad about a guy cautioning his cheating lover that getting back together "ain't gonna be easy." It's a really long song. Too long, some might say.

6. **"Part-Time Love"** (3:16, R) This was a big hit for Elton and one of his better collaborations with Gary Osborne. It's a terrific rocker with Elton and the band in fine form. The song works well. (This was also banned in Russia for the song's meaning, i.e., cheating.)

Terry O'Neill via Getty Images

7. **"Georgia"** (4:50, B) This is a great, underrated song with wonderful lyrics by Gary Osborne. It is also one of Elton's best musical compositions, i.e., it's a *classic* Elton-esque tune. In terms of the lyrics, any writer would be proud of the first verse: "When it's springtime down in Georgia, it's winter time up in Maine,

you can go from snow to sunshine, if you board a southbound train." And the chorus is one of Elton's best. Not to mention that the background vocals come in like a SWAT team with a no-knock warrant: BAM! We're big fans of this one.

8. **"Shooting Star"** (2:44, B) This ballad is a slow, jazzy love song that's pleasant enough. There's a nice horn interlude throughout, and Elton's vocals are very understated. Osborne's lyrics are good.

9. **"Madness"** (5:53, R) "Um, Elton, I've got these lyrics that are about what some might interpret as terrorist bombings, and fire, and death, and a child screaming, and conflict, and a world gone mad." "What's it called?" "Madness." "Bring it on!" This song is *dark*. On first listening, it's as though we're inside the mad mind of a lunatic who blows stuff up and kills people. Other interpretations, however, lean toward it being a didactic call to "stop the madness," essentially. Musically, it's up-tempo, and in a minor key (D minor). But any time spent listening carefully to the lyrics makes one come away…let's say…unsmiling.

10. **"Reverie"** (0:53, I) Elton has talked about his early classical piano lessons and his practicing of Chopin Études and other classical pieces. This under-a-minute instrumental bespeaks his training and composition skills. It's lovely.

11. **"Song for Guy"** (written by John) (6:35, I, R) The sum total of the lyrics to this (mostly) instrumental are "Life isn't everything." All righty then. But seriously, this song has a sad backstory. Guy Burchett was a seventeen-year-old messenger who worked for Elton's company Rocket Records. He was killed in a motor vehicle accident and Elton named the song in his honor. Elton did not write the song after Burchett's death. He wrote it the night before after being inspired (and depressed) and only titled it after learning of the accident.

BEST SONG: "Georgia"

13. *Victim of Love* (1979)

This was Elton's thirteenth studio album and it was released on October 13, 1979, and produced two singles. *Rolling Stone* did not like this Elton John album, which isn't surprising considering there are no Elton John songs on the album, he doesn't play the piano on any track, nor are any of his band members on the record. All Elton provides for *Victim of Love* is vocals. Stephen Holden wrote, "Elton John's entry into the rock-disco sweepstakes comes a year too late to make much of an impact. Moreover, *Victim of Love* doesn't contain any John songs: producer Pete Bellotte, best known for his work with Donna Summer, did most of the writing here, except for a mummified version of 'Johnny B. Goode' that's too slow for dancing. Only two of the new numbers, the title tune and 'Thunder in the Night,' have catchy melodies. Otherwise, the album is empty of ideas. The style here is anonymous, derivative, Los Angeles-cum-Munich pop disco with no climaxes, no interesting instrumental breaks, no novel twists whatsoever. Either John and Bellotte couldn't think of anything better to do than echo the synthesizer hook of Rod Stewart's 'Da Ya Think I'm Sexy?' or they just wanted to get the product out in a hurry. Doesn't matter. *Victim of Love* hasn't a breath of life." It's included in the canonical list of records discussed because it is considered one of his official thirty studio albums.

1. **"Johnny B. Goode"** (written by Chuck Berry) (8:06, R) This was the second single from *Victim of Love* and it's a disco-esque, slowed-down version of the Chuck Berry classic. Not much more to say about it.

2. **"Warm Love in a Cold World"** (written by Pete Bellotte, Stefan Wisnet, Gunther Moll) (4:30, 3:22 on older pressings, R) This is a dance track that Elton does a pretty good job on—with his vocals, at least.

3. **"Born Bad"** (written by Pete Bellotte, Geoff Bastow) (5:16, 6:20 on older pressings, R) This track shoots for a blatant disco sound and feel, and it's got a decent melody and harmonies. This would score big in an eighties club.

4. **"Thunder in the Night"** (written by Pete Bellotte, Michael Hofmann) (4:40, R) This is very disco and the pulsating bass line is one we've heard in countless songs of the era. Elton does a good job, again, with the vocals. Another song of its time.

5. **"Spotlight"** (written by Pete Bellotte, Stefan Wisnet, Gunther Moll) (4:24, R) Another club-ready eighties track with a signature disco bass line and drums. Well-produced but, ultimately, indistinguishable from a lot of songs of the era. This one, though, has the falsetto female background vocals that are always a lot of fun.

6. **"Street Boogie"** (written by Pete Bellotte, Stefan Wisnet, Gunther Moll) (3:56, R) What's a disco album without a song with "boogie" in the title? Other than that, though…

7. **"Victim of Love"** (written by Pete Bellotte, Sylvester Levay, Jerry Rix) (4:52, 5:02 on older pressings, R) This was the first single off the album and it did not make the top twenty anywhere in the world. This is the best song on *Victim of Love*. It's interesting and has some great moments. This one is a pleasure to listen to on an album of songs that sometimes don't always please.

BEST SONG: "Victim of Love"

14. *21 at 33* (1980)

This is an enjoyable album. It was Elton's twenty-first official release and fourteenth studio album. It was released on May 13, 1980, when he was thirty-three years old, thus, *21 at 33*. There is a myriad collection of lyric writers on this record, including Bernie Taupin, Tom Robinson, Gary Osborne, and Judie Tzuke. The music site *AllMusic.com* gave the album three out of five stars and wrote, "*21 at 33* is far from a complete washout.... The scattered nature and lack of cohesion on *21 at 33* would translate onto John's next few albums.... Not until the full-fledged reunion with Taupin and backing quartet on *Too Low for Zero* (1983) would John begin to reestablish himself as a central pop music figure."

1. **"Chasing the Crown"** (5:36, R) This song is apparently sung by Satan. It's a standard Elton-esque rocker, but the lyrics are less benign. The Devil brags throughout the song of building the Great Wall of China, sinking an ocean liner, spreading the Plague, participating in the Boston Tea Party, and more, and proclaiming proudly that he did all this because he was "chasing the crown." What crown? The crown signifying him as the king of the world and lord of all mankind? Probably. Great guitar break in the middle.

2. **"Little Jeannie"** (co-written with Gary Osborne) (5:14, B) This was the first single released from *21 at 33* and it hit Number 1 on the Billboard Adult Contemporary chart and was, up until that ranking, the only Number 1 Elton single not written with Bernie Taupin. It reminds us of "Daniel," doesn't it? The singer loves Little Jeannie, she has improved his life, and he wants her to be his acrobat. Hmm.

3. **"Sartorial Eloquence"** (co-written with Tom Robinson) (4:45, B) This was the second single from *21 at 33*. The piano intro to this song always reminds us of "Easy" by Lionel Ritchie. This is a terrific ballad about a woman who seems cut from the same cloth as Billy Joel's "Big Shot," who wears "Park Avenue clothes" and has "Dom Pérignon in [her] hand." In "Sartorial Eloquence," our heroine has (in what might be lyricist Tom Robinson's greatest image) "a self-sufficient swept-back hairdo" and "a style that's

almost of your own." This song was played on the BBC during the Snooker World Championship (even though its theme is not really relevant to a sporting match.)

4. **"Two Rooms at the End of the World"** (5:40, R) Bernie commented on this song: "The first song we wrote again together was a song called 'Two Rooms at the End of the World,' which was about us coming back together." Bernie and Elton had not written together from 1976 until *21 at 33* in 1980. The song is an up-tempo rocker with nary a hint of Elton's piano, but horns and powerful chords punching through each verse. Oh, and there's an awesome cowbell (you can never have enough cowbell). The lyrics are straightforward and discuss how they split up and got back together.

5. **"White Lady White Powder" (4:34, R)** This is an excellent rocker about cocaine. The Eagles sing background vocals. Not much more to say about it. Elton performed it live ten times in 1980, the year of *21 at 33*'s release, and then it never showed up again in concert.

6. **"Dear God"** (co-written with Gary Osborne) (3:47, B) This was the third and last single released from *21 at 33*. This is a powerful ballad with lyrics that challenge the Creator to "show some sign," "don't desert us," and asks "Are you there" and "Do you care?" Elton's music on this track is one of his better accompaniments, boasting his beloved descending chord progression as well as a heartfelt vocal. After a whole song beseeching the Lord, the song concludes with the ultimate answer to the seeking: "Love is the answer, so light up our way dear God…." This is an unusual Elton song, but it's one of his most moving. Reportedly, Elton only performed this song once in concert, in 1980 in Australia. (What's kind of funny is that in the original *21 at 33* track listing, this song follows an ode to cocaine—"White Lady White Powder," a Bernie Taupin lyric. So thematically, it's kind of like, "I've had enough, now I need help." It works when considered in that context.)

7. **"Never Gonna Fall in Love Again"** (co-written with Tom Robinson) (4:09, B) This is a great ballad with great lyrics, and great harmonies, as well as a great sax solo by Richie Cannata. Elton truly responded to great lyrics by Tom Robinson, and this is one of the best songs on *21 at 33*. One of the best lines: "I got a brand-new problem: pretty and she's five-foot-ten."

8. **"Take Me Back"** (co-written with Tom Robinson) (3:52, R) This is Elton writing and performing a country song. It's a reasonable facsimile of what a country song would sound like if it were written and sung by Elton John, which sounds weird, but you know what we mean. It's probably quite appealing to country fans; somewhat less so for Elton fans (so we've heard).

9. **"Give Me the Love"** (co-written with Judie Tzuke) (5:30, R) This is a Motown-y song with lyrics written by English singer/songwriter Judie Tzuke. It's somewhat "by the numbers" in its composition and performance, but pleasant enough to have on an Elton playlist and smile when it cycles around to it.

BEST SONG: TIE: "Two Rooms at the End of the World" and "Dear God"

15. *The Fox* (1981)

This was Elton John's fifteenth studio album and it was released on May 20, 1981. It produced three singles. Bernie Taupin only wrote lyrics for four songs on this album. *Rolling Stone* gave *The Fox* three out of five stars and wrote, "With *The Fox*, the king of Seventies mass-market pop-rock has finally found a comfortable balance between the churchy turgidity of 'serious' efforts like *Blue Moves* and the irresistible thrust of his finest singles. For a change, there's no glaringly obvious filler, and Elton John's lusty pop gospel singing eschews the earlier extremes of oratorical histrionics and rock & roll brattiness. Tune for tune, these eleven songs make up John's most consistently listenable collection in years." That's some seriously rococo writing, but the reviewer is right.

1. **"Breaking Down Barriers"** (co-written with Gary Osborne) (4:42, R) This is a standard Elton rocker with a truly strange genesis. The original version of this song was improvised by Elton in his living room for the August 1980 *Best of British* show. The difference, though, is that the living room version did not use Gary Osborne's lyrics. At the prompting of the interviewer, Elton wrote music to John Donne's poem "No Man is an Island." This version later became "Breaking Down Barriers." Elton seems to have only performed it once in concert.

2. **"Heart in the Right Place"** (co-written with Gary Osborne) (5:15, R) This is a heavy, blues-oriented,

No Man is an Island
By John Donne

No man is an island entire of itself; every man is a piece of the continent, a part of the main; if a clod be washed away by the sea, Europe is the less, as well as if a promontory were, as well as any manner of thy friends or of thine own were; any man's death diminishes me, because I am involved in mankind. And therefore never send to know for whom the bell tolls; it tolls for thee.

minor-key rocker about a hypocritical celebrity journalist. He assures the celeb that his "heart is in the right place" but that he won't hesitate to "move in for the kill" and "destroy your reputation." The celeb telling the story in this song hates journalists. Steve Lukather of Toto plays a blistering guitar solo and James Newton Howard makes his synthesizer sound like a full string section. Elton does not seem to have performed this live.

3. **"Just Like Belgium"** (4:10, R) This was the second single from *The Fox*, and it did not chart anywhere in the world, even though Elton performed it in concert a few times in 1981 and 1982. The song is about a guy reminiscing from an unnamed place about a vacation in Belgium. The place they're now in reminds him of that trip, and he cites examples of how it's "just like Belgium." It's a peppy number (supposedly originally written for Rod Stewart, who rejected it) with Bernie Taupin lyrics, but ultimately not a memorable number to fans. A sax solo by Jim Horn (who played on Beatles, Rolling Stones, and Beach Boys records) is a highlight.

4. **"Nobody Wins"** (co-written with Jean-Paul Dreau, Gary Osborne) (3:40, R) This was the first single from *The Fox*, and it peaked at Number 23 on the US Billboard Adult Contemporary chart. This has a very eighties sound to it and is about a kid reflecting on the breakup of his parents. The lyrics are sad and both the verses and choruses are, appropriately, in minor keys. Musically, the song consists of synthesizers, Elton's piano, and a drum machine. The synthesizers were programmed and played by Jeff Porcaro and Steve Porcaro of Toto. Elton played this a dozen times or so in concert in 1981 and 1982.

5. **"Fascist Faces"** (5:12, R) This is one of the songs on *The Fox* that has Bernie Taupin lyrics. And it's one of those songs we've called a "Cornflake Girl" song—a reference to the Tori Amos song "Cornflake Girl" that has lyrics that pretty much don't make sense to anyone but Tori. "Fascist Faces" comes off as a paranoid rant

by a guy who's, well, paranoid and believes he's being targeted and watched. And there's an allusion to the political red/blue split in American politics and culture (red shoes and blue pants), but, without Bernie to explain specifically what the song's about, it's a bit too vague to do anything but enjoy the music, which, by the way, reminds us of Everclear.

6. **"Carla/Etude"** (4:46, I) A really beautiful instrumental for piano and strings played with the London Philharmonic Orchestra conducted by James Newton Howard. Elton has performed this piece close to 175 times in concert.

7. **"Fanfare"** (co-written with James Newton Howard) (1:26, I) Another lovely instrumental that follows "Carla/Etude." This is more up-tempo. Elton has never gone right into this song from "Carla/Etude" when he performed that song in concert.

8. **"Chloe"** (co-written with Gary Osborne) (4:40, B) This was the third single from *The Fox*, and it was named for this book's author Steve's cat Chloe. (And because the internet is real, and the genesis story of Elton's song "Chloe" could, after the publication of this book, become that it is about some writer's cat, allow us to state firmly: We're just kidding.) This is a sad love song (not about a cat) that starts in a minor key and then roars into a great chorus with great backing vocals. This is an underappreciated classic from the Rocket Man, and Elton performed it live at least three dozen times in 1982. And it's got a great guitar solo. This song reached Number 16 on the US Billboard Adult Contemporary chart. (And isn't Chloe a pretty girl?)

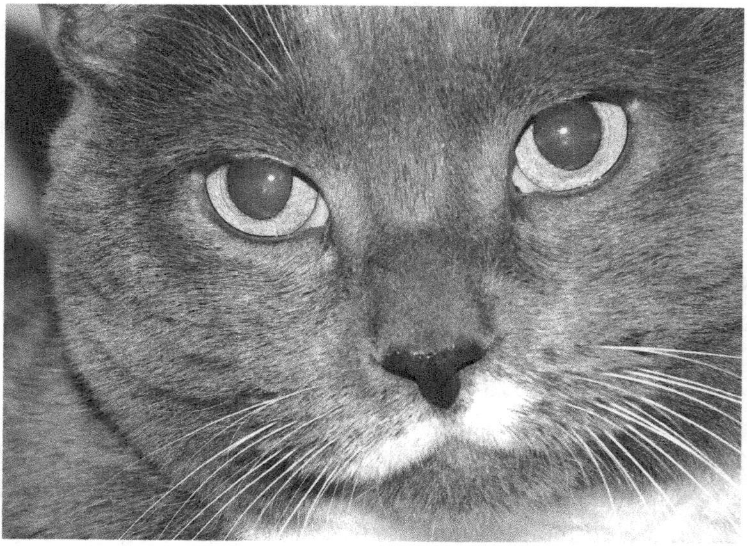

Chloe Spignesi Photo courtesy of Valerie Barnes

9. **"Heels of the Wind"** (3:35, R) This is one of the songs on *The Fox* with Bernie Taupin lyrics. It's a rocker about a broken relationship. It's a typical Elton John track, with the addition of gospel-y background vocals and James Newton Howard synthesizers. It's a bit ordinary to have made much of a mark upon its release, and it remains a deep cut that some fans like a lot. Elton does not seem to have ever performed this song live in concert.

10. **"Elton's Song"** (co-written with Tom Robinson) (3:02, B) This song caused all kinds of controversy when it was released, even though it had been recorded two years prior to *The Fox* and Elton had performed it in concert. Why? Because it's about a young boy's love for another boy. Some radio stations wouldn't play a song about gay love. But what's fascinating about the uproar is that nowhere in the lyrics are we told that the narrator is singing about another boy. The idolized "you" in the song is never assigned a gender, and the lyrics could apply to a girl as well as a boy: "your gypsy hair and dark brown eyes," "your grace and style cut me to the bone," etc. The reason everyone knew

it was about a gay crush is because of the title (i.e., Elton is a male singing about someone, and Elton is gay) plus the Russell Mulcahy-directed video (that was never shown on television). The video is set in a boy's school, and it's obvious from the first minute that it's about a boy who is in love with another boy. And confirmation comes in a scene early on when we see a young boy playing pool, being watched by the star of the video (the song's narrator) and the lyric is, "I watched you playing pool." Today, this song wouldn't garner even a raised eyebrow, but back then there was a hullabaloo. Musically, it's a complex piano ballad consisting of nothing but Elton on the piano and James Newton Howard on synthesizers. Elton played this several dozen times between 1979 and 1982, and brought it back in some 1999 concerts.

11. **"The Fox"** (5:20, B) This is a ballad that has the gravitas and classic Elton feel to it that makes it an appropriate closer to *The Fox*. This song would have fit nicely on *Tumbleweed Connection* or *Honky Château*, and it boasts James Newton Howard on the organ instead of the synthesizer and an all-star collection of background vocalists. Lyrically, it's a love song of sorts that uses the metaphor of the fox and the hunt to describe the vagaries of the couple's interactions: "It's an evergreen affair, as temptation taunts the fox into the hunter's waiting lair." "The Fox" is one of Elton and Bernie's more memorable ballads.

BEST SONG: "The Fox"

16. *Jump Up!* (1982)

This Elton John album, his sixteenth, is most notable for its song "Empty Garden (Hey Hey Johnny)," which is about the assassinated Beatle John Lennon. Bernie reportedly did not like this album and, in 2010, called it "one of our worst albums," which is, frankly, debatable. In our opinion, there's some good stuff on this record. It was released on April 9, 1982. *Rolling Stone* gave *Jump Up!* four out of five stars and wrote, "*Jump Up!* is the album that redeems Elton John from his famine years as a fallen superstar exiled to less verdant pastures. Showing more spunk than anyone might have expected at this late date, he's put himself back on top simply by making a tour de force of a record that says he knows he's worth it. Even if he never again comes close to inciting the mass hysteria of the mid-Seventies, the sheer stylistic breadth of *Jump Up!* should secure Elton John's reputation as a rare master of pop form."

1. **"Dear John"** (co-written with Gary Osborne) (3:28, R) This is the opening track to 1982's *Jump Up!* and is about a guy returning home to find a "Dear John" letter after his girl leaves him. The narrator claims he doesn't care and was about to write *her* a "Dear John" letter. The twist, perhaps, is that his "Dear John" letter to her would likewise be addressed to "John." Musically, it's another Elton rocker with some kick-ass piano playing by Elton.

2. **"Spiteful Child"** (4:11, R) This is another disgruntled boyfriend song. It's a jaunty rocker with interesting chord changes. The narrator is pissed at apparently being "shaken down" (and presumably dumped) and proclaims angrily, "You'd better be ready to run, now I've got you under the gun…" and assures her(?) that he has his money on vengeance and scolds her for "breaking the spirit in [him]."

3. **"Ball and Chain"** (co-written with Gary Osborne) (3:27, R) This is an Elton John song with members of The Who and Toto playing. That alone makes it notable, right? Musically, it's a countrified rocker that's pleasant enough. Pete Townshend of The Who plays acoustic guitar on it and Jeff Porcaro of Toto plays drums. Lyrically, it's about a guy bitching about a bad

relationship and accusing his lover of being a "ball and chain around [his] heart."

4. **"Legal Boys"** (co-written with Tim Rice) (3:08, R) This song, co-written with Tim Rice (with whom Elton wrote "Can You Feel the Love Tonight" and *Aida*), is about lawyers, accountants, and getting a divorce. It sounds like it could be part of a Broadway musical. (For example, the scene in Act I where the husband sings to his ex-wife about the tribulation of dealing with the "legal boys" in order to be granted an official divorce.)

5. **"I Am Your Robot"** (4:42, R) Elton and Bernie do science fiction. This song is fun, and we cannot help but think that it seems to have been somewhat influenced by Fleetwood Mac's "Rhiannon."

6. **"Blue Eyes"** (co-written with Gary Osborne) (3:25, B) This song hit Number 1 on the Billboard Adult Contemporary list when it was released as a single. It's one of Elton's more notable collaborations with Gary Osborne and is musically quite sophisticated, changing keys throughout and boasting some really beautiful melodic lines. While the lyrics are good, this song is more an example of the musical talent Elton possesses, as well as evidence of his early classical training. This song does not offer a standard pop ballad song progression.

7. **"Empty Garden (Hey Hey Johnny)"** (5:05, B) John Lennon's horrible murder created an impossible situation for his musical friends who wanted to pay tribute to him. How can you write a song about your relationship with *John Lennon*? Well, some of them did it and succeeded in communicating not only the unfathomable loss, but also their love for their friend. Paul McCartney did it with "Here Today," George Harrison did it with "All Those Years Ago," and Elton and Bernie did it with "Empty Garden." This song is *heart wrenching*. Bernie uses the metaphor of John as a gardener, and after his death, his garden is empty and will not be tended to again. Bernie says the image of the

garden came from seeing the piles of flowers outside the Dakota after John's death. He doesn't mention John's murderer by name, but does include the line, "It's funny how one insect can damage so much grain." (George Harrison called the killer the "devil's best friend" in "All Those Years Ago.") The song is in E and is a stately ballad with an unforgettable chorus. Jeff Porcaro of Toto provided drums that can be accurately described as "powerful," but that adjective doesn't even come close to describing their effect on the song. The line "Won't you come out to play?" is a nod to John's *White Album* song "Dear Prudence." Elton performed "Empty Garden" at just about every performance of his residency at Caesars Palace in Las Vegas from April 2016 through October 2017. He also performed it at Madison Square Garden throughout his many appearances there. The song hit Number 13 on the Billboard Hot 100 chart in the US.

8. **"Princess"** (co-written with Gary Osborne) (4:55, R) This is a love song to the narrator's "Princess." She makes his life "seem worthwhile" (that "seem" is an odd choice, no?). The song feels a little disjointed, as some of Elton's songs do when he tries to jam lyrics into a pre-conceived chord pattern (particularly for the verses). We don't think there's any argument that Elton's best lyricist is Bernie Taupin. But it's a pleasant enough song, and it's got a catchy chorus.

9. **"Where Have All the Good Times Gone?"** (3:58, R) This song is a lament for the old days that even includes a shout-out to The Four Tops (and it's got a very Motown-y opening with Elton on the electric piano). Bernie waxes nostalgic in the lyrics, missing a time when "our hearts could fly without wings" and those "crazy summers…would never end." Great song.

10. **"All Quiet on the Western Front"** (6:00, B) Elton and Bernie are serious artists and, thus, they are not averse to tackling weightier topics, as in this song that concludes the album, which is an antiwar ballad about World War I. This is a powerful song that captures and personalizes the horror of war. The lyrics

were inspired by the Erich Maria Remarque novel of the same name. Elton asked Bernie to change one line: "thin white men in stinking tents." He said, "It's not an attractive line to sing." Bernie changed it, but the entire line was eventually deleted from the song. The song has a big, majestic ending—with synthesizer strings repeating—like in a marching anthem.

BEST SONG: "Empty Garden (Hey Hey Johnny)"

17. *Too Low for Zero* (1983)

This album was released on May 30, 1983, and heralded the reconstitution of Elton John and Bernie Taupin as a songwriting team. It reached Number 25 on the Billboard 200 chart. *Rolling Stone* gave it three out of five stars and wrote, "Elton John and Bernie Taupin have written some great hit singles, but since the early *Elton John* LP, they have never produced an album of consistently first-rate material. And although *Too Low for Zero* is a big step up from losers like *Blue Moves* and *A Single Man*, it doesn't hang together, either." *AllMusic.com* gave it four-and-a-half stars out of five and wrote, "*Too Low for Zero* [is] a full-fledged reunion with his best collaborator, Bernie Taupin, and his classic touring band. Happily, this is a reunion that works like gangbusters, capturing everybody at a near-peak of their form....It's a terrific record, an exemplary illustration of what a veteran artist could achieve in the early '80s." In a 1984 interview with Paul Gambaccini, Elton said of *Too Low for Zero,* "I was so proud of that album....I felt that was the first album I'd done for a long, long time where it was a great, great album. I was happy with everything. I said to my manager, 'If this one doesn't happen, I will give up, and I'll become a greengrocer.'"

1. **"Cold as Christmas (In the Middle of the Year)"** (4:19, B) This was the fourth single from *Too Low for Zero* and it didn't chart in the US or the UK. It did hit Number 16 in Ireland. It's a typical Elton ballad with Bernie's lyrics telling the story of an estranged couple who go on vacation to the Caribbean in hopes (the guy's hopes, actually) of repairing the relationship and the marriage. Spoiler alert: It doesn't work. In a place where it's ninety-five degrees, he says, "I dreamed of love in a better climate...but there's an icy fringe on everything." He might be talking to one of his kids about the problem at one point ("there's a winter look in your mother's eyes..."), and the song concludes with him wondering why "the frost in the summertime." This is a sad but melodic song about yet another failed relationship in the Elton/Bernie lyrical universe.

2. **"I'm Still Standing"** (3:02, R) This song was the second single from *Too Low for Zero,* and it was a big hit for Elton and got a big boost thanks to the music video on heavy rotation on

MTV, one of Elton's first forays onto the medium. It peaked at Number 1 on the Canada Top Singles and Switzerland singles charts, Number 4 on the UK Singles Chart, and at Number 12 on the Billboard Hot 100 chart. Elton has performed this song more than 1,500 times in concert from the year of its release through today. Elton has said the song is a commentary on him still being relevant. This song rocks, and it's got an unforgettable (and immediately memorized) chorus and some blazing guitar from Davey Johnstone. This song has *longevity*: they did it on *Glee* and *The X Factor*, it was in the movie *Sing*, and it's in the video game *Just Dance 2019*. According to Bernie, the song was not written about Elton's resilience. It was a kiss-off to an old girlfriend: "It's perhaps one more example of the original idea being interpreted by everyone into something quite different," he said in an interview. "I think people see it as an anthem based on Elton's strong sense of survival in the face of adversity. Which, believe me, is perfectly fine by me. In fact, it's probably infinitely more interesting, perhaps, than what it was initially written about." On January 30, 2018, Lady Gaga and several other artists performed in an Elton John tribute concert at Madison Square Garden called *Elton John: I'm Still Standing*.

3. **"Too Low for Zero"** (5:46, R) This was the fifth and final single off the album, and it did not chart in either the UK or US (it did hit Number 52 on the Australian chart). This song is in the voice of the guy who is described by both the title of the album and the song. He's hung over, he's lost money gambling, he's too tired to work, he has insomnia, and he even puts "the cat out two hours early." Nothing works and the chorus is the I'm "too low for zero" refrain. Musically, it's got a rhythmic bongo (via drum machine) underpinning the melody and an interesting piano solo by Elton. It's a bit less than Elton and Bernie's best, and yet the boys liked it enough to name the album after the song and, perhaps, also make a statement about the message of the song? Elton has played this song around three dozen times in concert.

4. **"Religion"** (4:05, R) In an interview in *Music Monthly* magazine on November 11, 2006, Elton John said the following about

organized religion: "Religion promotes the hatred and spite against gays. From my point of view, I would ban religion completely. Organized religion doesn't seem to work. It turns people into really hateful lemmings and it's not really compassionate." Twenty-three years before this interview, Elton recorded this song about different people finding God and coming to religion (granted, Bernie wrote the words, but it can be argued that Elton tacitly endorsed the theme of the song by recording it). The song is about a gambler, an alcoholic, and a hooker all finding religion. The chorus basically says that we all make the same mistakes and suggests that if we don't embrace religion, then we'll end up with "the man" (and not Jesus). The song is a typical guitar-driven Elton rocker with slide guitar riffs throughout. Elton's piano is barely a presence on this track.

5. "I Guess That's Why They Call It the Blues" (co-written with Davey Johnstone) (4:41, B) This was the first single off *Too Low for Zero*, and it peaked at Number 2 on the US Billboard Adult Contemporary chart. It was also a Platinum seller. Lyrically, it's a love song; musically, it's one of Elton's best ballads. This is one of those Elton songs that came easily, as Davey Johnstone describes the writing and recording process in the Sidebar. There's a cool harmonica solo by none other than Stevie Wonder in it, too. Elton has performed this song in concert almost 1,900 times.

Davey Johnstone, in *Rolling Stone* in 2019: "Elton said, 'I've got this lyric and I think it's a guitar song.' I said, 'OK.' He showed me the lyric and I went, 'Oh, what a beautiful lyric.' We wrote the song right there in about 20 minutes. He said, 'That's it. Let's record it.' The next day, I think, we invite the whole band in the room. We played them the song and we proceeded to record it and that was it. I mean, when you start with a lyric like that, you're already halfway there. So I really can't emphasize enough how important Bernie's contribution has been over the years through this whole thing."

6. **"Crystal"** (5:05, R) This song lends itself to multifaceted interpretations. First, "Crystal" is the nickname Elton had for a former lover named Gary Clarke who was much younger than him. Second, "Crystal" can refer to crystal meth. And third, the lines "If she leaves me, handle her with care…if she calls you long distance just be there" makes it sound like Crystal is a runaway daughter. If the lyrics are reviewed with each of those possible subtexts in mind, they work in all cases. Musically, it's an up-tempo, minor-key rocker with a great vocal performance by Elton. He has performed this in concert fewer than ten times.

7. **"Kiss the Bride"** (4:22, R) This was the third single off *Too Low for Zero*, and it hit Number 25 on the US Billboard Hot 100 chart. This song is about a guy who attends the wedding of a former lover and is upset that she's getting married to someone else. Elton has performed this more than seventy times in concert. It's a great Elton rocker with the irresistible "I wanna kiss the bride!" chorus. (Calm down, brother. You missed your chance.)

8. **"Whipping Boy"** (3:43, R) This rocker is about a guy who's having an affair with someone much too young ("But you're way too young, I could do time if they found out, look out, San Quentin here I come"), and who mistreats him. He even blatantly describes this taboo, sexually assaultive relationship as an "illegal kind of loving." One great lyric is when he says he's thirty, looks like fifty, and feels like sixty-three. (The specificity of "sixty-three" is what makes it genius.) It's got a fast-paced tempo that almost feels like the guy's being chased. This is a unique song that Elton seems to have never performed in concert.

9. **"Saint"** (5:17, B) This is a powerful ballad about a young woman with a mind of her own. "No one's gonna stare you down," we're told. And "You took the whole world by surprise." Elton's vocal taps his full range, with a high-pitched melody that lets us hear him singing at the top of his voice. Elton plays a Yamaha synthesizer and a clavinet on this song, and it's got classic Elton

melodic riffs as well as a hot Davey Johnstone guitar solo. Elton doesn't seem to have performed this in concert.

10. **"One More Arrow"** (3:34, B) Elton sings in a high falsetto for part of this compelling and emotional piano ballad that closes *Too Low for Zero*. It reads like it's about Bernie's father, although it could be about a friend who died too soon. However, lyrics like, "We argued once, he knocked me down, and he cried when he thought he'd hurt me" sound like it's a father/son relationship being described. The segment describing a grave is one of the more beautiful lyrics Bernie has written. He uses the metaphor of his father's soul being an arrow landing "in a shady spot somewhere" and tells us the "soft brown earth holds him." Very moving, indeed. Elton did perform "One More Arrow" in concert a few dozen times in 1984, but hasn't since. This is probably because his voice deepened after his throat surgery and he's aged, and falsetto is difficult to sing live under those circumstances.

BEST SONG: "One More Arrow"

18. *Breaking Hearts* (1984)

Breaking Hearts was a successful record for Elton and Bernie, and it garnered four Top 40 hits around the world. The album, released on June 18, 1984, is notable for its marking the final musical performance on an Elton John recording of Elton's longtime bassist Dee Murray, who died of skin cancer in 1992. The album reunited Elton's original band—Davey Johnstone, Murray, and Nigel Olsson. Interestingly, the album featured a photo of Bernie Taupin taken by the legendary photographer Herb Ritts. *AllMusic.com* wrote, "Without question this is one of John's most consistent efforts during his half decade on Geffen Records ('81–'86). However, the shift in pop music styles since 1975, as well as lack of edgy material, seemed to stifle the band's return to full form circa *Goodbye Yellow Brick Road* (1973) or *Captain Fantastic and the Brown Dirt Cowboy* (1975)."

1. **"Restless"** (5:17, R) A fun, somewhat formulaic rocker with Elton using his rough-edged rock 'n' roll voice. It's about a guy who's broke and can't get a job and we learn that everybody's restless. It's okay, but it's not a track most fans would probably put on repeat. You hear it once, you've heard it.

2. **"Slow Down Georgie (She's Poison)"** (4:10, R) The narrator is trying to prevent his friend from getting involved with a woman whose reputation is about "as nasty as the Berlin Wall." He tries to convince him throughout the song to back away, but we never find out if he's successful. Musically, it's an above average Elton/Bernie rocker. (See: "Li'l 'Frigerator.")

3. **"Who Wears These Shoes?"** (4:04, R) This is an up-tempo rocker in the key of G that is, once again, about a romantic breakup. The singer wants to know who now walks in his footsteps, thus "who wears these shoes?" It starts a bit "stalker-y" with the narrator standing outside his former lover's house and seeing two silhouettes in the window, which "tell[s] me it's over." We guess the album was called *Breaking Hearts* for a reason (maybe *Broken Hearts* would have been more on the nose).

4. **"Breaking Hearts (Ain't What It Used to Be)"** (3:34, B) This sounds like something from a musical. It consists of a contemplative set of lyrics about people aging and relationships failing. Elton plays keyboards, and there is a quiet string accompaniment. We can't help but wonder if this was going to be in one of Elton's musicals and ended up here instead. That's how Broadway-esque this song is.

5. **"Li'l 'Frigerator"** (3:37, R) This is a mean-spirited rocker about an "empty shell" young hooker with a "geisha smile" and "cherry bombs inside her eyes." The narrator is instructing others about the woman, stating quite clearly that she's an "empty shell" and that "you're a piece of meat." Damn. Why so bitter, Bernie?

6. **"Passengers"** (co-written with Davey Johnstone, Phineas Mkhize) (3:24, R) Elton does Bob Marley? This reggae-inspired song is commonly either beloved or despised. It's both playful and dark, and the opening refrain "Deny the passenger who want to get on" is both hypnotic and annoying at the same time. We can't help but sense a deeper meaning, though, when hearing lines like "There's wheels upon the jail, a black train built of bones." Trains have certainly been used for nefarious purposes throughout history, so maybe we're meant to dig deeper. A sad and sorry tale masked in a childish tune, perhaps?

7. **"In Neon"** (4:19, B) The intro to this song sounds like "A Natural Woman" to our ears. The song is about a failed actress who apparently had some minor success (she was on a billboard, after all) but when we meet her she's a waitress ("behind the counter she stares out the window" at her own image). It's a bit plodding musically, and in this case, the lyrics are more memorable and more powerful than Elton's music.

8. **"Burning Buildings"** (4:02, B) This starts out as a quintessential Elton ballad but then soars with an extraordinary chorus. Once again, Bernie visits the theme of failed relationships with his lyrics, and, yes, we know it's a metaphor, but the "lovers leap off

burning buildings" in the chorus is *dark,* especially today, after the tragedy of 9/11, which was seventeen years away when this song was written. Nonetheless, we endure, just to get to a truly great chorus.

9. **"Did He Shoot Her?"** (3:21, R) The narrator hates his ex-girlfriend's new boyfriend and wants to know if the guy shot her (metaphorically, of course), and he challenges him to a shoot-out (literally). It's a decent rocker with a great drum part.

10. **"Sad Songs (Say So Much)"** (4:55, R) This song was a moderately successful single that hit Number 4 on the Billboard Hot 100 chart and Number 2 on the Billboard Adult Contemporary chart. The message of the song is to listen to old songs on the radio when you're sad. This is still somewhat popular among fans, yet musically it's one of Elton's lesser efforts. It uses the hoary three-chord 1-4-5 progression found in so many other songs, but it's a great dance and karaoke track because everyone knows and can sing the chorus.

BEST SONG: "Burning Buildings"

19. *Ice on Fire* (1985)

This album was released on November 4, 1985, and produced four singles. *Rolling Stone* did not like this record: "It's too much to expect a substantial album from Elton John at this point, but with the return of his longtime producer, Gus Dudgeon, for *Ice on Fire*, there was the hope that he might at least whip up a few frothy singles. Though the riffs abound, they're warmed over from other hits—most of them not his own—without any foundation of personal style." *Rolling Stone*'s excoriation notwithstanding, a great many fans like this album.

1. **"This Town"** (3:56, R) This is an up-tempo synth- and bass-driven rocker that opens the *Ice on Fire* album. The lyrics are bleak and speak of layoffs and old veterans tapping their canes because too much in this town reminds them of war. The party feel to the track belies the depressing lyrics, and we come away nodding our heads to the relentless beat while trying not to think of the forlorn milieu that Bernie paints so effectively. "This Town" featured the awesome Sister Sledge on background vocals. A relentless, throbbing bass line seems to suggest the inexorable decline everyone in this town just, oh well, has to live with. Elton has played this more than fifty times in concert, mainly in 1985 and 1986.

2. **"Cry to Heaven"** (4:16, B) This was the third single from *Ice on Fire*, and it didn't chart in the US or the UK. It's a classic minor-key Elton-and-Bernie ballad. The song is about a generic beleaguered town besieged by war, told through the point of view of the children who have to live through it and try to survive. "Cry to Heaven" is a sad song, and speaks to the horrors of war for everyone who experiences it, but especially the children. It's a departure from the other techno-driven songs on the album. Elton has only played this a dozen or so times in concert, and almost solely in 1986.

3. **"Soul Glove"** (3:31, R) This was the fourth single from *Ice on Fire*, but it was only released in Spain. This is an old-school soul song, something the Four Tops, the Temptations, or even Earth,

Wind & Fire might do. The song has a horn and synthesizer part, and old friend Kiki Dee sings backing vocals. Lyrically, it's about a guy coming home to his love and asking her to slip into his "soul glove." We're not sure what that means. If *she* were singing the song, then there's an easily arrived at, vulgar interpretation of the euphemism, but in the song, he's the one with the "glove." This is a less than memorable Elton/Bernie song, and he may not have ever performed this in concert.

4. **"Nikita"** (5:43, B) This was the first single from *Ice on Fire*, and it was an international success. "Nikita" is an irresistible pop hit that has the same appeal as "Daniel" and others of its ilk: a great melody, great chord changes, great lyrics, and terrific background vocals, which included Elton's friend, the late George Michael. Elton has played "Nikita" three hundred or so times in concert and it reached Number 3 on the US Billboard Adult Contemporary chart. None other than Ken Russell directed the video for the song. This is unquestionably an Elton John "Greatest Hit."

5. **"Too Young"** (5:12, B) This is a song about another guy in love with a girl who, we are told, is "too young." How young is too young? That's not revealed, but young enough for the girl to still be living with her parents. It's a pretty-enough ballad, with an obvious Beach Boys "Wouldn't It Be Nice?" inspiration. Lyrically, it's a very straightforward message, and the young man knows the odds are against him; "We could try it for awhile," he tells her, "but they'd get us in the long run." The fadeout refrain is "Baby, you're too young," and we never learn the ultimate status of their relationship.

6. **"Wrap Her Up"** (co-written with Davey Johnstone, Fred Mandel, Charlie Morgan, Paul Westwood) (6:21, R) This was the second single released from *Ice on Fire*, and it reached Number 12 on the UK Singles Chart and Number 20 on the US Billboard Hot 100 chart. In the track, Elton John and George Michael swap vocals, with George singing his lines in a high-pitched falsetto. The

song is about the love of women, and the end includes a list of some memorable ladies, including fictional characters like Elsie Tanner from *Coronation Street*. This is the list of women named in the song: Marlene Dietrich, Marilyn Monroe, Brigitte Bardot, Doris Day, Billie Jean King, Samantha Fox, Joan Collins, Kiki Dee, Katharine Hepburn, Vivien Leigh, Grace Jones, Priscilla Presley, Vanessa Williams, Dusty Springfield, Nancy Reagan, Rita Hayworth, Material Girl, Julie Andrews, Superwoman, Annie Lennox, Mata Hari, Anouska Hempel, Shirley Temple, Tallulah Bankhead, Linda Lovelace, Little Eva, Nastassja Kinski, Princess Caroline of Monaco, Miss Pat Fernandez, Elsie Tanner. This is a fun, novelty song that pays tribute to some legendary ladies. Elton performed this song in concert several times in 1985 and 1986.

7. **"Satellite"** (3:57, R) This is a weird love song with a head-nodding, toe-tapping beat. Bernie uses the metaphor of love being like a satellite and tells the woman he's writing to, "I want you to surround me like a satellite." He uses the symbol of a comet in the first line, telling her, "You come on like a comet, ideas in your head," but that outer space/satellite/comet/imagery throughout falls somewhat flat. It's a listenable song with a typical Elton melody infused with eighties sounds and production, including Elton playing a synthesizer instead of a piano.

8. **"Tell Me What the Papers Say"** (3:40, R) This is a fun dance song with a starkly fatalistic attitude. Shortly after this peppy song begins (seemingly as a rant against the media?), we're told "Everybody's got to die someday." The song then goes on to recite a litany of negative societal and global developments: coal mines closed, more jails, Japanese still killing whales, dope, pills, and guns kill, etc. But then the ultimate blame is planted firmly on the media. "Lipstick boys all look like queens…least that's what the papers say." That's the refrain throughout and the obvious conclusion is, don't believe everything you read and make your own decisions. So, with that kind of subtextual empowerment, maybe it's not such a fatalistic song after all? However, the irony

is blatant: everything mentioned in the song is real, and *not* just media hype. So we're left with a song that basically says, "Attitude is everything." This song boasts a very clever set of lyrics with a somewhat mundane musical underpinning.

9. **"Candy by the Pound"** (3:56, R) This song is about a guy thrilled with his new girlfriend and happy that he's now getting "candy by the pound," which, of course, means he and the new girlfriend are testing the suspension on a regular basis. The boyfriend is a tad obvious: "With you underneath it's like candy by the pound." My, my. He tells us that his new girlfriend is "sweeter than the grapes hanging from the vine." We're happy for this braggart throughout the song until we learn at the end that he's "hiding from the claws" of his old girlfriend who's "screaming murder" and beating his door down while, right behind it, he's—you guessed it—"eating candy by the pound." This is a well-done rocker that's actually pretty comical. The characters and scenarios are funny and faithful to how things sometimes go in the real world.

10. **"Shoot Down the Moon"** (5:09, B) *Ice on Fire* concludes with this pretty but sad piano and strings (synthesizer) ballad about a breakup. This is a quintessential Elton John/Bernie Taupin song and it would not have been out of place on almost any of his other albums. Elton played this a dozen or so times in concert in 1985 and 1986. The song resolves with a gloomy conclusion: "We can build a bridge between us, but the empty space remains."

BEST SONG: "Nikita"

20. *Leather Jackets* (1986)

Leather Jackets was recorded in Austria and released on October 15, 1986. It did not produce any Top 40 chart hits, even though five songs were released from the album as singles. This is not a beloved record to Elton and Bernie and, apparently, Elton was in the midst of indulging his cocaine addiction when the album was recorded. Ironically, this album is significant for including contributions from notables such as Cliff Richard, members of Queen, and even Cher. It peaked at Number 91 on the US Billboard 200 chart. *AllMusic.com* wrote, "Even the most ardent enthusiasts freely admit that *Leather Jackets* was nothing more or less than a final fulfillment of his six-album deal with Geffen Records. On top of the half-hearted material and less-than-inspired performances is increasing evidence that John's voice—which would require a potentially career-ending surgery less than a year later—is beginning to show signs of extreme fatigue and strain."

1. **"Leather Jackets"** (4:10, R) Is this song about the death of rock 'n' roll? It sounds like Bernie is lamenting the loss of fifties rock 'n' roll and the ubiquitous presence of just plain rock (or at the least, what passed for rock in the eighties). He asks "Do you pray to someone new when you're locked up in the *rock*?" and even asks "Is the golden age dead and gone?" He then name-checks "Buddy" (as in Holly) and references the "king," which can only be Elvis, right? His targets are "them boys in leather jackets." Musically, the song is a synth-driven rocker with a great beat—and you can dance to it!

2. **"Hoop of Fire"** (4:14, B) This is a pretty ballad with great backing vocals. It was the fourth single released from *Leather Jackets*. It's got a country-ish swing to it, and we can easily hear this performed by—pick a country star. Lyrically it's about a relationship in which one partner claims to want "simple things" like "long walks on lonely beaches" and "guitars with nylon strings" and the other partner sees right through them and thinks they'd really rather "leap though a hoop of fire." We suppose the underlying message is a simple "lighten up," right?

3. **"Don't Trust That Woman"** (co-written with Cher, and Elton John writing as "Lady Choc Ice") (4:58, R) Elton wrote this song with Cher, who wanted to be listed first as songwriter, so Elton used the pseudonym Lady Choc Ice, which was actually his nickname for his then-wife Renate. It's a standard rocker musically, but lyrically it's about a woman who we learn in the first line is a "ball-breaker." We're instructed not to untie her (is she tied up because someone wanted to "rear-end" her?—first verse), and throughout the song, the woman is described in less than flattering terms: liar, mean sister, tongue-twister, two-fister, man-eater, a woman half-crazy, and lazy. Considering a woman was the co-writer for this song, we can't help but suspect that it's a misogynistic revenge song against a woman Cher hated. Just wondering.

4. **"Go It Alone"** (4:26, R) A disco-tinged rocker with a fierce bass line. Once again, it's about a breakup and failed relationship. It's in F minor and has the great line "The cars you drive to buy your friends, they don't ever come back clean."

5. **"Gypsy Heart"** (4:46, B) Another Elton ballad, this one in the key of G. A guy misses his woman, who we're told has a gypsy heart. He tells us she comes and goes, but the song's question is, will she come back again? It's very pretty and the quintessential slow song to dance to (if it were played in clubs, which is unlikely these days).

6. **"Slow Rivers"** (3:06, B) This is a duet with Cliff Richard, and it was performed on a Noel Edmonds Christmas special on the BBC in 1986 and was the second single released from *Leather Jackets.* It's a rather ordinary ballad about, yes, a failed relationship and unrequited love: "One foot in your door, that's all I ever got." It has the great line, "The winter here don't believe in God…", and the chorus is pretty catchy.

7. **"Heartache All Over the World"** (4:01, R) Is this the worst song Elton John has ever recorded? At one point, he seemed

to think so. He said precisely that in a 2001 interview with the UK magazine *Uncut* which, its title notwithstanding, is not a porn mag, but a magazine about music and movies. So what's so bad about "Heartache All Over the World," anyway? This song, the first single released from *Leather Jackets*, is a lament about not being able to get a date for a Friday or Saturday night. It's a song that doesn't know what it wants to be, an '80s rocker or a *Footloose*-esque dance anthem. It succeeds at neither, frankly. The lyrics are rather trite; the music is "less than." And who are we to argue with the master, anyway?

8. **"Angeline"** (co-written with Alan Carvell) (3:55, R) Any song that features two members of Queen—Roger Taylor on drums and John Deacon on bass—playing for their friend Reg is notable. And the song is worthy of their participation. It's a kick-ass rocker, and the opening repeated "oh-oh-oh-oh-oh" refrain can't help but remind us of Matthew McConaughey's chest-pounding chant/mantra in Martin Scorsese's 2013 hit, *The Wolf of Wall Street*. The lyrics are, well, one more set of somewhat misogynistic lyrics from Bernie Taupin in which he wants to treat Angeline like a "sex machine," and tells us that she "just loves it when I treat her mean." The narrator also assures us that he talks tough and acts rough. Overall, though, "Angeline" is one of the more memorable tracks on *Leather Jackets* and was the fifth and final single released from the album.

9. **"Memory of Love"** (co-written with Gary Osborne) (4:08, B) This ballad with lyrics by Gary Osborne is oddly paced, with a pounding beat that can sometimes feel draggy. Also, Elton uses a really weird singing style, dramatically clipping each word. It's pleasant enough, though, and its message is essentially don't take love for granted. (And the chorus uses "The Canon," Elton and many fans' favorite chord progression. See the Sidebar "The Canon" at the end of the song reviews.)

10. **"Paris"** (3:58, B) This is a ballad about a guy being depressed about having broken up with someone, and it was the third

single released from *Leather Jackets.* The first line tells us "Without you I no longer swim upstream…." The song uses an interesting metaphor of the narrator feeling "shipwrecked," and the song is essentially about suffering. Musically, it's lovely, and Elton delivers a heartfelt vocal. He performed "Paris" in concert almost three dozen times in 1986.

11. **"I Fall Apart"** (4:00, B) This song, a sad ballad, seems to be about a guy who lost his woman to another woman and isn't taking it very well. The lyrics point to this inevitable conclusion: "For every rose you give her, I'll give her three, but in the meantime, I'll just wish that she was me." Elton may not have performed this in concert (yet). It's pretty and perfect for slow dancing, regardless of your gender identity. Or dance partner choice.

BEST SONG: "Hoop of Fire"

21. *Reg Strikes Back* (1988)

> *"My album* Reg Strikes Back *did very well in England. It's just gone cardboard."*
>
> —Elton John

This album was released on June 24, 1988, and produced four singles. It is notable for being Elton's self-proclaimed comeback album and also for being bassist Dee Murray's final album with Elton. Dee didn't play bass on the album, though; he only sang background vocals. Dee Murray died on January 15, 1992, of a stroke following a long battle with skin cancer. Drummer Nigel Olsson said of Murray, "We will never again create anything as wonderful—as inspirational—without Dee's presence." In March 1992, Elton performed two tribute concerts at the Grand Ole Opry to raise money for Dee Murray's family. *Rolling Stone* gave this album three out of five stars and wrote, "Okay, folks, here's the real comeback. After a successful throat operation, Elton John is back with urgent shouting and playful crooning. The forty-one-year-old songster has also discarded his flamboyant image, including the dandy outfits. A throwback to his inspired pop rock of the Seventies, *Reg Strikes Back* is cathartic for Elton John."

1. **"Town of Plenty"** (3:40, R) This was the second single released from *Reg Strikes Back* (but only in the UK—it was not released in the US), and it was the first time we fans heard what Elton's voice sounded like following his successful January 1987 throat surgery to remove what was described by his Australian publicist Patti Mostyn as a "non-malignant lesion." Elton spent six weeks in Australia recovering and had to cancel a thirty-two-concert tour of the United States. (He sounded the same after the surgery as he did before, frankly.) This is a classic 1-4-5 blues-inspired rocker with Pete Townshend playing acoustic guitar, with lyrics that bespeak the travails of tour traveling ("We had no media, only art survived there"). Even with the depressing image of band

luggage spread out on an airport airstrip, there is a renewed spirit in the sound and in Elton's singing. "Town of Plenty" charted for one week at Number 74 and then dropped off. Elton only played this in concert a few times in 1988 and 1989.

2. **"A Word in Spanish"** (4:39, B) This was the third (second in the US) single from *Reg Strikes Back*, and it was a US Top 40 hit. It's a classic love song with the paramour singing to the one he loves, pleading "If only I could tell you, if only you would listen…." The lyrical hook is that he thinks she'll understand if he could tell her how he feels using a word in Spanish that he had heard but doesn't know its meaning. It's "love," of course, but the song seems to end with his love not being returned. This isn't a bad song, but it seems somewhat somnolent for a global single release from Elton John. Since it was a single, Elton performed it a few dozen times in concert in 1988 and 1989.

3. **"Mona Lisas and Mad Hatters, Part Two"** (4:12, R) This was the fourth single released from *Reg Strikes Back*, but only as a twelve-inch single that was different from the album version. It is a sequel of sorts to the beloved ballad "Mona Lisas and Mad Hatters" from the *Honky Château* album, but other than a similarity in meaning, it couldn't be more different. It is still somewhat as cynical lyrically as the original, but musically it's the polar opposite. This is a hard-edged rocker with a searing trumpet solo by Freddie Hubbard. Also, there's a nod to the Beatles's "Drive My Car" with a "beep beep beep beep yeah" at the end of the song. Bottom line, it's a serious rocker that provides an aural counterpoint to the original, but ultimately delivers a somewhat more optimistic tone than does version one. Especially with lyrics like, "When I walk along the West Side… searching for the city that took away the kid in me." The *Honky Château* "Mona Lisa" hardened the boy, but she's gotten older and seems to have mellowed. Elton has been known to perform both songs in concert in a very powerful extended session.

4. **"I Don't Wanna Go On with You Like That"** (4:35, R) This was the first single released from *Reg Strikes Back* and it peaked at Number 1 on the US Billboard Adult Contemporary chart (it only reached Number 30 on the UK Singles Chart). This is one of Elton's best dance tracks and is about a guy whose girlfriend wants him to be "one of four or five." Between the title and the lyrics, it's a fairly straightforward message. The Shep Pettibone dance remix is killer and a fan favorite. The Russell Mulcahy-directed video was likewise very popular.

5. **"Japanese Hands"** (4:40, B) This song is about an encounter with a geisha in Kyoto in the Kansai region of Japan. We're not sure of when it takes place, but the lyrics do mention an earthquake. The most recent earthquake prior to the release of *Reg Strikes Back* was in 1984 in Otaki, so it's unclear if the earthquake in the song was an artistic device or was referring to a real quake. Elton wrote the song on a synthesizer and it has an eerie feel to it. The narrator is certainly ensorcelled by his geisha. We're told, "You forget the western woman when you're sleeping on Kyoto time," and "Flesh on silk looks different than on a cotton sheet back home, where no one wears their hair like yours beneath those oriental combs." The song is an interesting cultural study of sorts, but the lack of a catchy melody or chorus hook makes it a bit of a struggle to get through. Elton only performed this live a couple of times in 1988, the year the album was released.

6. **"Goodbye Marlon Brando"** (3:30, R) This is an unusual rocker with a "Saturday Night's Alright (for Fighting)" feel to it. In it, the narrator has had it up to *here* with the nonsense permeating every minute of every day. In fact, he even asks if the listener would like to rent a room in a sanitarium or "crawl back to the womb." The lyrics are a list of what we need to say goodbye to. This list is voluminous, yet justifiable. Included are Glasnost, the morning news, prime time (and the "fools that choose to view"), the clowns in Congress, the tabloids, gridlock, evangelists, "geeks with power tools," and even New Age music and Rocky Five, Six, Seven, and Eight. Elton performed this song around

twenty times in the year the album was released and it does not seem to have reared its head live since. Interestingly, Billy Joel, Elton's good friend, released "We Didn't Start the Fire" a year later in 1989, which, like "Goodbye Marlon Brando," rattles off a list of historical and cultural events and people, eschewing, on behalf of his generation, blame for the mess. Perhaps this song was an influence?

7. **"The Camera Never Lies"** (4:36, R) This rocker is about a guy who is apparently dating either a model or an actress. It's about betrayal, and he finds out she's lying to him when he sees her pictures in newspapers and magazines and on TV. Thus, the camera never lies. Musically, it's probably an average Elton song; i.e., it's a bit ordinary. The lyrics are more interesting than the music. Elton does not seem to have performed this in concert.

8. **"Heavy Traffic"** (co-written with Davey Johnstone) (3:30, R) Life in the inner city. There's Shakey, and "Jane Doe," Snake Hips Joe, and the flyboys on the corner, and Judy, Billy, Cindy, and, of course, Mack the PCP cook, living on "apple juice and cocaine." This shuffle-beat story-song is an Elton John and Davey Johnstone collaboration, and it's a fun song with a dark underbelly. "Heavy traffic" is the metaphor for lives of sex, drugs, and violence. The title would seem to be a nod to the 1973 Ralph Bakshi adult animated film of the same name.

9. **"Poor Cow"** (3:50, R) This up-tempo rocker is *bleak*, as well as being somewhat misogynistic. Also, the title is a tad insulting. The song is about a woman who is pregnant (again)—the "poor cow" of the title—and apparently she has a lowlife husband not averse to raising a hand to her on occasion, a la "You'll see your whole life coming at you in the back of his hand." She'll work some overtime, but Frank will still complain about how little they earn. Her mother's no help: she visits every Monday and all she does is "nag about the world" and then bitch about how much she hates Dallas, Texas. The working class poor are represented here as cynical and depressed, but maintaining their

pride and their health. The "rich bitch girls" ain't got "no spine for labor." This is a dark song in a minor key that has an ironically peppy beat with a big production sound and some Ray Cooper percussion sweetening thrown in for flavor.

10. **"Since God Invented Girls"** (4:54, B) This ballad has Bruce Johnston and Carl Wilson of the Beach Boys singing background vocals, and Brian Wilson is mentioned in the lyrics: "Now I know what Brian Wilson meant, every time I step outside, I see what Heaven sent." It's a celebration of women, with some regrettable focus on their physicality, using tacky euphemisms: "The mother of invention made it good for me, tighter in the rear, longer in the seam…." It's a pretty song, though, its sexist lapses notwithstanding. It's not on Elton's concert playlists.

BEST SONG: "I Don't Wanna Go On with You Like That"

22. *Sleeping with the Past* (1989)

This album was released on August 29, 1989, and produced four singles. The *Los Angeles Times* called it "a savvy piece of smooth pop craft resplendent with as consistently strong a sequence of tunes as John has put together since his mid-'70s days as the dominant force on the pop charts." The music website *AllMusic.com* wrote, "The past Elton John has in mind is the era of soul music of the mid-1960s to the mid-1970s, and although all the songs are new, he recreates it well here. The album's most notable selection is the ballad 'Sacrifice,' which amazingly became his first-ever number one hit in the U.K." Elton called it "the strongest record we've ever made," and Bernie told *Music Connection*, "This is a songwriting salute. It's all inspired and it says that on the album, and due to that it's really given the album a cohesiveness. It's not a concept album, but there's a concept in the idea. More than any other record we've made, this sounds like an album. It sounds like it all belongs together, and I'm really, really proud of that. We worked really hard on this record, and we worked hand-in-hand on this one." *Sleeping with the Past* peaked at Number 23 on the Billboard 200 chart, but hit Number 1 on the UK charts. It also went Platinum.

1. **"Durban Deep"** (5:29, R) The *Los Angeles Times* wrote of this song, "The strongest song here is 'Durban Deep,' a catchy, reggae-beat number that eschews the soapbox sloganeering of most songs about the plight of South African blacks, focusing instead on the apolitical but deeply felt blues of a hard-pressed miner." We're not sure we'd agree with it being the strongest song on the album, but it is definitely evidence of Elton and Bernie pushing the boundaries of their songwriting. Instead of the Old West, though, we see life through the eyes of a Durban, South Africa, miner. It's not a pretty picture, the song's up-tempo jauntiness notwithstanding.

2. **"Healing Hands"** (4:31, R) This is a soul song by two British white guys and was the first single off *Sleeping with the Past.* Apparently inspired by the Four Tops's "Reach Out I'll Be There," it reminds some listeners more of "Philadelphia Freedom" than the Tops classic, but, as is said, it's all in the eye of the beholder

(listener). The song does work as a tribute to Motown, and Elton does some fancy key changing in the song, starting in B flat and moving to D for the chorus. This is a fun song.

3. **"Whispers"** (5:28, B) This was the third single off the album and is a very pretty ballad that begins with an irresistible percussion break. Lyrically, it reads like a poem and is another "love betrayed" song from Elton and Bernie. Elton performed this song live twice in 1989, the year *Sleeping with the Past* was released and, apparently, one time four years later in 1993 at a concert in Canada.

4. **"Club at the End of the Street"** (4:52, R) This is Elton and Bernie honoring the Drifters. In 2013, Elton told *Rolling Stone*, "We wanted to write a song like the Drifters would record, one of those Goffin-King, Brill Building songs. It's the closest we ever got to one." Fifteen years earlier, Bernie said, in an interview with *Music Connection*, "What I would do is I'd take a song like a Drifters song and I'd try to write a Drifters-type lyric....'Club at the End of the Street'...is probably the straightest emulation of one of those songs. When you hear it, it has the feel of a song like 'Under the Boardwalk.'...[W]hat I would do is I'd make notes for Elton at the bottom of the lyric sheet, like 'Think Drifters, think this, or think that.'" We can easily imagine the Drifters themselves doing this song. They also-name check Otis Redding and Marvin Gaye in the song. This is an enjoyable song, and it comes complete with a wailing sax solo by Vince Denham. It was the fifth and final single off *Sleeping with the Past*.

5. **"Sleeping with the Past"** (4:54, R) This is a rocker with a "Philadelphia Freedom" feel to it. The message of the song is "dump the loser you're with, honey." There's some scolding going on: "You're proud to love him, it's a foolish sign...you're a broken heart at the scene of the crime." Obviously, the lyrics are blatant and the narrator is trying to help a friend—and perhaps a love interest of his own?: "He's just an iceman honey, ain't got no heart of gold...come on and shake this shadow that you're

clinging to...." The song begins with an instantly memorable riff, the kind that Elton is so good at writing. Many of his riffs stick with us. An example would be the opening of a wildly disparate song from "Sleeping with the Past": the song "House" from *Made in England.* Once you hear Elton sing "This is my house..." you never forget it. This title song is a cool rocker that Elton played in concert in 1989 a couple of dozen times.

6. **"Stone's Throw from Hurtin'"** (4:45, R) This is a song inspired by the songs of Marvin Gaye, plus Bernie said that he knew it would be like a "Sam & Dave thing." If you did not know this was Elton singing, you'd never guess it. Elton's weird sounding, high-pitched voice was achieved by him whispering into the microphone during the rough take of the lead vocal. Elton wanted this to be a single release, but it wasn't. Lyrically, the song is about a failing relationship. The "stone's throw from hurtin'" of the title is how far the narrator is from destroying "everything we put together." There's a guitar solo at the end that sounds like a slide guitar but is actually an electric guitar with a vibrato arm played by Davey Johnstone. Elton performed this close to twenty times in 1989 and 1990 and then revisited it in 1993. It must have been quite something to hear Elton sing this song live.

7. **"Sacrifice"** (5:06, B) This very popular ballad was the second single released from *Sleeping with the Past.* It reached Number 1 on the UK Singles Chart and Number 18 on the US Billboard Hot 100. Bernie and Elton are both on record as saying this is one of their all-time favorite songs. In a 1989 interview, Bernie said, "It's a simple lyric, but it's an intelligent, adult lyric. It's basically about the rigors of adult love, and it's a million miles away from 'Your Song.' Elton came up with a brilliant melody, and his performance on it gives it a lot of integrity and meaning." Musically, the chord changes are simple, but beautiful. Elton does a fantastic job with the vocal, and the band is subtle, yet a definite presence. Elton fans love this song, and he has performed it over five hundred times in concert from 1989 through today. And that doesn't count the live TV performances, many of

which are considered some of his finest performances of the song. The video for "Sacrifice" was directed by Alek Keshishian, the director of the Madonna documentary *Truth or Dare*, and it also starred supermodel Yasmeen Ghauri and singer/songwriter Chris Isaak.

8. **"I Never Knew Her Name"** (3:29, R) This song is about a guy who falls for the bride at a wedding he's attending: "The congregation gathered, but in darkness I remained, in love with the bride of a handsome man, but I never knew her name." Elton and Bernie have both said they wanted this be like an Aretha Franklin song. Elton's piano part was inspired by the piano in Aretha's song, "Don't Play That Song," a shuffling, back and forth rhythmic part that propels the song through each verse. Its "soul song" inspiration is obvious and true to the sources Elton and Bernie listened to growing up.

9. **"Amazes Me"** (4:37, B) This was the fourth single released from *Sleeping with the Past*, and it reached Number 3 on the US Adult Contemporary chart. This is a bluesy ballad with a gospel chorus singing backup. Bernie has said of this song, "This is one of my favorite tracks, simply because it has a Southern swampy feel that I feel was really captured in the recording." Lyrically, it's about the narrator's fascination with a woman he describes as a "mystery of ebony." And she may or may not be a sorceress—he talks about drifting in her "hoodoo" (which means voodoo). It's a stately song with a searing guitar solo by Davey Johnstone. This is an interesting excursion into Southern blues/R&B, perhaps not so much musically, but definitely lyrically. Elton has only played this song live a few times.

10. **"Blue Avenue"** (4:33, B) Elton closes *Sleeping with the Past* with this contemplative ballad about a relationship falling apart. The title "Blue Avenue" serves as the metaphor for the emotional zone where everything went bad: "Looks like we gotta wreck, babe, up on Blue Avenue." This song is *sultry*, and speaks to how what started as almost an addiction, an obsession, went bad

because "it takes more than hocus pocus to save us from Blue Avenue." It's a fairly traditional Elton ballad. Elton has said of the song, "'Blue Avenue' isn't exactly an R&B type song…but I felt comfortable with it. It's a very Elton John type song, but it kind of fits in with the rest." Elton played this live around fifteen or so times in 1992 and 1993.

BEST SONG: "Sacrifice"

Elton John's "Blue" Songs

"Blue Avenue"
"Blue Eyes"
Blue Moves (album)
"Blue Wonderful"
"Blues for Baby and Me"
"Blues Never Fade Away"
"I Guess That's Why They Call It the Blues"
"Out of the Blue"
"Screw You (Young Man's Blues) "
"Someday Out of the Blue"

23. *The One* (1992)

This was Elton's twenty-third studio album, and it was released on June 22, 1992, with a cover designed by Gianni Versace. The album peaked at Number 8 on the US Billboard 200 chart and Number 2 on the UK Albums chart. Elton has said that this was the first album that he recorded without using drugs or alcohol. *Rolling Stone* said of *The One*, "Buying an Elton John album these days is like investing in a mutual fund: You won't get a huge payoff, but you probably won't get burned either.... [A]udiences buy into John's work at this point for a familiar sense of craft, not for stinging creativity. Which means that at the very least *The One* stands as the musical equivalent of comfort food."

1. **"Simple Life"** (6:25, R) This was the fourth and final single off *The One*, and it hit Number 1 on the Billboard Adult Contemporary chart. Elton has performed "Simple Life" over two hundred times in concert. Lyrically, the song is about conquering addictions (metaphorically, of all kinds) and reprioritizing your life so that it's more "simple." It's a great Elton rocker, with some interesting production: the opening sax-like riff was played on a Roland RD-1000 digital electric piano. The beginning of the studio version of the song sounds a little like the Beatles's "Baby, You're a Rich Man." This song is an undeniable Elton and Bernie classic.

2. **"The One"** (5:53, B) This was the first single released from *The One*, and it reached Number 9 on the Billboard Hot 100 chart and Number 1 on the Billboard Hot Adult Contemporary Tracks chart. Elton was nominated for Best Male Pop Vocal Performance for this song at the 1993 Grammy Awards. He lost to Sting, who won for "If I Ever Lose My Faith In You." The song is a classic Elton ballad, with an instantly memorable chorus and equally memorable Elton-esque chord changes. Lyrically, the song is about knowing you've found your one true love, and Elton was clearly in that place in his life. As Elton makes that clear in the chorus, "Baby, you're the one." Lyrically, it's probably one of the greatest love songs Bernie has ever written. This song is an Elton concert staple. He reportedly has performed this live close to six hundred times from 1992 through 2016. "The One" was a huge success for Elton and Bernie, and it remains a fan favorite.

3. **"Sweat It Out"** (6:38, R) This is a rocking empowerment anthem in a minor key. But before we get to the "Don't kowtow, don't bow down…back's up, sweat it out" chorus, we're treated to a litany of bad stuff to overcome: we're told there's "no ceiling on hard living," and "she-devils [are] ruling Britain," and that it's "hard to handle when the bank's broke." But then the emboldening chorus does come, and the hope of Elton and Bernie is obviously that listeners come away from the song with a new sense of ambition and confidence. There doesn't seem to be a record of Elton performing this song in concert.

4. **"Runaway Train"** (5:23, R) This duet with Eric Clapton was the second single released from *The One*. It peaked at Number 10 on the Billboard Mainstream Rock chart. This is a great rock song, and Elton and Eric both make it clear why they are charter members of rock royalty. Lyrically, the song is about lost love and is expressed in the lines "Love is lost like a runaway train, oh I'm out of control and out of my hands." They affirm the song's message "Nothing hits harder than a runaway train," powerfully using the metaphor of the train to talk about just how screwed up the narrator actually is. Eric Clapton sings on this track, as well as delivers a blistering guitar solo. Elton performed this concert ten times or so in 1992, and Eric Clapton performed it at least once on his own.

5. **"Whitewash County"** (5:30, R) This song talks about, somewhat obliquely at times, racism in the American South. The title is blatant, though. The concept of "whitewashing" intolerant behavior is common in certain areas, right? The lyrics speak of the "fear behind your name," as though the mere mention of Whitewash County could instill terror in certain…*ethnicities*. The last line tells Whitewash County that it has "changed your face so often but you never change your name." Bernie Taupin has always been interested in the sociocultural characteristics of certain parts of America. Musically, the song rocks and its major key and good time feeling belie the underlying darker message of the song. Elton has played this a few times in concert. The song ends with a rollicking piano solo by the Rocket Man.

6. **"The North"** (5:15, B) This is another great ballad with Elton's (and many other songwriters') beloved chord progression, "The Canon." (See the sidebar about "The Canon" at the end of the song reviews.) Lyrically, it's multifaceted. It could be about Bernie being a transplanted Northerner (from Northern England), and it could also be a metaphorical commentary on Elton's addiction and recovery, with the "north" serving as a symbol for that cold place where the addictions live. But could it also have what could be a UFO reference? Can these lines be referring to a sighting? "In the Northern Skies, there was a steel cloud, it used to follow me around, but I don't see it now." Whatever Bernie's intended meaning of the lyrics, the variegated text and legitimate subtext illustrate the poetic talent of Bernie as a writer. Fantastic song, with a superb production and great harmonies. Elton has played this a dozen or so times in concert.

7. **"When a Woman Doesn't Want You"** (4:56, B) This is a song that can serve as an anthem for the Me Too movement, but it was released a couple of decades before that social crusade sprang into existence. We can finish the title on our own: "When a woman doesn't want you," *leave her alone*. The lyrics are unambiguous: "The things that she wants, the things that she needs…the choice is hers," and "You can't take a woman when she doesn't want you, and you can't be a man if you're blind to reason…." Musically, it's a classic Elton piano ballad with poignant chord changes and harmonies. Elton has only performed this a few times in concert.

8. **"Emily"** (4:58, R) This is one of the most bittersweet songs in Elton and Bernie's songography. The story is simple: elderly Emily visits her sisters' graves one last time, clutches a framed picture of her war-veteran husband, then goes home to die. "Tonight's the night they let the ladder down," we're told, and Emily's gold canary then sings to an empty room. Emily has climbed up to heaven to be with her loved ones. Musically, it's got a "Daniel" feel to it. Elton does not seem to have performed this live. If he hasn't, he should have. It's a wonderful deep cut. This song could be played at funerals—and it would be appropriate.

9. **"On Dark Street"** (4:43, R) A marriage collapses. Layoffs and pay cuts have crippled the husband, and he plaintively asks, "What will it take to make you stay?" and states "I get to see my family slipping through my hands." Once again, Bernie successfully captures the persona of a character who is struggling. Musically, the tune is something the Four Tops or Marvin Gaye could have written and recorded. It has a very Motown and, yes, "Philadelphia Freedom" feel to it. Elton does not seem to have performed this in concert prior to his Farewell Tour.

10. **"Understanding Women"** (5:03, R) This song is about precisely what the title says it is: understanding—or trying to understand—women. The narrator doesn't, but really wants to: "Some men reach beyond the pain of understanding women." His motivation seems legit, and heartfelt, but the musical tone of the song is dark with lots of minor chords and an insistent, repeated opening riff that bespeaks frustration, impatience, and perhaps, ultimately, anger? This is not a song Elton has been known to perform in concert.

11. **"The Last Song"** (3:21, B) This was the third single released from *The One* and it reached Number 23 on the US Billboard Hot 100. This was an important song for Elton and Bernie. It's about a son dying of AIDS who doesn't know how to tell his father, and the narrative is told in the voice of the son. He admits he thought he was invulnerable—"I never dreamed I'd feel this fire beneath my skin"—and that he completely misjudged his father: "I never thought you'd come, I guess I misjudged love between a father and a son." It's a very sad song, and musically Elton is restrained and elegiac with his writing and performance. He's performed it almost two hundred times in concert from 1992 through today.

BEST SONG: "The One"

24. *Made in England* (1995)

Other than the title track, *Made in England,* which was released on March 20, 1995, consists of songs with one-word titles. And other than "Believe," all the titles are nouns. Does this mean anything? Do the titles tell an underlying story? Maybe? This is a popular album with some great songs which, other than "Believe" (which was a huge hit), are now mostly considered deep cuts. Of the album, *Rolling Stone* said, "*Made in England* is a startlingly fine album, one that shows a newly committed artist tapping into the essence of his creative flow."

1. **"Believe"** (4:55, B) This is undeniably one of Elton and Bernie's greatest ballads and was the first single released from *Made in England.* Everything about it is incredible: the music, the melody, the lyrics, the Paul Buckmaster instrumental break, the performance, the official video...it's great in the caliber of "Don't Let the Sun Go Down on Me" and "Someone Saved My Life Tonight" great. Elton and Bernie were *on* when they wrote this classic. Elton was nominated for a Grammy for Best Male Vocal Performance for "Believe" in 1996 (Seal won for "A Kiss From a Rose"). "Believe" hit Number 1 on *Billboard*'s Adult Contemporary chart. A classic.

2. **"Made in England"** (5:09, R) This is an iconic song dripping in irony that, for us, is made all the better for its opening "Hard Day's Night"-sounding guitar chord. Although the lyrics are by Bernie Taupin, they tell Elton's story, and the "forty years of pain" he endured in a country where "you can still say 'homo' and everybody laughs." The song is also an anti-paparazzi screed with Elton singing, "You had a scent for scandal, well here's my middle finger." Take that, tabloid scum. But in the end, all the abuse and disrespect doesn't matter because, as we're told, "If you're made in England, you're built to last." The track rocks and also has a Beatles-esque fade out ending. Great song, which he hasn't performed live since 1998. This was the second single released from *Made in England.*

3. **"House"** (4:27, B) This is a lovely song that elevates a mundane itemization of the narrator's life into an existential musing on the nature of his soul. He checks them off: This is my house, floor, bed, and then moves on to this is winter, trees, dark, dreams, and culminates this musing with "What is my soul?" and "Where is the answer?" before coming to the conclusion that the answer is "inside my house." The house is a metaphor for his true self. This is an extraordinary song, with a lovely melody, wrapped in the seductive cloak of a beautiful ballad.

4. **"Cold"** (5:37, B) Why is he cold? Because she broke up with him. "Love hurts so much," and "'I don't love you' is like a stake being driven through your heart." No wonder he's cold. This is a beautiful ballad with a great production (it's got a *Madman Across the Water* feel to it). The lyrics are heartbreaking.

5. **"Pain"** (3:49, R) When we hear a song like "Pain," we can't help but wonder if the lyricist, Bernie Taupin in this case, has experienced the type of agony he describes in the song. Because the words are dead-on, balls accurate about what pain is, and what it means (and yes, we cannot help but insert a *My Cousin Vinny* reference when it is necessary to do so). We all know pain; some of us know excruciating pain. Ultimately, we do know the underlying context of "Pain": Bernie wrote it while his father was dying of cancer. The lyrics are presented as a dialogue between a reporter and the amorphous entity, Pain. "What's your plan?" the reporter asks. "My plan is pain," Pain replies. "When will you leave?" the reporter asks. "I'll never go away," Pain replies. Musically, this sounds like a Rolling Stones song. The guitar riffs are clearly drawn from the Stones and the rocking rhythm belies the seriousness of the lyrics. Elton has done this ironic musical interpretation of some of Bernie's darker lyrics before, an example being "Poor Cow" from *Reg Strikes Back*. It pretty much always works.

6. **"Belfast"** (6:29, B) This is an orchestral ballad about the ceaseless fighting and bloodshed in Belfast, Ireland. The lyrics paint a

dark, dispirited picture of life in a de facto war zone. "Rocks and tanks go hand in hand with madness." It's a bleak song with an uplifting assurance at the end that "No bloody boots or crucifix can ever hope to split this emerald island…I never saw a braver place, Belfast."

7. **"Latitude"** (3:34, B) This song sounds like a folk ballad that someone—say Podrick (or Ed Sheeran, with or without eyelids)—might sing on a *Games of Thrones* episode. It's about the disruption caused by distance and a reminder that it "gets to us all." The narrative is set in London, and the narrator tells us it is his "time to write" and "your time to call." The notion of "latitude" is used as a direct representation of the distance between people, although the deeper subtext referring to emotional distance is quite obvious. It's in the key of G and is a bit ordinary in its musical structure. (Note: We apologize for the *GOT* references to those who don't know the show. We couldn't resist.)

8. **"Please"** (3:52, R) This song is a country-flavored rocker about a troubled relationship. The singer asks "please, please, please, oh please, let me grow old with you." But we learn later that he is concerned about "how many more times can we lay on the line, watching our love hang by a thread?" The song's also got a Beatles feel to it. "Please" was the fourth and final single released from *Made in England*.

9. **"Man"** (5:16, B) This is a powerful ballad about self-empowerment and having a true sense of your own identity. Self-definition permeates the lyrics, shifting from the macro—"Man stands in all his glory"—to the micro—"I'm a man…." As he always achieves with these types of ballads, Elton does a superb job with the vocal of this song. The gospel-like chorus and ending add a real depth of feeling. This song should be more popular among fans. From what we can tell, Elton has never performed this song in concert. Pity.

10. **"Lies"** (4:25, R) The narrator tells us just about everything that he, and other people, lie about. The list is long. It includes lying about who they love; lying about the truth; lying to save their lives; lying about their youth, their age, and beauty; lying about the night before; lying in the face of death; lying about their fame, about their name; and even lying for a drug or two. After this motley recitation of venality and deception, the narrator tells us, "I've lied about most everything, but I've never lied to you." What's significant about "Lies" is Bernie Taupin's shout-out to Tennessee Williams, and Williams's plays *A Streetcar Named Desire* and *Sweet Bird of Youth*. Bernie is obviously a Tennessee Williams fan and tells us "I could be great like Tennessee Williams if I could only hear something that sounds like the truth." This is a terrific song that Elton has rarely performed in concert. The last time seems to be on his 1995 tour when he performed it in Norway, France, and elsewhere.

11. **"Blessed"** (5:01, B) This is one of Elton and Bernie's loveliest and most touching ballads and was the third single released from *Made in England*. Bernie had remarried and was ready to have a child when he wrote these lyrics. "Hey you, you're a child in my head," he begins. He then talks to his unborn child and assures him or her they'll be blessed. A perfect grace note is the nod to "Your Song" with the lyric, "Your eyes might be green, or the bluest that I've ever seen." Many fans have said that this is their favorite "I love my child" song and many talk about singing it to their baby. Elton obviously likes this song. He performed it live consistently from 1995 through 2010. The video was directed by David and Raphaël Vital-Durand and is kind of weird. Elton's head is in an orb that floats through different worlds and landscapes.

BEST SONG: TIE: "Believe" and "Blessed"

This is a typical 2019 Elton John set list. These are the songs he played at the Amway Center in Orlando, Florida, on Monday, March 18, 2019. One hell of a show, eh?

1. "Bennie and the Jets"
2. "All the Girls Love Alice"
3. "I Guess That's Why They Call It the Blues"
4. "Border Song"
5. "Tiny Dancer"
6. "Philadelphia Freedom"
7. "Indian Sunset"
8. "Rocket Man (I Think It's Gonna Be a Long, Long Time)"
9. "Take Me to the Pilot"
10. "Someone Saved My Life Tonight"
11. "Levon"
12. "Candle in the Wind"
13. "Funeral for a Friend/Love Lies Bleeding"
14. "Burn Down the Mission"
15. "Daniel"
16. "Believe"
17. "Sad Songs (Say So Much)"
18. "Don't Let the Sun Go Down on Me"
19. "The Bitch Is Back"
20. "I'm Still Standing"
21. "Crocodile Rock"
22. "Saturday Night's Alright (for Fighting)"

Encore

23. "Your Song"
24. "Goodbye Yellow Brick Road"

25. *The Big Picture* (1997)

The Big Picture was released on September 22, 1997, and produced four singles. The album reached Number 9 on the US Billboard 200 chart and Number 3 on the UK Official Albums Chart. It was certified Platinum in the US by the Recording Industry Association of America (RIAA). *Entertainment Weekly* gave it a C; the *Los Angeles Times* said "the album lacks the character, the freshness, and the moody theatricality that you find in the songwriting team's classic early work." *Rolling Stone* said, "John's latest album is state-of-the-artist pop, heavy on the grand balladry, low on raw stress. It is the work of a man—two men, really, including lyricist Bernie Taupin—content in the knowledge that passing fashion and fickle celebrity are no match for a well-crafted love song."

1. **"Long Way from Happiness"** (4:47, B) *The Big Picture* starts off with this beautiful ballad about a guy who's in love with someone who is apparently in the friend zone. But he's right there, watching out for her, "looking out for you all the time." There's an interesting lyrical nuance where he tells her she's a long way from happiness, but then also acknowledges "*we're* a long way from happiness." Wishful thinking about their ultimate reuniting? There is some lovely piano and acoustic guitar in this song. Elton only performed this song in concert a few times in 1997.

2. **"Live Like Horses"** (5:02, B) This stunning ballad was the first single released from *The Big Picture* and it truly was a milestone release for Elton. The album version was Elton performing the song solo. The single, however, was a duet with the legendary tenor Luciano Pavarotti, accompanied by a moody video shot in black and white by Peter Demetris in Austria. Lyrically, the song is about the death of Bernie Taupin's father and how life goes on. It's a very poetic lyric and Elton's music serves it well. Elton performed this song in concert a couple of dozen times between 1994 and 1999, which is interesting because the *The Big Picture* album didn't come out until 1997. There is an explanation: "Live Like Horses" was originally intended for the *Made in England* album (which came out in 1995), but there wasn't the

opportunity to include it. So Elton had the song in his arsenal from 1994.

3. **"The End Will Come"** (4:53, B) The end of *what* will come? Our love, of course. This Beatles-esque ballad is about the inevitable end of love. Yes, it is a rather pessimistic view of relationships. It starts off optimistically: "And when we start we say forever, we say, 'We care, we need, we feel.'" But it isn't long (still in the first verse, actually) before "We just accept that love must die." Musically, this song has the appeal of some of Elton's best ballads.

4. **"If the River Can Bend"** (5:23, R) This was the fourth single released from *The Big Picture* and it's a radio-friendly rocker complete with searing guitar and a gospel choir. It's about a search for self, for God, for peace and, early on in the song we're told, "I don't know where we go, I sure feel there's something out there." A "great awakening" and a "new beginning" are heralded, and the metaphor of the title bespeaks optimism. Rivers can and do bend, and the seeker tells us that if said river can bend, then "I'll find you waiting." Who will be waiting? God? One's true self? True love? This song is a reflective discussion of the search for faith and enlightenment with a great musical underpinning. Elton performed this in concert several dozen times in 1998, including a few times with Billy Joel.

5. **"Love's Got a Lot to Answer For"** (5:02, B) Elton John knows how to write ballads. He may be the single singer/songwriter who has consistently written a slew of lovely piano ballads throughout his career. And here's an excellent test for whether or not a ballad is pure unto itself: can a piano player/singer sit down at the keyboard and perform the song and not lose any

Elton and Billy: The "Face to Face" Concerts

Elton John and Billy Joel mounted very successful tandem concerts in 1994, 1995, 1998, 2001, 2002, 2003, 2009, and 2010. Their playlists consisted of the two of them performing Elton John songs and Billy Joel songs together. The crowds went wild.

of the power of the original full-band release? Sure, "Let It Be" has guitar, drums, harmonies, etc., but a singer and a piano can communicate to the listener the power and beauty of the song without John, George, or Ringo. Not all ballads are like that. Some need the band. "Love's Got a Lot to Answer For" passes the test. Lyrically, the song is about yet another lover's betrayal. "I guess I must have been dreaming to think that I believed in you at all." The narrator describes he and his lover as "two hearts gone to war." Ultimately, he demands answers from the personified "love," which, of course, aren't forthcoming.

6. **"Something About the Way You Look Tonight"** (5:13, B) This was the second single released off *The Big Picture*, and it hit Number 1 on the Billboard Adult Contemporary chart. It's a classic love song of the kind that Elton and Bernie have done so well over the years. The lyrics are blatant ("You light up every second of the day") and the music makes good use of "The Canon" for certain passages. To us, it's the kind of song that still makes the goosebumps rise, even on repeated listening. *Billboard* described the song as "a grandly executed ballad that washes John's larger-than-life performance in cinematic strings and whooping, choir-styled backing vocals." That sounds about right, doesn't it? The video for this song—one of Elton's best—has supermodels in it, particularly Kate Moss and Sophie Dahl. Elton has performed this song almost 150 times in concert between 1997 and 2016, and it's been covered by artists as wide-ranging as One Direction and Engelbert Humperdinck.

7. **"The Big Picture"** (3:45, B) This beautiful ballad (with a rocking middle) has a very post-Beatles-Paul McCartney feel to it. It's got a great, creative melody, and the lyrics are about a guy who really wants to be part of the "big picture" of the woman he loves but is concerned she considers him just a friend. He even asks her, "Have I got a future in the big picture?" This would have made a very interesting release as a single from the album (it's the title track, after all) but it ended up remaining a deep cut that many fans truly love.

8. **"Recover Your Soul"** (5:18, B) This was the third single released from *The Big Picture*. It reached Number 5 on the Billboard Adult Contemporary chart. This is a classic Elton ballad and it bespeaks the Elton of "Daniel," "Candle in the Wind," and even "Border Song." The verses use the beloved "Canon" chord progression and it's got a catchy chorus that's perfect for the radio and for singing along. Lyrically, the narrator encourages someone who has lost in love to recover their soul, and to find the path to healing. "Love was a fire but it stopped burning," but so what? "Release, relax, let go." This is a great song, and we wonder what would have happened if it had been the first single from the album.

9. **"January"** (4:02, R) "January is the month that cares," we're told in this rocking love song. It's a pleasant-enough song, but a bit by-the-Elton-numbers. There doesn't seem to be a record of him ever performing "January" live, but he may have slipped it in during a set at some point.

10. **"I Can't Steer My Heart Clear of You"** (4:10, B) This is a musically complex ballad with an equally sophisticated set of lyrics. Sometimes, as in the case of this song, Bernie Taupin's lyrics push Elton to some of his most intricate songwriting. Lyrically, the song is about unrequited love, using the metaphors of weather, storms, rough seas, and the stars. It seems that Elton hasn't played this live, and it remains a lesser-known deep cut, but one worth seeking out.

11. **"Wicked Dreams"** (4:39, R) Elton and Bernie conclude *The Big Picture* with an all-out rocker in the

> In 2016, a UK *Guardian* journalist visited Elton's home and was surprised that there were no pianos in the house. Elton explained: "I play 107 shows a year, why am I going to go home and play the fucking piano?... God, I couldn't think of anything worse. I have leisure, and I have work. And I do enough work. When I get home, the last thing I want to do is play the piano."

key of C. The song has a killer bass, drum, and guitar foundation, and the song has some "Saturday Night's Alright (for Fighting)"-esque riffs throughout. True to form, though, the musical break in the middle of the song is Elton waling away on the 88s. Lyrically, the song is about a guy dreaming of his one true love. She may or may not be in attendance in reality, but he loves her in his wicked dream. This is a great rocker in Elton's classic style.

BEST SONG: "Live Like Horses"

26. *Songs from the West Coast* (2001)

Songs from the West Coast, which many fans and critics praised as a return to the "Classic Elton" sound, was released on October 1, 2001 (a little over two weeks after the tragedy of 9/11, not that that has anything to do with it. It's just a reminder of what the culture was like at the time.). *Rolling Stone* gave the album four out of five stars and wrote, "John can't always send his music soaring the way it used to, but its spirit and ambition have finally come back home." The album produced three singles. *AllMusic.com* wrote, "[T]his is the richest, best record he's released in a long time, an album where it feels like a hit single is secondary to the sheer pleasure of craft, whether it's crafting a song or an album.... His songwriting hasn't been this diverse or consistent since the early '80s, and he hasn't made a record better than this in years. No, *Songs from the West Coast* won't make you forget *Tumbleweed Connection*, but it often recalls those peaks, which, frankly, is enough." *Songs from the West Coast* reached Number 6 on the Billboard Adult Contemporary chart and was certified Gold by the RIAA. This album was welcomed by fans and critics alike for Elton's return to his piano-based roots.

1. **"The Emperor's New Clothes"** (4:28, R) What are the "emperor's new clothes"? They're no clothes at all. The title of this song comes from a short story written by Hans Christian Andersen in 1837, which is about a vain and pompous emperor who demands new clothes be made for him. His tailors don't make *any* garments for him, but tell him that they did, but that they're invisible to anyone who is unsuited for their job, or just plain stupid. Not wanting to appear as either, the emperor walks among his subjects naked, and no one will tell him he's not wearing anything for fear of appearing stupid. A little kid finally blurts out, "But he isn't wearing anything at all!" The song title phrase has become an idiom and euphemism suggesting pompous arrogance and pretentiousness. If someone is said to be wearing the "emperor's new clothes," they are presumed to be a delusional narcissist who believes what they want to believe, regardless of empirical reality. In this song, it's Elton and Bernie who, in the early days of their career, enduring a period of poverty, holes in their shoes, and overdue rent, Elton sings, "We refused to admit that we wore

this disguise, every inch of us growing like Pinocchio's nose, as we walked around in the emperor's new clothes." This is a terrific song that would have easily felt at home on *Madman Across the Water* or *Tumbleweed Connection*. It's no wonder *Songs from the West Coast* is a fan favorite. Elton performed "The Emperor's New Clothes" in concert about a dozen times in 2009 and 2010.

2. **"Dark Diamond"** (4:26, R) This irresistible, shuffling, reggae-esque rocker is classic Elton. Plus, it's got a timeless and legendary musician onboard: none other than Stevie Wonder plays harmonica and clavinet on the track. Lyrically it's about perseverance and, of course, having your heart broken. This would have made for an interesting single release. Elton doesn't seem to have performed this in concert. (Without Stevie, how could he have, right?)

3. **"Look Ma, No Hands"** (4:22, R) This is another great song from the west coast (the album was mixed in Hollywood, California). It's got a Bob Dylan feel to it and Elton has never sounded better. Once again, he harkens back to the glory days of *Tumbleweed Connection* with the writing and sound of the track. The lyrics are rich with reference as well. "Top of the world, ma!" is from the 1949 James Cagney film *White Heat*. Plus, Bernie's lyrics reference Roswell and the purported UFO crash of 1947, as well as Mandeville, Louisiana, Philadelphia, New Orleans, and the Midas touch. This is a fantastic track from the album.

4. **"American Triangle"** (4:49, B) This song is about Matthew Shepard, the twenty-one-year-old who was tortured and murdered in 1998 for being gay. Several lines of the song refer specifically to Shepard, particularly "I've seen a scarecrow wrapped in wire, left to die on a high ridge fence," which was drawn from a comment made by a cyclist who first discovered Shephard's body and initially thought it was a scarecrow. Shepard was in a coma and never regained consciousness. He died six days after the attack, on October 12, 1998. Musically, this is one of Elton's most heartbreaking songs (and includes

background vocals by Rufus Wainwright). Bernie's lyrics paint a picture of the intolerance and hatred some people manifest toward gay people, and Elton's melody, especially the "cold, cold wind" section, is emotionally devastating. Wyoming, Shephard's home state and the site of his torture and murder, does not fare well in this song. Elton performed "American Triangle," perhaps the most important song he and Bernie have ever written, many times in concert from 2000 to 2002, and then again in 2009, 2010, and 2011.

5. **"Original Sin"** (4:49, B) This lovely, mellow ballad with a great chorus was the third single released from the album. Is it about unrequited love? Or star worship? The official video has Elton as a photographer on prom night and stars Elizabeth Taylor and Mandy Moore. Mandy Moore is the kid sister of the prom girl and we immediately know that she's a huge Elton John fan. She has Elton John posters and pictures up in her room and is listening to an Elton John record when she is magically transported by Glinda the Good Witch through the *Goodbye Yellow Brick Road* poster to an Elton John concert in the seventies, where she's received like she's a pop star herself. Actors play doppelgängers of celebrities, including Bette Midler and Sonny and Cher, and a guy who is supposed to be Elton gives her a flower from the stage. And then, back in her bedroom, the record ends. So who or what's the original sin of the title? In the video, it's apparently Elton himself. But the lyrics leave lots of room for interpretation. Elton has performed "Original Sin" in concert many times between 2001 and 2004, and then again in 2009.

6. **"Birds"** (3:51, R) A metaphorical rocker that sounds like something from the early seventies. It's got the great line, "How come birds don't fall from the sky when they die?" and the lyrics then explain that they always find a quiet place to hide to die. The message of the song is then made clear with the line, "Like birds I need a quiet place to hide." It's basically a song about self-knowledge and insecurity, belied by a rocking tune you can tap

your foot to. Elton performed this song more than a dozen times in concert in 2001.

7. **"I Want Love"** (4:35, B) This is one of Elton's best ballads, and a song that harkens back to the sounds of many tracks from his glory days in the seventies—not to mention the obvious and blatant Beatles influences throughout the track. (There are moments where it actually sounds like a Beatles song, complete with John Lennon-like piano chords and George Harrison-like slide guitar. In this song, Elton nods to the best.) The message is absolutely in your face, from the title through the lyrics: this guy wants love. He wants love on his "own terms" and acknowledges he has a lot of "baggage" that he carries around, preventing him from achieving that goal. In a May 26, 2019, essay by Elton in the UK *Guardian*, he said, "'I Want Love' is a song Bernie wrote, I think, about himself: a middle-aged man with a few divorces, wondering if he's ever going to fall in love again." It's a great song, and was rightly released as the first single from the album. There was, of course, an accompanying music video that some feel could have been better than it was. The entire video, shot in one continuous shot by Sam Taylor-Wood, consists of Robert Downey Jr. walking through the empty Greystone Mansion in Beverly Hills, California, lip-synching to the song (they shot sixteen takes and used the last one). Elton knew how good this song was and has played it solo over two hundred times in concert between 2001 and 2017, as well as more than sixty performances of the song with Billy Joel. "I Want Love" reached Number 6 on the Billboard Adult Contemporary chart, and it got Elton nominated for a Grammy in 2002 for Best Male Pop Vocal Performance. (John Mayer won for "Your Body Is A Wonderland." We think Elton deserved it.)

8. **"The Wasteland"** (4:21, R) This is an ass-kicking, bluesy rock song that illustrates quite powerfully Elton's education in all things rock and blues. It begins with a classic blues riff and moves into a fantastic hybrid song that utilizes blues structure combined with Elton's melodic turns and a rock momentum.

"I Want Love" makes an incredibly powerful appearance in the movie *Rocketman* when, early on in the movie, eleven-year-old Elton and his whole family sing "I Want Love" (yes, years before it was written, but that doesn't matter—if you've seen the movie, you know what we mean) in Elton's childhood home. The lyrics are meaningful to all of them, who each lack any meaningful love or connection between them. As we note in our review of the movie in this volume, *Rocketman* is a movie musical that would have worked just as well on Broadway and the "I Want Love" moment is a perfect example of such a Broadway-esque moment.

Elton and Bernie acknowledge the roots of this song with the lines, "Come on Robert Johnson, though we're worlds apart, you and I know what it's like with the devil in our heart." They're referencing the legend that country-blues guitarist Robert Johnson sold his soul to the Devil at a crossroads in exchange for his musical talent (Johnson never talked about the story, and the Devil had no comment). The legendary Billy Preston plays organ on this tune. Elton has performed this song solo dozens of times in concert, and also did it when he toured with Billy Joel, totaling close to a hundred live performances. He obviously likes this song. So do we.

9. **"Ballad of the Boy in the Red Shoes"** (4:52, B) This is a song about AIDS. It's a classic Elton ballad that would have fit nicely on the *Madman Across the Water* album. Elton has performed this song many times in concert and commonly introduces it by telling the audience that the title character and narrator is a dancer who had AIDS. The lyrics are touching and painful—"Gonna miss the sunlight when I lose my eyesight"—and they are also scathing toward the American administration in power at the time of the beginnings of the AIDS crisis. Ronald Reagan is "that old man who wouldn't listen" and who "was ignorant." At the end, the singer tells us "Take my red shoes, I can't wear them anymore," evoking Bob Dylan's line "put these guns in the ground, I can't shoot them

anymore" from his classic ballad "Knocking on Heaven's Door." Like "American Triangle," this song is another example of the work Elton does with his Elton John AIDS Foundation.

10. **"Love Her Like Me"** (3:58, R) A rich guy has married an ex of the narrator, and this song is a message to the guy that no matter what he gives her, he'll never "love her like me." You can "make her change her name," he tells him, "you and your old money," but you'll never love her like me. The song has a nice swing to it and a great chorus with some unusual instruments being used throughout the song. What is that opening buzz-like instrument, anyway? Is it a Mellotron? A bouzouki? A dobro? This eclectic instrumentation makes for an interesting, enjoyable song—even though the theme is one of lost love and, possibly, regret. Elton doesn't usually perform this song in concert.

11. **"Mansfield"** (4:56, B) Bernie Taupin has a way of recapturing moments of a life, of a love affair, of a tragedy, of a "paradise lost," flawlessly with his lyrics. "Mansfield" is one of those songs. As he tells us in the song, "Sometimes the magic of the past is all we've got." The song is about two "old friends" who end up in a "romantic novel" of their own. And it all takes place "in that little house on Mansfield." The song is a pretty ballad that Elton only performed a few times live in 2001.

12. **"This Train Don't Stop There Anymore"** (4:39, B) This song, an Elton John classic, was the second single released from *Songs from the West Coast*, and Elton performed it in concert more than a hundred times from 2001 through 2004. The piano opening reminds us of "Goodbye Yellow Brick Road," and the first verse seems to be Bernie speaking: "The sentimental things I write never meant that much to me." And the chorus seems to be Elton contemplating his career path, or perhaps the realization that the end was closer than the beginning: "I used to be the main express...but this train don't stop there anymore." Some have suggested it's about Elton giving up a cocaine habit. Whether or not that's actually 100 percent true, the lyrics can

easily be interpreted to be solely about an artist reflecting back on his career, complete with memories and regrets. It's a melancholy ballad that we can imagine was written at a bad time in an artist's life. The video for this song starred a convincing Justin Timberlake as a young Elton John. The theme of the video is one of what Tony Soprano called the life of the "sad clown." Elton is swarmed by sycophants and hangers-on, and yet for all the pomp of his feather boas and striped suit, he walks the final corridor to the stage alone. The video is very effective, and was directed by David LaChapelle.

BEST SONG: "American Triangle"

27. *Peachtree Road* (2004)

This album—what some fans call the "ballad album"—was released on November 9, 2004, and was named after a street in Atlanta, Georgia, where one of Elton's homes is located. *Peachtree Road* was certified Gold by the Recording Industry Association of America (RIAA) in December 2004, barely a month after its release. Elton was sole producer on the record and Nigel Olsson (who, with Dee Murray, was dismissed from Elton's band after *Captain Fantastic and the Brown Dirt Cowboy*) played drums on all tracks, and was now, again, a permanent member of Elton's band. The album, which garnered mostly positive reviews, also featured the horn section from Chicago, James Pankow, Lee Loughnane, and Walter Parazaider, as well as gospel vocalist Adam McKnight. This is a great album that stands as one of Elton and Bernie's best.

1. **"Weight of the World"** (3:58, B) This contemplative ballad in G is one of Elton and Bernie's finest. It's got a classic "Elton" sound and, as the opening track of *Peachtree Road*, it sets the stage for the fine songs to follow. Thematically, the lyrics speak to an acknowledgment that a new stage of life is beginning, perhaps exemplified by the line, "These days I'm happy to see a sunset instead of a line." The narrator tells us he's "happy to play with the weight of the world off [his] back." This is an evocative, deeply felt song with great lyrics. Elton performed this in concert four dozen times or so between 2004 and 2010.

2. **"Porch Swing in Tupelo"** (4:38, B) This is another beautiful ballad from this album, and even though it begins with the narrator musing about the old South and just spending time swinging on a porch swing in Tupelo, it's ultimately about Elvis. Elvis was born in Tupelo and appears in the final verse as a "truck drivin' boy" with a "grease monkey look and a rock 'n' roll voice." Turns out Elvis sat in that swing in Tupelo "singin' 'ah, praise to god,' through poverty's tears." Lovely song with haunting lyrics. Elton performed this more than forty times in concert in 2004 and 2005.

3. **"Answer in the Sky"** (4:03, R) This song uses the practice of looking into the *sky* and possibly seeing celestial "light" as a metaphor for the contemplative practice of looking into *yourself* and possibly seeing...God? Your true self? It's a laid-back rocker with some interesting keyboard voicings by Elton. The ultimate message is that we all need something to believe in and we should all hope that "good can still control the hearts of men," with "good" standing in for "love." This is essentially an "All You Need Is Love" song from Elton and Bernie (even though that sentiment, of course, had been stated before). Elton performed this song in concert close to eighty times in 2004 and 2005.

4. **"Turn the Lights Out When You Leave"** (5:02, B) This countrified ballad is yet another breakup song with a great chorus. His woman—who "may look pretty in that lacy little dress"—is leaving him, and he wants her to know that he "ain't gonna die" and he "ain't gonna cry." And then he asks her to turn the lights out when she leaves. This is a very appealing song, especially upon repeat listens. Elton performed this song in concert close to eighty times in 2004 and 2005.

5. **"My Elusive Drug"** (4:12, B) This is a truly great Elton ballad. It's amazing how Elton can look at a set of Bernie's lyrics and intuitively know what's a ballad and what's a rocker. This song, about a guy who gets clean and sober and trades his addictions for *her*, is a classic. And Elton again impresses with his musical skills, moving from unlikely chord to unlikely chord with ease, and always shaping the melody to the changes. This is an all-time great song and should be better known. Elton played it in concert three dozen times in 2004 and 2005, but that was it.

6. **"They Call Her the Cat"** (4:27, R) This honky tonk rocker starts off generic and typical, but the second half of the verses suddenly definitively sound like an Elton song, if that makes any sense. This song is about a transsexual club performer who they call the cat, and who was "just plain mister, once" and a "little boy lost in the land of the free." She had a sex change and now "she's so fine

that the water line don't separate hot and cold." The cat's name was Billy, and now "Billy got a kitty." Fun song. Elton performed this song live around eighty times from 2004 through 2006.

7. **"Freaks in Love"** (4:32, B) Another great *Peachtree Road* ballad, and this one has real soul. We can easily imagine the Four Tops or the Temptations, or even Earth, Wind & Fire doing this song. This song is beloved by a lot of fans, and Elton performed it live in concert almost forty times in 2004 and 2005. Hold up those lighters and go ahead and sway to the music.

8. **"All That I'm Allowed (I'm Thankful)"**(4:52, B) This is a heartfelt ballad with one of Elton's catchiest, most memorable choruses. The song and the chorus sound fresh and appealing today, almost two decades after the song was written. It's essentially a "gratitude anthem," with lines like "I've got all that I'm allowed, it'll do for me, I'm grateful" and "I see hope in every cloud." This is another stellar song from this album. Elton performed it in concert close to sixty times from 2004 through 2006.

9. **"I Stop and I Breathe"** (3:39, B) This is a ballad extraordinaire that illustrates quite effectively how Elton's songwriting is unquestionably (at times) quite musically sophisticated. The chord changes in this song are complex and stylish, and he moves gracefully in and out of different keys as well. Lyrically it's a love song that tells the story of a couple that had a fight but made their way through it and survived: "We are still alright. We took it on the chin." The narrator stops and breathes because "you wanted me." This song is a superb musical achievement, but it seems that Elton has yet to perform it live.

10. **"Too Many Tears"** (4:14, R) This song is about the assassinations of John F. Kennedy and Martin Luther King Jr., and it includes references to man landing on the moon and, possibly, Gandhi ("The barefoot man lived a simple life…"). The message is that there have been too many tears cried because of tragedies that affected everyone and that we should just work for peace and

brotherhood. Musically, it's a lesser effort, considering the caliber of songwriting on the rest of this album. It sounds like it could have been on *Elton John*, and Elton's songwriting had evolved from there by this point in his career. It seems Elton has never performed this in concert.

11. **"It's Getting Dark in Here"** (3:50, B) This is an archetypal Elton John ballad, but this one is not about a breakup, a love affair, or any type of relationship, except for the relationship between the narrator and his sanity. This song is about paranoia and depression. The title "It's Getting Dark in Here" is a metaphor for the bleak state of mind he's being consumed by. He's afraid of his shadow, and of strangers on the street, and feels that "the world's so ugly" and "rooms are spooky." Imagistically, Bernie's lyrics nail the state of mind where one feels "close to tears" and "sometimes I feel I'm on fire." The song is pretty, but doesn't end positively. How can it when one of the last lines is "the sun's always setting on my life"? Whoever the narrator was talking to in "Don't Let the Sun Go Down on Me" isn't listening now, is the message of this somber song. There's no record of Elton performing this one live. It would make an interesting two-song set with the aforementioned "Don't Let the Sun Go Down on Me."

12. **"I Can't Keep This from You"** (4:34, B) There's a reason *Peachtree Road* is known as the "ballad album" among some fans. It's because there are a lot of ballads on it, and the record concludes with this lovely track. (The fact that it is, indeed, an album of mostly ballads is the reason one of your co-authors ranks this in his top ten Elton favorite albums. Hint: It's Steve.) This song is about a guy who decides he has to tell the woman he loves that he loves her. It's a beautiful love song, and Elton performed it in concert a few times in 2004 upon the release of the album. Appropriately, it has musical callbacks to "Don't Let the Sun Go Down on Me" in certain lines.

BEST SONG: TIE: "It's Getting Dark in Here" and "I Can't Keep This from You"

28. *The Captain & the Kid* (2006)

This studio album, Elton's twenty-eighth, was released on September 18, 2006, and serves as a sequel of sorts to *Captain Fantastic and the Brown Dirt Cowboy*. It reached Number 18 on the US Billboard 200 chart and Number 7 on the US Rock Albums chart. There was no actual single released from the album. The intent was to have it received and perceived as a single work, a concept album. They did, however, release "The Bridge" as a song for radio play only. This album was well-received, and *Entertainment Weekly* called it "Elton's best album in decades."

1. **"Postcards from Richard Nixon"** (5:15, R) This song, for all its implied meaning as suggested from a strict read of the title, is a reminiscence, specifically of the years when Elton and Bernie were new to America. It opens with Richard Nixon welcoming the boys, and Bernie describes them as "twin spirits soaking up a dream, fuel to feed the press machine." They were here to conquer America. And they did. Bernie's lyrics play with irony, especially in the chorus when we're told that Nixon "sent so many overseas," but apparently wanted Elton and Bernie to serve as a bit of a distraction from the negative press about the Vietnam War: "A small diversion caused by two, pale kids come to play." Musically, the opening is Elton and the piano, and then the drums kick in, pumping up this melodic rocker. Elton performed this song a couple of dozen times during his fall 2006 tour.

2. **"Just Like Noah's Ark"** (5:33, R) This is a great traditional Stones-influenced rock 'n' roll song, spiced up with Elton-esque chord changes. The song is about the music business, and they pull no punches: "Pretty girls and boys in drag"; "Italian promotion men chomping a big cigar"; "Radio boss dipping his nose in a little white packet", etc. Elton assures us, though, that "we're not as dumb as we might look," thus proclaiming dominance over the sleazier, more corrupt aspects of the business. At the end of the song, Elton's dog Arthur barks in time to the music. Who's a good boy? Elton only performed this song live five times or so during his fall 2006 tour.

3. **"Wouldn't Have You Any Other Way (NYC)"** (4:38, B) This is a nostalgic ballad about New York City, summed up by the line, "This city's got a thing about it, don't try to understand it." Images of New York abound: Grand Central, skaters, black limos, taxis, the subway, Joey Gallo, Studio 54. It's a nice-enough song, but a little less memorable than it could have been considering the subject. Elton only performed this song live a few times during his fall 2006 tour.

4. **"Tinderbox"** (4:25, B) This is a memorable song from this album. Bernie Taupin's lyrics reminisce about his and Elton's personal and creative relationship over the years. It's very honest in its depiction of interpersonal tensions, especially with lines like, "We've been living in a tinderbox, and two sparks can set the whole thing off," and "Pressure's gonna cook us if we don't unlock it, gun's going off if we don't uncock it." Damn, boys. Were things really that fraught at times? Based on this lovely ballad (which makes creative use of "The Canon"), we'll take your word for it. Elton performed this song a couple of dozen times during his fall 2006 tour.

5. **"And the House Fell Down"** (4:48, R) The "house" is Bernie's life because of a cocaine addiction, and it also describes his and Elton's career, because of Elton's own addictions and him not working with Bernie. This song is a terrific rocker that paints a really dark picture of addiction and collapse. Bernie pulls no punches: "With a rolled up note I'm hovering on that line, three days on a diet of cocaine and wine, and a little weed just to level me sometime." And, "When you're high as this you think you know it all, when you're this deep in there's no place else to fall." Lots of minor chords, which is, y'know, fitting. Apparently, Elton hasn't performed this song live in concert.

6. **"Blues Never Fade Away"** (4:45, B) This is a touching ballad about Ryan White, John Lennon, and AIDS and OD victims. The theme is that the "blues" (the pain of loss) never goes away. This song was a staple during his 2006 tour, and he resurrected it a few times during performances in 2009.

7. **"The Bridge"** (3:38, B) Is this "Your Song 2.0"? This was the only song from the album released as a radio single. The opening, and parts of the song, harken back to the piano intro and other parts of "Your Song." It's primarily Elton and his piano, but there is a lovely interlude which consists of harmonies by the band members and Elton's lyrical piano playing. The song, as Elton has said, can "apply to anyone," and it's about making a decision to cross the metaphorical "bridge" separating progress and the void. It's a self-empowerment anthem: "And every one of us has to face that day, do you cross the bridge or do you fade away?" We're told that the bridge is telling us "come and risk it all or die trying." Elton performed this song live in concert around sixty times from 2006 through 2008.

8. **"I Must Have Lost It on the Wind"** (3:53, R) This is a countrified, slow-paced rocker about past loves, but, we're told, "I'm no longer counting, I'm not keeping score." This is one more Elton/Bernie song about failed relationships, in a sense. Especially when the last verse tells us "[I] swore the heart I was reeling in was perfect at the time, you couldn't tell me I was wrong, you couldn't tell me anything…." It seems Elton only performed this song live a couple of times in 2006. Also, the first episode of season eleven of *Grey's Anatomy* in 2014 was titled "I Must Have Lost It on the Wind." The show always titled episodes with a song title and have used, in addition to this Elton track, titles from the Beatles, REM, Billy Joel, Simon & Garfunkel, Cyndi Lauper, and others.

9. **"Old '67"** (4:01, B) This is a nostalgic ballad that reminisces about Elton and Bernie's life together back in old 1967. The song and conversation take place in the south of France, where the two old friends talk about what it was like back in the day. "What a time of innocence, what a time we've lost," Elton sings, and then toasts, "Here's to old '67 and an older me and you." Musically, it's a traditional Elton ballad with glorious chord changes and a beautiful melody. It would have fit well on *Tumbleweed Connection* or even *Honky Château*. He performed this song several times during his 2006 tour.

10. **"The Captain and the Kid"** (5:03, R) This is another autobiographical song that wraps up the connection between this album and *Captain Fantastic and the Brown Dirt Cowboy*, confirming its role as a sequel or follow-up to that classic record. The lyrics were written by Bernie The Kid, but from Captain Elton's point of view; the first couple of verses, though, are Bernie talking about himself. Sometimes it's a tad blatant: "We stuck around for the battle, waiting for a plan to turn you into the brown dirt cowboy, and me into a rocket man…" The lyrics juxtapose the differences between Bernie and Elton, using shoes, for example as an image: "six-inch heels" and "old cowboy boots." Musically, the song has a country influence, and ends suddenly, perhaps leaving the door open for more on the John-Taupin relationship? Elton performed this song in concert a couple of dozen times in 2006.

BEST SONG: "The Bridge"

29. *The Diving Board* (2013)

This album, released on September 13, 2013, is what Elton has called the "most piano-oriented album of my career." The UK *Guardian* loved this superb album, calling it "a lovely union of craftsmanship and artistry." They cite both the Oscar Wilde and Blind Tom songs as especially notable, and say, "John gives each song the space it deserves, ruminating in a baritone that evokes golden autumn light. He also revels in playing his piano…." Reviews were generally positive for this album and it is, as some critics noted, a return to form. *American Songwriter* wrote, "*The Diving Board* proves that Elton John is on the right musical path once again, sounding so energized by the familiar trappings that a career renaissance, which seemed a long shot a few years back, now seems thrillingly possible." The album produced three singles.

1. **"Oceans Away"** (3:58, B) This stunning piano/vocal ballad opens *The Diving Board* with a serious message, and a tribute. The message is, cherish the old veterans for they won't be with us for long. The tribute is to Bernie Taupin's father Robert who fought in Burma and North Africa during the Second World War. Bernie Taupin (and, of course, Elton as well) has always had boundless respect and admiration for veterans, especially WWII vets. He's written about soldiers as far back as *Tumbleweed Connection*'s "Talking Old Soldiers." "Oceans Away" references overseas cemeteries where American soldiers are buried, with the powerful lyric, "Those that flew, those that fell, the ones that had to stay, beneath a little wooden cross oceans away." This is a beautiful and touching song and one of Elton and Bernie's most significant works. Elton played "Oceans Away" more than fifty times in concert in 2013 and 2014.

2. **"Oscar Wilde Gets Out"** (4:35, R) This song is an historical accounting of the life of Oscar Wilde, specifically, his being jailed for homosexual offenses, being let out, and moving to France under an assumed name. Musically, the song is a minor key rocker with a pounding drum line. The chorus has a nice string accompaniment. This is one of the more interesting entries in Elton and Bernie's songography and speaks to their elevation of

the common pop song to a work that makes an historical and pro-tolerance statement. This could have fit on *Madman Across the Water*. In September 2013, Elton played this song six times in concerts.

3. **"A Town Called Jubilee"** (4:30, R) This is a country-themed rocker that Bernie Taupin said, "is a perfect example of how a song just grows from the first line. I just got the image of a farm being sold, and all the junk lying around, and the first stanza just came to me in one thought, as it were." It's tinged with sadness as the lyrics describe the forlorn environment and the hopelessness of the farming poor. Musically, it's pleasant enough, but not anything we haven't heard Elton do many times before. To date, reportedly, he has not performed this song in concert.

4. **"The Ballad of Blind Tom"** (4:12, R) This song is about a former slave who is blind and a piano savant. The verses describe Tom and how he can play anything—"Say, that boy's a wonderment, no, the kid's a freak"—and his job is "entertaining royalty all points, east, west, and between." The chorus, however, brilliantly shifts the point of view to Blind Tom. The final verse returns the point of view to observers who talk about Tom as though he were just a performing fool, with one of them stating, "He weren't no use for slaving, wouldn't want him in my yard." This song, set as it is in the Jim Crow era, paints a dark portrait of what life was like for freed slaves and blacks in general in America during that period.

5. **"Dream #1"** (0:40, I) This is a pretty, sad solo piano interlude.

6. **"My Quicksand"** (4:47, B) This is an extraordinary ballad that Elton thinks is one of his best, if not his all-time best. He told *Rolling Stone*: "When I did 'My Quicksand,' I thought, 'That's the best track I've ever recorded, right there. Piano-wise, vocalwise, everything about it. I've never played the piano like that on a record before—the solo was improvised. It's just a very musical moment that I was very proud of on this record. I knew that I'd

moved forward—this is the kind of song that I never thought I'd be singing when I started out. My days of making pop records like *Goodbye Yellow Brick Road* and *Don't Shoot Me I'm Only the Piano Player*, they were when I was younger. I'm not that guy anymore. I'm this guy. It's the most honest record I've ever made." The solo he's referring to is a very jazzy break that also has classical influences. Lyrically, the song is about a guy moving to France and ending up in metaphorical quicksand, and that brief description does not do Bernie Taupin's lyrics justice. You have to hear it for the full experience. This is a major artistic achievement by Elton and Bernie. Interestingly, considering Elton's fondness for this song, he does not seem to have performed it live in concert.

7. **"Can't Stay Alone Tonight"** (4:48, R) This song was the third single released from *The Diving Board*. It's a rather ordinary, slow-paced rocker that is a surprising choice for a single release. It's a less-than-typical Elton John song and it's one more song about a troubled relationship. There are other songs on *The Diving Board* that probably would have garnered more attention from fans if released as a single. We would have loved to have seen "My Quicksand" released as a single, for example. We suspect *that* song would have garnered attention and more radio play. Elton only performed this song a couple of times in concert in 2013.

8. **"Voyeur"** (4:16, B) Stephen King was once described by horror writer J.N. Williamson as a "noticer." This song, "Voyeur," could be his theme song. It's a well-written—both musically and lyrically—ballad about a guy who tells us, "Yes, I see things." It's a perfect fit for this album. Elton reportedly only performed it live three times, all in 2013, the year of the record's release.

9. **"Home Again"** (5:01, B) This was the first single released from *The Diving Board*. It is a great ballad with Elton's writing and playing at his best and Bernie's lyrics at his most poignant. It's got a classic "Elton" sound and feel, and once again, we can feel

a nod to the *Madman Across the Water* vibe and know that this would have fit beautifully on that album. The song peaked at Number 14 on the Billboard Adult Contemporary chart and spent twenty weeks on the chart. It was a daring move to release a ballad as the first single from the record. Fans hoping for a rocker were probably surprised. But it was a confident move as well. Elton and Bernie knew how good "Home Again" is. Elton performed this song in concert close to seventy times in 2013 and 2014.

10. **"Take This Dirty Water"** (4:25, R) This is a gospel-y rocker about perseverance, stamina, and doing the right thing. The lyrics use "dirty water" as a metaphor for the crap that permeates lives when people turn to lies and taking risks that could result in "break[ing] some bones." It's a pleasant-enough, standard Elton rocker with roots in Americana and the blues. This was not on Elton's concert playlist.

11. **"Dream #2"** (0:43, I) A lovely, very classically inspired piano solo. We tend to forget, amidst the raucous presence of Bennie, and the Rocket Man, and Levon, that Elton is a classically-trained pianist. This short piece reminds us.

12. **"The New Fever Waltz"** (4:38, B) This evocative ballad is a song about World War I, specifically trench warfare and European imperialism. In a video interview, sitting next to producer T Bone Burnett, Bernie said he "liked to throw a curveball" into things he wrote, and that his main goal with certain songs was to make people think. It's stately and melodic and definitely one of the superior tracks on the album. Elton's songwriting is Elton at his best. Bernie's lyrics are compelling, yet historically significant. This is a great song. It seems he's only performed this song once in concert, in September 2013 at the University of Southern California.

13. **"Mexican Vacation (Kids in the Candlelight)"** (3:34, R) This was the second single released from *The Diving Board* and it's a

bluesy rocker that's kind of appealing, but isn't anything special. We think there were probably better choices for the second release from the album, but that's a purely subjective opinion. Elton performed this song less than five times in concert in 2013.

14. **"Dream #3"** (1:37, I) This is a longer piano instrumental that is quite accomplished and features drums as well as piano. It's got almost an Aaron Copland feel to it. Elton is a gifted instrumental composer and his instrumentals, though few and far between on his albums, are fantastic.

15. **"The Diving Board"** (5:59, B) This torch-song-like ballad is about the price of fame. The diving board is a metaphor for what celebrities use to dive into "a crowd," i.e. fans, appearances, etc. Elton has spoken publicly about this song, saying it's about the younger generation of stars—Lindsay Lohan and Justin Bieber were mentioned in particular—

How an Elton John Concert is Cancelled

"Dear friends in Verona, it is with regret that we have to announce that Elton's show in Verona tonight (Thursday 30th May) has been cancelled.

Yesterday Elton was battling a cold. He was struggling with his vocal warm ups before last night's Verona show and although he battled through it was touch and go if he would be able to complete the show. The cold, damp conditions at the outdoor arena also exacerbated the condition. Unfortunately, after a night's rest and consultation with a doctor today, his singing voice has gone with inflamed vocal chords and he has now been advised he shouldn't attempt to complete the show tonight. As such, it with a heavy heart that we have announce [sic] that tonight's show in Verona is cancelled. We are currently investigating rescheduling options for the show.

With medication prescribed we expect Elton to be well enough to perform in Wiesbaden on Saturday 1st June."

who Elton describes as "all these kids who are out there now not knowing what the hell is going on." He continued to comment on his own celebrity: "I was twenty-three when I got famous. And I made every mistake in the book. But whatever was going on, the drinking, the drugs, whatever, I was still making music, I kept making music and I never stopped." It's a powerful song and, as sometimes happens in the John/Taupin creative partnership, the lyrics are more impactful then the music. Surprisingly, considering it's the title track of the album, Elton seems to have not performed this song live in concert.

BEST SONG: TIE: "Oceans Away" and "My Quicksand"

30. *Wonderful Crazy Night* (2016)

This is Elton's most recent album as of this writing. It was released on February 5, 2016, and it reached Number 8 on the US Billboard 200 album chart. *Rolling Stone* liked *Wonderful Crazy Night*, giving it four out of five stars. They wrote, "There is a matured pacing and weight to the music and John's vocal performances that make this record one of his finest in its own right. *Wonderful Crazy Night* is about what happens after those loose clothes and cool drinks [referencing the title song]. The final tally: It's all worth it." *Wonderful Crazy Night* produced five singles.

1. **"Wonderful Crazy Night"** (3:13, R) Elton opens the album with an irresistible rocker that reminisces about one wonderful night from long ago when it seemed the "clocks [had] stopped" and they "grabbed that magic just because." Elton lets loose on a great piano solo in the middle, and Nigel Olsson's drums just don't stop. This track was the second single from the album (the first was "Looking Up"). Elton performed this in concert about a dozen times in 2016 and 2017.

2. **"In the Name of You"** (4:33, R) The beginning of this always reminds us of Fleetwood Mac's "Tusk" even though they're totally different songs. It's probably the foot-stomping rhythm of the opening of each song. It's a standard Elton ballad with great chord changes and a classic Elton melody. Once again, we're awed by the superb songwriting, and Bernie's lyrics are likewise lyrical and evocative. Elton has played this in concert, notably in 2016 when the album was released. This song was the fourth single released from the album.

3. **"Claw Hammer"** (4:22, R) This is a superb example of really well-written lyrics matched with a great song construction. The verses are in a minor key; the chorus is in a major key and is one of Elton's best. Not to mention that this may be one of the only (if not *the* only) pop songs with the word "ontological" in it, as in "You're an ontological soul…." (Ontology is the branch of metaphysics that deals with the nature of being.) The play-out ending has Elton doing an eerie jazzy piano solo that fits the

song perfectly. Apparently, Elton has never performed this song in concert. Maybe he'll bring it out on the *Farewell Yellow Brick Road Tour*. It's a great song.

4. **"Blue Wonderful"** (3:37, B) This is a beautiful love song that uses the beloved "Canon" for the verses (see the sidebar "The Canon" at the end of the albums section). It's about (possibly) a lost love in whose blue eyes the narrator would get lost. There's also probably a dual meaning in "blues." In addition to referencing her beautiful blue eyes, he says, "addicted as I am to the blues..." which could be a nod to the sad songs and the blues genre of music Elton and Bernie have always said they loved. This is a memorable tune and Elton performed it dozens of times live during his 2016 concerts. The music video for this song is similarly memorable. It was directed by Thibaut Duverneix and was shot in Canada. The sequence was choreographed by Victor Quijada, with Lydia Bouchard and James Gregg as the dancers. The girl ("blue wonderful" herself?) dances and flies (literally) with her lover, or does she? The video ends with her standing alone in the night under a streetlight, enwrapped in mist. "Blue Wonderful" was the third single released from the album.

5. **"I've Got 2 Wings"** (4:35, R) This is a song about a guitar-playing Louisiana preacher named Elder Utah Smith who performed with two wings attached to his back. Bernie wrote it as a tribute and, when asked about his motivation, he said, "I have this terrible tendency in my work to resurrect the neglected. It's great ammunition for songs. I mean, a Louisiana guitar-playing evangelist who wears a pair of wings? What's not to love about that?" The song has a hint of country to it, but it's too rock 'n' roll to be called a country or bluegrass song. The lyrics are Utah speaking in the first person about his goals as a preacher ("I was a light for the living and I spoke of peace and love") and the chorus has the poignant lines, "I was here and I was gone, just a heartbeat from the past, but I went from paper wings, to the real thing at last." This song seems to have not been performed in concert by Elton.

6. **"A Good Heart"** (4:50, B) This song was the fifth single released from the album. It's a quintessential Elton piano ballad, the type of song that has ensorcelled his fans for five decades. The lyrics are multidimensional. Bernie said he wrote it about his kids; Elton feels it could be about his husband David; Elton also said it could be about him and Bernie because they had been together almost fifty years when Bernie wrote the lyrics. There are lines that sound like a father singing to his kids: "Don't be afraid of all my years, what you see or what you hear. It's all yours and yours and yours alone, yours for the taking, so take it home." Bernie told *Rolling Stone*, "I think we have a mirror image on that because we both have young kids. Mine are a little older than his, but it's interesting. That ties us together because we're such radically different characters, but the one thing that ties us together is the kids. We can both understand the perils, pitfalls and joys of raising kids." This is a classic song

Elton ended up in an intensive care unit in a hospital in the UK in May 2017 after contracting a life-threatening bacterial infection in Chile during a tour with James Taylor. "I went to South America," he told UK's *The Sun*, "had a wonderful tour with James Taylor, came back from Chile, felt bad on the plane, got home on a Tuesday night. I was in intensive care on Thursday and stayed there for two days. I was very, very close to death.... I knew I was sick but I didn't know I had such a dangerous thing inside of me until I had a scan, which was after nine shows, 24 flights and a summer ball." Elton said this experience impacted his thinking about touring, and ultimately he decided to mount a huge farewell tour and then stay off the road to work on creative projects (including writing the musical *The Devil Wears Prada*) and to spend more time with his and his husband David Furnish's two young sons, Elijah and Zachary. "You think about your mortality and think, 'God, I want to spend more time with the boys,'" he said.

that goes deep. As evidence of its importance in the Elton John canon, Elton has performed it live over a hundred times between 2016 and 2018.

7. **"Looking Up"** (4:06, R) This was the first single released from *Wonderful Crazy Night*. It's an old school, upbeat Elton rocker reminiscent of "Saturday Night's Alright (for Fighting)" and even "Crocodile Rock." The theme of the song is summed up in the first line of the chorus: "Now I'm looking up more than I look down...." Bernie Taupin told *Rolling Stone* that the positive vibe was intentional: "[I] wanted to do something that exuded positive energy." And so it does. Elton performed this song live in concert more than 125 times between 2016 and 2018.

8. **"Guilty Pleasure"** (3:38, R) This is a rocker about possibly unrequited love. *Does she love me or is she using me?* is the question, as evinced by the lyric, "Am I the lover you'd like my love or just a guilty pleasure?" It's a fast-paced foot stomper that has some great guitar playing by Davey Johnstone. Elton played this song several times during his 2016 *Wonderful Crazy Night* tour.

9. **"Tambourine"** (4:17, B) This is a metaphorical love ballad of sorts. Early on, it's obvious: "It feels like flying when I see your face." But then the tambourine of the title itself becomes the singer: "Smack it in the middle, toss it in the air, I don't care, you can play me everywhere...." And then we're back to extolling his love for her: "You got my head ringing like a tambourine." This is a pretty song that has legendary percussionist Ray Cooper on it playing, yep, the tambourine. Elton seems to have not played this one live.

10. **"The Open Chord"** (4:04, B) An open chord is a chord played on a stringed instrument in which two or more strings are left unfingered and, thus, "open." What, specifically is this open chord? This song uses the metaphor of an open chord as a change element, and in the song it can be interpreted as either a person, a burst of self-knowledge and creativity, or both. The singer in this song describes a "sense of wonder" and a "new direction looking down the lens." The "lens" can be literal, as in a camera, or it can be a symbol for a new sense of focus, the cited "new broom." The chorus proclaims, "You're an open chord I want to play all day." "The Open Chord" also talks about writing and about hearing a song in his head and writing it down. Bernie seemed to have been newly motivated when writing these lyrics. Elton does not seem to have performed this song live in concert.

BEST SONG: "Blue Wonderful"

THE CANON

One of Elton John's favorite chord progressions (and one of ours as well) is what has come to be known as "The Canon," named after Pachelbel's "Canon in D."

It consists of a chord sequence in a descending diatonic scale. It's the "Let It Be" chord sequence (C-G/B-Am-C/G-F-C/E-Dm-G); the "A Whiter Shade of Pale" chord sequence, the "All the Young Dudes" chord sequence, the verses of "I Dreamed a Dream" from *Les Misérables*, ELO's "When I Was a Boy," etc.

You've heard it, and you know it.

Elton uses this sequence in "Skyline Pigeon," "Harmony," "Chameleon," "The North," "Goodbye Yellow Brick Road," "Man," and elsewhere.

It's a lovely progression. John Lennon used it in "Mind Games" and "A Day in the Life."

2

ELTON JOHN SONGS NOT ON THE THIRTY STUDIO ALBUMS

THIS SECTION PROVIDES info about B-sides, bonus tracks, songs from musicals, oddities (like the "Microwave Oven Song," for example), and other songs by Elton John that are not on the canon of his thirty classic studio albums. Note: Covers by Elton John of songs by other songwriters or musicians are not included on this list. (This is not a complete list of these oddities and rarities. See Eltonography.com for what is probably the most complete list of non-canon songs available.)

1. "71-75 New Oxford Street" Instrumental, released as a 1971 single by the group Mr. Bloe with Elton playing piano
2. "16th Century Man" From the musical *The Road to El Dorado*
3. "A Dream Come True" Duet with Leon Russell, available on the album *The Union*
4. "A Step Too Far" From the musical *Aida*
5. "Across the River Thames" Bonus track download for *The Captain & the Kid*
6. "Act of War" Bonus track for *Ice on Fire*, available on the 1985 CD and 1992 reissue
7. "After All This Time" From the musical *Lestat*

8. "All Across the Havens" Appears on 1992's *Rare Masters* and the 1995 reissue of *Empty Sky*
9. "Amneris' Letter" From the musical *Aida*
10. "And the Clock Goes Round" Never officially released, demo available on YouTube
11. "Angry Dance" From the musical *Billy Elliot*
12. "Another Pyramid" From the musical *Aida*
13. "Are We Laughing?" From the 1999 movie soundtrack *The Muse*
14. "Baby I Miss You" Never officially released, demo available on YouTube
15. "Back to Paramount" From the 1999 movie soundtrack *The Muse*
16. "Back to the Aquarium" From the 1999 movie soundtrack *The Muse*
17. "Bad Side of the Moon" B-side of "Border Song"; appears on *11-17-70*
18. "Be Prepared" From the musical *The Lion King*
19. "Beautiful Boy" From the musical *Lestat*
20. "Better Have a Gift" From the 1999 movie soundtrack *The Muse*
21. "Born to Boogie" From the musical *Billy Elliot*
22. "Can I Put You On" From the 1971 movie soundtrack *Friends*
23. "Can You Feel the Love Tonight" From the musical *The Lion King*
24. "Cartier" B-side of "Sartorial Eloquence"
25. "Children's Song" Bonus track for *Wonderful Crazy Night*
26. "Circle of Life" From the musical *The Lion King*
27. "Cold Highway" Written for *Caribou*; released on the 1985 and 2001 reissues of the album
28. "Come Back Baby" Bluesology track released on *To Be Continued...*
29. "Dancing in the End Zone" Bonus track on 1999 reissue of *Sleeping with the Past*
30. "A Dandelion Dies in the Wind" Never officially released, demo available on YouTube
31. "Deep into the Ground" From the musical *Billy Elliot*
32. "Did Anyone Sleep with Joan of Arc?" B-side of "This Train Don't Stop Here Anymore"
33. "Don't Go Breaking My Heart" Released as a single with Kiki Dee in 1976; bonus track on 1995 UK reissue of *Rock of the Westies*; on *Elton John's Greatest Hits Volume II*; *Greatest Hits 1976-1986*
34. "Donner Pour Donner" On *To Be Continued...*
35. "Dreamboat" Bonus track on the 1998 reissue of *Too Low for Zero*
36. "Driving Home" From the 1999 movie soundtrack *The Muse*

37. "Driving to Jack's" From the 1999 movie soundtrack *The Muse*
38. "Driving to Universal" From the 1999 movie soundtrack *The Muse*
39. "Earn While You Learn Instrumental" B-side of the 1983 UK single "I'm Still Standing" and a bonus track on the 1998 reissue of *Too Low for Zero*
40. "Easier to Walk Away" On the 1990 albums *To Be Continued…* and *The Very Best of Elton John*
41. "Easy as Life" From the musical *Aida*
42. "Ego" Bonus track on the 1998 reissue of *A Single Man*
43. "Eight Hundred Dollar Shoes" Duet with Leon Russell, available on the album *The Union*
44. "Elaborate Lives" From the musical *Aida*
45. "El Dorado" From the musical *The Road to El Dorado*
46. "Electricity" From the musical *Billy Elliot*
47. "Embrace It" From the musical *Lestat*
48. "Enchantment Passing Through" From the musical *Aida*
49. "England and America" Bonus track for *Wonderful Crazy Night*
50. "Expressing Yourself" From the musical *Billy Elliot*
51. "Fat Boys and Ugly Girls" Bonus track for *The One*
52. "Finale" From the musical *Billy Elliot*
53. "Flintstone Boy" B-side of 1978 single "Ego"
54. "Free and Easy" Bonus track for *Wonderful Crazy Night*
55. "Friends" From the 1971 movie soundtrack *Friends*
56. "Friends Never Say Goodbye" From the musical *The Road to El Dorado*
57. "From the Dead" From the musical *Lestat*
58. "Get Out (of This Town)" Never officially released, demo available on YouTube
59. "Gone to Shiloh" Duet with Leon Russell, available on the album *The Union*
60. "Grandma's Song" From the musical *Billy Elliot*
61. "Hakuna Matata" From the musical *The Lion King*
62. "He Could Be a Star" From the musical *Billy Elliot*
63. "Hearts Have Turned to Stone" Duet with Leon Russell, available on the album *The Union*
64. "Hello Hello" From the 2011 movie soundtrack *Gnomeo & Juliet*
65. "Here's to the Next Time" B-side of "I've Been Loving You"

66. "Hey Ahab" Duet with Leon Russell, available on the album *The Union*
67. "Ho! Ho! Ho! (Who'd Be a Turkey at Christmas)" B-side of the 1973 single "Step into Christmas"
68. "Honey Roll" From the 1971 movie soundtrack *Friends*
69. "Hour Glass" Never officially released, demo available on YouTube
70. "House of Cards" Bonus track on the 2005 30th Anniversary Deluxe Edition of *Captain Fantastic and the Brown Dirt Cowboy*
71. "How I Know You" From the musical *Aida*
72. "(I'm Gonna) Love Me Again" Duet with Taron Egerton; available on the 2019 movie soundtrack *Rocketman*
73. "I Can't Go on Living Without You" Never officially released, demo available on YouTube
74. "I Cry at Night" Bonus track on the 1998 reissue of *A Single Man*
75. "I Get a Little Bit Lonely" Never officially released, demo available on YouTube
76. "I Just Can't Wait to Be King" From the musical *The Lion King*
77. "I Know the Truth" From the musical *Aida*
78. "I Love You and That's All That Matters" Never officially released, demo available on YouTube
79. "I Meant to Do My Work Today (A Day in the Country)" From the 1971 movie soundtrack *Friends*
80. "I Should Have Sent Roses" Duet with Leon Russell, available on the album *The Union*
81. "I Swear I Heard the Night Talkin'" From *To Be Continued...*
82. "I Want More" From the musical *Lestat*
83. "I'll Never Have That Chance" From the musical *Lestat*
84. "I've Been Loving You" Elton's first single; available on YouTube
85. "If It Wasn't for Bad" From *The Union*
86. "In Paris" From the musical *Lestat*
87. "In the Hands of Angels" From *The Union*
88. "In the Morning" Never officially released, demo available on YouTube
89. "Into the Old Man's Shoes" B-side of "Your Song" in the UK; originally written for and recorded for *Tumbleweed Connection* but not included on the album; released on the 1985, 2001, and 2008 reissues of the album

90. "It's Me That You Need" B-side of "Lady Samantha" single
91. "It's Tough to Be a God" From the musical *The Road to El Dorado*
92. "Jack Rabbit" B-side of "Saturday Night's Alright (for Fighting)" single; bonus track on the 1995 and 1996 reissue of *Don't Shoot Me I'm Only the Piano Player*
93. "Jimmie Rodgers' Dream" Duet with Leon Russell, available on the album *The Union*
94. "Just Like Strange Rain" On *Rare Masters*; on 1995 reissue of *Empty Sky*
95. "Lady Samantha" Single released before *Empty Sky*
96. "Let Me Be Your Car" On *Rare Masters*
97. "Like Father Like Son" From the musical *Aida*
98. "Love Builds a Garden" From the 2011 movie soundtrack *Gnomeo & Juliet*
99. "Love is a Cannibal" Bonus track on the 1999 reissue of *Sleeping With the Past*
100. "Lovesick" Bonus track on the 1998 reissue of *A Single Man*
101. "Made for Me" On *To Be Continued…*
102. "Make Me as You Are" From the musical *Lestat*
103. "Mandalay Again" Duet with Leon Russell, available on the album *The Union*
104. "Meet Christine" From the 1999 movie soundtrack *The Muse*
105. "Merry Christmas Maggie Thatcher" From the musical *Billy Elliot*
106. "Michelle's Song" From the 1971 movie soundtrack *Friends*
107. "Microwave Oven Song" Improvised song using lyrics from a microwave oven instruction manual; written and performed on the 1997 show *An Audience with Elton John*; video available on YouTube
108. "Monkey Suit" Duet with Leon Russell, available on the album *The Union*
109. "Morality Play" From the musical *Lestat*
110. "Multiple Personality" From the 1999 movie soundtrack *The Muse*
111. "My Heart Dances" From the musical *The Road to El Dorado*
112. "My Kind of Hell" Duet with Leon Russell, available on the album *The Union*
113. "My Strongest Suit" From the musical *Aida*
114. "Never Too Late" From the 2019 reissue of *The Lion King* movie

115. "Never Too Old (To Hold Somebody)" Duet with Leon Russell, available on the album *The Union*
116. "Nice and Slow" On *The Complete Thom Bell Sessions*
117. "Nicolas' Song" From the musical *Lestat*
118. "No Monsters" Bonus track for *Wonderful Crazy Night*
119. "No Valentines" On *Love Songs*
120. "Not Me" From the musical *Aida*
121. "Once We Were Kings" From the musical *Billy Elliot*
122. "Orchestral Finale" From the musical *Aida*
123. "Planes" Bonus track for 1996 reissue of *Rock of the Westies*
124. "Queen of Cities (El Dorado II)" From the musical *The Road to El Dorado*
125. "Regimental Sgt. Zippo" Never officially released, demo available on YouTube
126. "Reminds Me of You" Never officially released, demo available on YouTube
127. "Right Before My Eyes" From the musical *Lestat*
128. "Rock and Roll Madonna" Released a single in the UK in 1970; appears on 1992's *Rare Masters* album
129. "Rock Me When He's Gone" Appears on 1992's *Rare Masters* album
130. "Rope Around a Fool" Bonus track on 1998 reissue of *Reg Strikes Back*
131. "Sail Me Away" From the musical *Lestat*
132. "Sarah Escapes" From the 1999 movie soundtrack *The Muse*
133. "Sara's Coming Back" Never officially released, demo available on YouTube
134. "Scarecrow" Never officially released, demo available on YouTube; first song Elton and Bernie ever wrote together
135. "Screw You (Young Man's Blues)" B-side of "Goodbye Yellow Brick Road" single
136. "Seasons" From the 1971 movie soundtrack *Friends*
137. "Shine" From the musical *Billy Elliot*
138. "Sick City" Written for *Caribou*; released on the 1985 and 2001 reissues of the album
139. "Sing Me No Sad Songs" Never officially released, demo available on YouTube

140. "Sitting Doing Nothing" Never officially released, demo available on YouTube
141. "Snow Queen" The B-side to the 1976 "Don't Go Breakin' My Heart" single, available on YouTube
142. "Solidarity" From the musical *Billy Elliot*
143. "Someday Out of the Blue" From the musical *The Road to El Dorado*
144. "Step into Christmas" Written for *Caribou*; released on the 1985 and 2001 reissues of the album
145. "Steven Redecorates" From the 1999 movie soundtrack *The Muse*
146. "Strangers" Written for *A Single Man*, appears as bonus track on 1998 reissue
147. "Sugar on the Floor" B-side of "Don't Go Breaking My Heart"
148. "Suit of Wolves" Bonus track for *The One*
149. "Swan Lake" From the musical *Billy Elliot*
150. "Take a Walk with Me" From the 1999 movie soundtrack *The Muse*
151. "Taking the Sun from My Eyes" Never officially released, demo available on YouTube
152. "Tartan Coloured Lady" Never officially released, demo available on YouTube
153. "Thank You for All Your Loving" Never officially released, demo available on YouTube
154. "The Angel Tree" Never officially released, demo available on YouTube
155. "The Aquarium" From the 1999 movie soundtrack *The Muse*
156. "The Best Part of the Day" Duet with Leon Russell, available on the album *The Union*
157. "The Cookie Factory" From the 1999 movie soundtrack *The Muse*
158. "The Crimson Kiss" From the musical *Lestat*
159. "The First Kiss" From the 1971 movie soundtrack *Friends*
160. "The Flowers Will Never Die" Never officially released, demo available on YouTube
161. "The Gods Love Nubia" From the musical *Aida*
162. "The Last to Arrive" Never officially released, demo available on YouTube
163. "The Letter (Billy's Reply)" From the musical *Billy Elliot*
164. "The Letter (Mum's Letter)" From the musical *Billy Elliot*

165. "The Man Who Never Died" B-side of "Nikita"
166. "The Messenger" From the musical *Aida*
167. "The Muse" From the 1999 movie soundtrack *The Muse*
168. "The Panic in Me" From the musical *The Road to El Dorado*
169. "The Retreat" B-side of "Princess"
170. "The Stars Look Down" From the musical *Billy Elliot*
171. "The Thirst" From the musical *Lestat*
172. "The Tide Will Turn for Rebecca" Never officially released, demo available on YouTube
173. "The Trail We Blaze" From the musical *The Road to El Dorado*
174. "The Wrong Gift" From the 1999 movie soundtrack *The Muse*
175. "There is Still a Little Love" Never officially released, demo available on YouTube
176. "There's No Tomorrow" Duet with Leon Russell, available on the album *The Union*
177. "There's Still Time for Me" Never officially released, demo available on YouTube
178. "To Kill Your Kind" From the musical *Lestat*
179. "To Live Like This" From the musical *Lestat*
180. "To the Guesthouse" From the 1999 movie soundtrack *The Muse*
181. "Trust Me" From the musical *The Road to El Dorado*
182. "Turn to Me" Never officially released, demo available on YouTube
183. "Two Fingers of Whiskey" Written for *Music from The American Epic Sessions: Original Motion Picture Soundtrack*
184. "Variation on Friends" From the 1971 movie soundtrack *Friends*
185. "Variation on Michelle's Song (A Day in the Country)" From the 1971 movie soundtrack *Friends*
186. "Velvet Fountain" Never officially released, demo available on YouTube
187. "Walk of Shame" From the 1999 movie soundtrack *The Muse*
188. "Welcome to the New World" From the musical *Lestat*
189. "What Should I Do?" From the 1999 movie soundtrack *The Muse*

> "Leon Russell told me that when he saw Elton, after two songs, he thought, 'OK, my career's over.'"
>
> —T Bone Burnett

190. "When the First Tear Shows" Never officially released, demo available on YouTube
191. "When I Was Tealby Abbey" Never officially released, demo available on YouTube
192. "When Love Is Dying" Duet with Leon Russell, available on the album *The Union*
193. "Whenever You're Ready (We'll Go Steady Again)" B-side of "Saturday Night's Alright (for Fighting)" single; bonus track on the 1995 and 1996 reissue of *Don't Shoot Me I'm Only the Piano Player*
194. "Where It's At" Never officially released, demo available on YouTube
195. "Without Question" From the musical *The Road to El Dorado*
196. "Written in the Stars" From the musical *Aida*
197. "Year of the Teddy Bear" Never officially released, demo available on YouTube
198. "You Can Make History (Young Again)" From the 1997 album *Love Songs*; also released as a 1996 cassette single
199. "You Gotta Love Someone" From the *Days of Thunder* soundtrack; also on *The Very Best of Elton John*
200. "You'll Be Sorry to See Me Go" Never officially released, demo available on YouTube

3

ELTON JOHN'S FORTY BIGGEST BILLBOARD HOT 100 SINGLES

1. "Candle in the Wind 1997"

Highest Position: No. 1 on October 11, 1997

2. "That's What Friends Are For" (Dionne & Friends)

Highest Position: No. 1 on January 18, 1986

3. "Philadelphia Freedom" (The Elton John Band)

Highest Position: No. 1 on April 12, 1975

4. "Crocodile Rock"

Highest Position: No. 1 on February 3, 1973

5. "Don't Go Breaking My Heart" (Elton John & Kiki Dee)

Highest Position: No. 1 on August 7, 1976

6. "Bennie and the Jets"

Highest Position: No. 1 on April 13, 1974

7. "Island Girl"

Highest Position: No. 1 on November 1, 1975

8. "Little Jeannie"

Highest Position: No. 3 on July 19, 1980

9. "Goodbye Yellow Brick Road"

Highest Position: No. 2 on December 8, 1973

10. "Lucy in the Sky with Diamonds"

Highest Position: No. 1 on January 4, 1975

11. "Daniel"

Highest Position: No. 2 on June 2, 1973

12. "I Don't Wanna Go on with You Like That"

Highest Position: No. 2 on August 27, 1988

13. "Can You Feel the Love Tonight"

Highest Position: No. 4 on August 6, 1994

14. "Someone Saved My Life Tonight"

Highest Position: No. 4 on August 16, 1975

15. "Don't Let the Sun Go Down on Me"

Highest Position: No. 2 on July 27, 1974

16. "I Guess That's Why They Call It the Blues"

Highest Position: No. 4 on January 28, 1984

17. "The Bitch Is Back"

Highest Position: No. 4 on November 2, 1974

18. "Sorry Seems to Be the Hardest Word"

Highest Position: No. 6 on December 25, 1976

19. "Don't Let the Sun Go Down on Me" (George Michael /Elton John)

Highest Position: No. 1 on February 1, 1992

20. "Candle in the Wind"

Highest Position: No. 6 on January 23, 1988

21. "Nikita"

Highest Position: No. 7 on March 22, 1986

22. "Sad Songs (Say So Much)"

Highest Position: No. 5 on August 11, 1984

23. "Rocket Man"

Highest Position: No. 6 on July 15, 1972

24. "Mama Can't Buy You Love"

Highest Position: No. 9 on August 25, 1979

25. "Your Song"

Highest Position: No. 8 on January 23, 1971

26. "The One"

Highest Position: No. 9 on September 19, 1992

27. "Saturday Night's Alright (for Fighting)"

Highest Position: No. 12 on September 15, 1973

28. "I'm Still Standing"

Highest Position: No. 12 on July 9, 1983

29. "Honky Cat"

Highest Position: No. 8 on September 23, 1972

30. "Blue Eyes"

Highest Position: No. 12 on October 2, 1982

31. "Sacrifice"

Highest Position: No. 18 on March 31, 1990

32. "Healing Hands"

Highest Position: No. 13 on October 28, 1990

33. "Empty Garden (Hey Hey Johnny)"

Highest Position: No. 13 on May 29, 1982

34. "Believe"

Highest Position: No. 13 on May 13, 1995

35. "Wrap Her Up"

Highest Position: No. 20 on December 7, 1985

36. "Who Wears These Shoes?"

Highest Position: No. 16 on November 3, 1984

37. "Grow Some Funk of Your Own" / "I Feel Like a Bullet (In the Gun of Robert Ford)"

Highest Position: No. 14 on February 28, 1976

38. "Through the Storm" (Aretha Franklin & Elton John)

Highest Position: No. 16 on May 27, 1989

39. "A Word in Spanish"

Highest Position: No. 19 on November 12, 1988

40. "Circle of Life"

Highest Position: No. 18 on December 15, 1994

Source: *Billboard*

4

ONE-OF-A-KIND ALBUMS

THIS SECTION LOOKS at Elton's live albums, plus an album of duets and a memorable collaboration. True one-of-a-kind stuff.

• *Here and There* (1976) •

This live album is in two parts: "Here," which was recorded at the Royal Festival Hall in London in summer 1974, and "There," which was recorded at Madison Square Garden on November 28, 1974.

Here

1. "Skyline Pigeon" (4:34)
2. "Border Song" (3:18)
3. "Honky Cat" (7:15)
4. "Love Song" (5:25)
5. "Crocodile Rock" (4:15)

There

1. "Funeral for a Friend/Love Lies Bleeding" (11:11)
2. "Rocket Man (I Think It's Going to Be a Long, Long Time)" (5:13)
3. "Bennie and the Jets" (6:09)
4. "Take Me to the Pilot" (5:48)

• *11-17-70* (1970) •

This live album was taken from an A&R Recording Studios radio broadcast on November 17, 1970, on WABC-FM in New York City.

1. "Take Me to the Pilot" (6:43)
2. "Honky Tonk Women" (4:09)
3. "Sixty Years On" (8:05)
4. "Can I Put You On" (6:38)
5. "Bad Side of the Moon" (4:30)
6. "Burn Down the Mission," "My Baby Left Me," "Get Back" (18:20)

• *Live in Australia with the Melbourne Symphony Orchestra* (1987) •

This album is from a live concert with the Melbourne Symphony Orchestra at the Sydney Entertainment Centre on December 14, 1986.

1. "Sixty Years On" (5:41)
2. "I Need You to Turn To" (3:14)
3. "The Greatest Discovery" (4:09)
4. "Tonight" (5:58)
5. "Sorry Seems to Be the Hardest Word" (3:58)
6. "The King Must Die" (5:21)
7. "Take Me to the Pilot" (4:22)
8. "Tiny Dancer" (7:46)
9. "Have Mercy on the Criminal" (5:50)
10. "Madman Across the Water" (6:38)
11. "Candle in the Wind" (4:10)
12. "Burn Down the Mission" (5:49)
13. "Your Song" (4:04)
14. "Don't Let the Sun Go Down on Me" (6:06)

• *Duets* (1993) •

This album consists of Elton singing duets of his songs with notable artists.

1. "Tear Drops" (4:55), with k.d. lang

2. "When I Think About Love (I Think About You)" (4:34) with P.M. Dawn
3. "The Power" (6:25) with Little Richard
4. "Shakey Ground" (3:51) with Don Henley
5. "True Love" (3:34) with Kiki Dee
6. "If You Were Me" (4:26) with Chris Rea
7. "A Woman's Needs" (5:18) with Tammy Wynette
8. "Don't Let the Sun Go Down On Me" (5:46) (live) with George Michael
9. "Old Friend" (4:15) with Nik Kershaw
10. "Go On And On" (5:50) with Gladys Knight
11. "Don't Go Breaking My Heart" (5:00) with RuPaul
12. "Ain't Nothing Like the Real Thing" (3:36) with Marcella Detroit
13. "I'm Your Puppet" (3:36) with Paul Young
14. "Love Letters" (4:01) with Bonnie Raitt
15. "Born to Lose" (4:33) with Leonard Cohen
16. "Duets for One" (4:52)

• *One Night Only* (2000) •

This live album was recorded on October 20 and 21, 2000, at Madison Square Garden.

1. "Goodbye Yellow Brick Road" (3:18)
2. "Philadelphia Freedom" (5:21)
3. "Don't Go Breaking My Heart" (4:19)
4. "Rocket Man (I Think It's Gonna be a Long, Long Time)" (5:43)
5. "Crocodile Rock" (4:13)
6. "Sacrifice" (5:20)
7. "Can You Feel the Love Tonight" (3:59)
8. "Bennie and the Jets" (5:02)
9. "Your Song" (4:17)
10. "Sad Songs (Say So Much)" (3:54)
11. "Candle in the Wind" (3:45)
12. "Saturday Night's Alright (for Fighting)" (4:38)
13. "I'm Still Standing" (3:04)

14. "Don't Let the Sun Go Down on Me" (5:59)
15. "I Guess That's Why They Call It the Blues" (5:10)

• *The Union* (2010) •

This album is a collaboration between Elton John and Leon Russell.

1. "If It Wasn't for Bad" (3:43)[2]
2. "Eight Hundred Dollar Shoes" (3:23)[1]
3. "Hey Ahab" (5:39)[1]
4. "Gone to Shiloh" (4:50)[1]
5. "Hearts Have Turned to Stone" (3:47)[2]
6. "Jimmie Rodgers' Dream" (3:42)[3]
7. "There's No Tomorrow" (3:45)[4]
8. "Monkey Suit" (4:46)[1]
9. "The Best Part of the Day" (4:45)[1]
10. "A Dream Come True" (5:07)[5]
11. "I Should Have Sent Roses" (5:21)[6]
12. "When Love Is Dying" (4:51)[1]
13. "My Kind of Hell" (3:16)[1]
14. "Mandalay Again" (4:54)[1]
15. "Never Too Old (To Hold Somebody)" (4:58)[1]
16. "In the Hands of Angels" (4:43)[2]

[1] Elton John, Bernie Taupin
[2] Leon Russell
[3] Elton John, Bernie Taupin, T Bone Burnett
[4] Elton John, Leon Russell, T Bone Burnett, James Timothy Shaw
[5] Elton John, Leon Russell
[6] Leon Russell, Bernie Taupin

5

GREATEST HITS COMPILATIONS

Terry O'Neill via Getty Images

THESE TRACK LISTINGS are of the initial releases, what we call the classic releases. Reissues and later albums with different song lineups are not included.

• *Greatest Hits* (1974) •

1. "Your Song" (4:00)
2. "Daniel" (3:53)
3. "Honky Cat" (5:12)
4. "Goodbye Yellow Brick Road" (3:14)
5. "Saturday Night's Alright (for Fighting)" (4:55)
6. "Rocket Man (I Think It's Going to Be a Long, Long Time)" (4:40)
7. "Bennie and the Jets" (5:10)
8. "Don't Let the Sun Go Down on Me" (5:33)
9. "Border Song" (3:19)
10. "Crocodile Rock" (3:56)

• *Elton John's Greatest Hits Volume II* (1977) •

1. "The Bitch Is Back" (3:39)
2. "Lucy in the Sky with Diamonds" (5:58)
3. "Sorry Seems to Be the Hardest Word" (3:43)
4. "Don't Go Breaking My Heart" (Duet with Kiki Dee) (4:23)
5. "Someone Saved My Life Tonight" (6:45)
6. "Philadelphia Freedom" (5:20)
7. "Island Girl" (3:43)
8. "Grow Some Funk of Your Own" (4:16)
9. "Levon" (5:21)
10. "Pinball Wizard" (5:10)

• *To Be Continued...* (1990) •

This is a 4-disc box set of seventy songs from Elton John's musical history.

Disc 1

1. "Come Back Baby" (Reg Dwight) (2:45)
2. "Lady Samantha" (3:03)
3. "It's Me That You Need" (4:04)
4. "Your Song" (demo) (3:33)

5. "Rock and Roll Madonna" (4:17)
6. "Bad Side of the Moon" (3:15)
7. "Your Song" (4:00)
8. "Take Me to the Pilot" (3:46)
9. "Border Song" (3:22)
10. "Sixty Years On" (4:57)
11. "Country Comfort" (5:07)
12. "Grey Seal" (original) (3:36)
13. "Friends" (2:20)
14. "Levon" (5:21)
15. "Tiny Dancer" (6:15)
16. "Madman Across the Water" (5:58)
17. "Honky Cat" (5:13)
18. "Mona Lisas and Mad Hatters" (4:59)

Disc 2

1. "Rocket Man" (4:43)
2. "Daniel" (3:53)
3. "Crocodile Rock" (3:54)
4. "Bennie and the Jets" (5:21)
5. "Goodbye Yellow Brick Road" (3:14)
6. "All the Girls Love Alice" (5:10)
7. "Funeral for a Friend/Love Lies Bleeding" (11:07)
8. "Whenever You're Ready (We'll Go Steady Again)" (2:53)
9. "Saturday Night's Alright (for Fighting)" (4:54)
10. "Jack Rabbit" (1:51)
11. "Harmony" (2:46)
12. "Screw You (Young Man's Blues)" (4:43)
13. "Step into Christmas" (4:30)
14. "The Bitch Is Back" (3:44)
15. "Pinball Wizard" (5:15)
16. "Someone Saved My Life Tonight" (6:45)

Disc 3

1. "Philadelphia Freedom" (5:39)
2. "One Day (At a Time)" (3:48)
3. "Lucy in the Sky with Diamonds" (6:16)

4. "I Saw Her Standing There" (duet with John Lennon, live) (3:43)
5. "Island Girl" (3:44)
6. "Sorry Seems to Be the Hardest Word" (3:47)
7. "Don't Go Breaking My Heart" (duet with Kiki Dee) (4:31)
8. "I Feel Like a Bullet (In the Gun of Robert Ford)" (live) (3:35)
9. "Ego" (3:59)
10. "Song for Guy" (6:40)
11. "Mama Can't Buy You Love" (4:03)
12. "Cartier" (0:54)
13. "Little Jeannie" (5:12)
14. "Donner Pour Donner" (duet with France Gall) (4:26)
15. "Fanfare/Chloe" (6:20)
16. "The Retreat" (4:45)
17. "Blue Eyes" (3:26)

Disc 4

1. "Empty Garden (Hey Hey Johnny)" (5:12)
2. "I Guess That's Why They Call It the Blues" (4:43)
3. "I'm Still Standing" (3:02)
4. "Sad Songs (Say So Much)" (4:10)
5. "Act of War" (duet with Millie Jackson) (4:44)
6. "Nikita" (5:44)
7. "Candle in the Wind" (live) (3:58)
8. "Carla/Etude" (live) (4:46)
9. "Don't Let the Sun Go Down on Me" (live) (5:39)
10. "I Don't Wanna Go on with You Like That" (Shep Pettibone remix) (7:18)
11. "Give Peace a Chance" (3:47)
12. "Healing Hands" 3:46)
13. "Sacrifice" (5:08)
14. "Made for Me" (4:22)
15. "You Gotta Love Someone" (US only) (4:59)
16. "I Swear I Heard the Night Talkin'" (US only) (4:30)
17. "Easier to Walk Away" (4:22)
18. "Suit of Wolves" (UK only) (5:46)
19. "Understanding Women" (UK only) (5:03)

• *Rare Masters* (1992) •

This is a double CD of thirty-seven songs, comprised of B-sides, outtakes, and the complete soundtrack of the movie *Friends*.

Disc 1

1. "I've Been Loving You" (3:16)
2. "Here's to the Next Time" (2:58)
3. "Lady Samantha" (3:02)
4. "All Across the Havens" (B-side of "Lady Samantha") (2:51)
5. "It's Me That You Need" (4:00)
6. "Just Like Strange Rain" (B-side of "It's Me That You Need") (3:44)
7. "Bad Side of the Moon" (3:12)
8. "Rock and Roll Madonna" (4:16)
9. "Grey Seal" (3:35)
10. "Friends" (2:33)
11. "Michelle's Song" (4:20)
12. "Seasons" (instrumental) (3:56)
13. "Variation on Michelle's Song (A Day in the Country)" (instrumental) (2:47)
14. "Can I Put You On" (5:57)
15. "Honey Roll" (B-side of "Friends") (3:07)
16. "Variations on 'Friends'" (instrumental) (1:43)
17. "I Meant to Do My Work Today (A Day in the Country)" (recitation with accompaniment) (1:36)
18. "Four Moods" (Buckmaster instrumental) (11:01)
19. "Seasons Reprise" (instrumental) (1:39)

Disc 2

1. "Madman Across the Water" (outtake) (8:50)
2. "Into the Old Man's Shoes" (outtake, B-side of UK "Your Song") (4:01)
3. "Rock Me When He's Gone" (outtake) (5:01)
4. "Slave" (outtake) (2:48)
5. "Skyline Pigeon" (re-recording) (3:51)
6. "Jack Rabbit" (1:51)
7. "Whenever You're Ready (We'll Go Steady Again)" (2:51)
8. "Let Me Be Your Car" (demo, written for Rod Stewart (4:52)

9. "Screw You" (later known as "Screw You (Young Man's Blues)" (4:41
10. "Step into Christmas" (4:30)
11. "Ho! Ho! Ho! (Who'd Be a Turkey at Christmas)" (B-side of "Step into Christmas") (4:03)
12. "Sick City" (5:23)
13. "Cold Highway" (3:26)
14. "One Day (At a Time)" (3:47)
15. "I Saw Her Standing There" (recorded live with Lennon at Madison Square Garden; this was Lennon's last concert appearance) (3:51)
16. "House of Cards" (3:09)
17. "Planes" (4:14)
18. "Sugar on the Floor" (1975)

• *Love Songs* (1995) •*

This is a compilation of, well, what Elton and company consider his "love songs." Is "Candle in the Wind" a love song? Regardless, it's a great collection.

1. "Can You Feel the Love Tonight" (4:02)
2. "The One" (5:55)
3. "Sacrifice" (5:09)
4. "Daniel" (3:55)
5. "Someone Saved My Life Tonight" (6:47)
6. "Your Song" (4:03)
7. "Don't Let the Sun Go Down on Me" (live duet with George Michael) (5:50)
8. "Believe" (4:44)
9. "Blue Eyes" (3:29)
10. "Sorry Seems to Be the Hardest Word" (3:50)
11. "Blessed" (5:03)
12. "Candle in the Wind" (live) (4:02)
13. "You Can Make History (Young Again)" (4:56)
14. "No Valentines" (4:11)
15. "Circle of Life" (4:50)

* North American version

• *Elton John's Greatest Hits 1970-2002* •*

This is a 2-CD compilation of Elton's hits spanning thirty-two years. It comes with a bonus third disk.

Disc 1

1. "Your Song" (4:03)
2. "Levon" (5:23)
3. "Tiny Dancer" (6:16)
4. "Rocket Man (I Think It's Going to Be a Long, Long Time)" (4:42)
5. "Honky Cat" (5:13)
6. "Crocodile Rock" (3:55)
7. "Daniel" (3:54)
8. "Saturday Night's Alright (for Fighting)" (4:54)
9. "Goodbye Yellow Brick Road" (3:14)
10. "Candle in the Wind" (3:50)
11. "Bennie and the Jets" (5:23)
12. "Don't Let the Sun Go Down on Me" (5:37)
13. "The Bitch Is Back" (3:45)
14. "Philadelphia Freedom" (5:20)
15. "Someone Saved My Life Tonight" (6:44)
16. "Island Girl" (3:43)
17. "Sorry Seems to Be the Hardest Word" (3:52)

Disc 2

1. "Don't Go Breaking My Heart" (with Kiki Dee) (4:35)
2. "Little Jeannie" (4:49)
3. "I'm Still Standing" (3:03)
4. "I Guess That's Why They Call It the Blues" (4:44)
5. "Sad Songs (Say So Much)" (4:10)
6. "I Don't Wanna Go on with You Like That" (4:32)
7. "Nikita" (5:45)
8. "Sacrifice" (5:06)
9. "The One" (5:53)
10. "Can You Feel the Love Tonight?" (4:02)
11. "Circle of Life" (4:52)
12. "Believe" (4:47)

13. "Blessed" (5:03)
14. "Something About the Way You Look Tonight" (4:00)
15. "Written in the Stars" (with LeAnn Rimes) (4:17)
16. "I Want Love" (4:36)
17. "This Train Don't Stop There Anymore" (4:39)

Bonus Disc

1. "Candle in the Wind" (live) (4:02)
2. "Don't Let the Sun Go Down on Me" (live) (with George Michael) (5:49)
3. "Live Like Horses" (live) (with Luciano Pavarotti) (5:08)
4. "Your Song" (live) (with Alessandro Safina) (4:19)

* American version

• *Diamonds* •

This is a 2-CD compilation of Elton's hits spanning thirty-six years. It was also released in a deluxe 3-disc edition. This listing is for all three CDs.

Disc 1

1. "Your Song" (4:03)
2. "Tiny Dancer" (6:16)
3. "Rocket Man (I Think It's Going to Be a Long, Long Time)" (4:42)
4. "Honky Cat" (5:13)
5. "Crocodile Rock" (3:55)
6. "Daniel" (3:54)
7. "Saturday Night's Alright (for Fighting)" (4:54)
8. "Goodbye Yellow Brick Road" (3:14)
9. "Candle in the Wind" (3:50)
10. "Bennie and the Jets" (5:23)
11. "The Bitch Is Back" (3:45)
12. "Philadelphia Freedom" (5:20)
13. "Island Girl" (3:43)
14. "Someone Saved My Life Tonight" (6:45)
15. "Don't Go Breaking My Heart (duet with Kiki Dee)" (4:35)
16. "Sorry Seems to Be the Hardest Word" (3:52)
17. "Little Jeannie" (4:49)

Disc 2

1. "Song for Guy" (6:34)
2. "Blue Eyes" (3:28)
3. "I'm Still Standing" (3:04)
4. "I Guess That's Why They Call It the Blues" (4:43)
5. "Sad Songs (Say So Much)" (4:48)
6. "Nikita" (5:44)
7. "I Don't Wanna Go on with You Like That" (4:34)
8. "Sacrifice" (5:05)
9. "Don't Let the Sun Go Down on Me (duet with George Michael) (5:48)
10. "Something About the Way You Look Tonight" (4:00)
11. "I Want Love" (4:37)
12. "Can You Feel the Love Tonight" (4:01)
13. "Are You Ready for Love" (3:32)
14. "Electricity" (3:32)
15. "Home Again" (5:02)
16. "Looking Up" (4:06)
17. "Circle of Life" (4:53)

Deluxe Edition Bonus CD

1. "Skyline Pigeon" (piano version) (B-side of "Daniel" single) (3:54)
2. "Lucy in the Sky with Diamonds" (6:16)
3. "Pinball Wizard" (5:14)
4. "Mama Can't Buy You Love" (4:04)
5. "Part-Time Love" (3:13)
6. "Victim of Love" (3:22)
7. "Empty Garden (Hey Hey Johnny)" (5:10)
8. "Kiss the Bride" (4:23)
9. "That's What Friends Are For" (quartet with Dionne Warwick, Stevie Wonder, and Gladys Knight) (4:15)
10. "The One" (5:53)
11. "True Love (duet with Kiki Dee)" (3:35)
12. "Believe" (4:47)
13. "Live Like Horses" (duet with Luciano Pavarotti) (5:07)
14. "Written in the Stars" (duet with LeAnn Rimes) (4:17)
15. "This Train Don't Stop There Anymore" (4:39)
16. "Good Morning to the Night" (with Pnau) (3:24)
17. "Step into Christmas" (4:29)

6

NOTABLE MOVIE AND TV APPEARANCES

THIS IS A look at some of Elton's TV and movie appearances. His appearances as a musical guest are not included. Music videos are not included. (There are just too many of both of them. And isn't that what IMDb.com is for anyway?)

1. 1972: *Born to Boogie* (himself)
2. 1975: *Tommy* (Pinball Wizard)
3. 1978: *The Muppet Show* (himself)
4. 1997: *Spice World* (himself)
5. 1997: *The Nanny* (himself)
6. 1997: *Elton John: Tantrums & Tiaras* (himself)
7. 1998: *South Park* (himself)
8. 1998: *The Simpsons* (himself)
9. 2000: *The Road to El Dorado* (The Narrator)
10. 2001: *Ally McBeal* (himself)
11. 2002: *The Country Bears* (himself)
12. 2002: *Will & Grace* (himself)
13. 2005: *Inside the Actor's Studio* (himself)
14. 2007: *Elton John: Me, Myself & I* (himself)
15. 2016: *Nashville* (season 4) (himself)
16. 2016: *Red Nose Day* (himself)

17. 2017: *The American Epic Sessions* (himself)
18. 2017: *Kingsman: The Golden Circle* (himself)
19. 2018: *Newsnight* (himself)
20. 2018: *Sir Bruce: A Celebration* (himself)

7

ROCKETMAN

A LOOK AT THE 2019 ELTON JOHN MOVIE

"People don't pay to see Reg Dwight! They pay to see *Elton John*!"
Elton John, *Rocketman*

Counselor: Did your marriage to Renate make you happy?
Elton John: Not really. I'm gay.

THE SINGLE

"(I'm Gonna) Love Me Again" (4:12, R) This is a Motown song not produced or released by Motown. Elton and Bernie love their soul music, that's for sure. This song was written by them for the *Rocketman* movie and is performed as a duet by Elton and Taron Egerton (who played Elton as an adult in the movie). It's a cool song with hints of "Philadelphia Freedom" influences, and it plays over the end credits of the movie. The theme of the song is the theme of the movie: it's an empowerment anthem in which the lyrics speak to the drive needed to achieve success at what you love to do. It's a quintessential Elton song in the sense that his musical props are front and center. The song is in the key of C, but the chorus is in C#, and it works beautifully. Many people leave the theater as soon as the credits start to roll. Those that do will not have heard this song. Pity.

Terry O'Neill via Getty Images

Rocketman—known as the "Elton John Movie" the way *Bohemian Rhapsody* is known as the "Queen Movie"—was released to theaters on Friday May 31, 2019, and was an immediate success. It achieved a score of 90 percent on *RottenTomatoes.com* and the reviews were consistently praising, particularly of Taron Egerton's performance as Elton. It is incredibly good, as is the film itself.

This is from an essay Elton John personally wrote for the UK *Guardian* about the movie:

> *I was in the cinema for about fifteen minutes before I started crying. Not crying as in the occasional tear quietly trickling down my cheek: really sobbing, in that loud, unguarded, emotionally destroyed way that makes people turn around and look at you with*

alarmed expressions. I was watching my family—my mum and dad, my nan—in my nan's old council house in Pinner Hill Road in the late 1950s, singing "I Want Love," a song Bernie Taupin and I had written in 2001. I knew it was in the film, but I didn't know how they were going to use it. Up until that point, I'd kept a discrete distance from the actual process of making a movie about my life. I gave some suggestions, saw a few daily rushes, said yay or nay to some important decisions and met two or three times with Taron Egerton, who plays me. But otherwise I'd kept well away from Rocketman, *letting my husband David [Furnish] be my eyes and ears on set every day. I figured it would be uncomfortable for everyone to have the person the film was about lurking around.*

This is from the UK *Guardian* review of the movie:

Rocketman *is a sucrose-enriched, biopic-slash-jukebox-musical hybrid which sometimes feels like it should be on the Broadway or London West End stage—and very possibly will. Sometimes the songs are woven realistically into the action, with Elton performing one of his nuclear-payload belters live on stage, or sometimes musingly trying out a song on the keyboard, giving us all goosebumps as we recognize a prototype of "Candle in the Wind." But sometimes the songs are part of a fantasy sequence, choreographed in such a way as takes us close to Lloyd Webber territory.*

And…

What the movie made an honest job of, was conveying the meaning of the song itself: the rocket pilot who is afraid and lonely and for whom the apparently mind-blowing business of space travel is all in a day's work. Rocketman *is an honest, heartfelt tribute to Elton John's music and his public image.*

Rocketman is a very well-done, quite surreal, magical-realism musical that serves as a skewed biography of sorts. We get to see—as if in reality—the scenarios and events that go on in Elton John's mind (*A*

Beautiful Mind, *Birdman*, and even *Pulp Fiction* come to mind as other examples of the genre).

However, don't go into your screening of *Rocketman* expecting chronological verisimilitude, or even factual accuracy. Taron "Elton" Egerton himself has made a point of reminding us that *Rocketman* is assuredly *not* an Elton John biopic.

Songs are played years before they were written (like Elton playing "Crocodile Rock" at the 1970 Troubadour show); people act unlike the way they did in real life (the harsh portrayal of Elton's father is at odds with family accounts of the man and his relationship with Elton); and events are out of order (Elton marries Renate in the late seventies when they didn't even meet until 1983), all for the sake of—according to director Dexter Fletcher—"capturing the moment cinematically and musically."

Also, we're told that the "John" in "Elton John" came from Elton's decision to name himself after John Lennon. When asked what his new last name is, his gaze falls on a photograph of the Beatles on the wall with John's face highlighted. His last name actually came from his long friendship with Long John Baldry.

The bulk of the film, and the movie's framing device, is a rehab facility, Alcoholics Anonymous, or Narcotics Anonymous meeting, which Elton joins at the beginning of the movie in full, red-feathered concert regalia. He introduces himself to the group, and as he speaks, his life is shown in flashbacks as he recounts his experiences. As we flash back and forth from his memories to the present, he strips away more and more of his stage persona, until at the end of the movie, he is in the meeting in his bathrobe. Artistically, the structure of the film works because the chronological and empirical "mistakes" could be "screen Elton" misremembering events. Again, as Taron Egerton said, it's not a biopic or a documentary. Liberties are taken for the artistic goal of honest portrayal of emotional and psychological truths and milestones.

The movie is about two people: young Reginald Dwight, and legendary musical icon Elton John. There are scenes from throughout Elton's life, as recalled and reported by Elton in group.

One of the fun scenes in the movie occurs after eleven-year-old Reg Dwight is awarded a scholarship to the Royal Academy of Music. He shows up for the first day, and a teacher is on stage playing a perfect rendition of Mozart's "Turkish Rondo" on a grand piano. She continues to play until she notices him and then stops and rises from the piano bench. She shakes his hand and asks him to play something for her. He sits down and plays, yes, "Turkish Rondo" flawlessly, but then stops abruptly. She asks him why he stopped, and we're to believe that she's suggesting perhaps he didn't know the rest of it. And then Reg says something along the lines of, "That's exactly where you stopped." And her eyebrows rise in surprise!

The success of *Rocketman* lies in what was ultimately the lesser artistic success of *Bohemian Rhapsody. Rocketman*—more *La La Land* than *Bohemian Rhapsody*—takes us inside the mind and psyche of this dual character of Reg and Elton. Events from Freddie Mercury's life were essentially reconstructed ad hoc in *Bohemian Rhapsody*, leaving the contemplating as to Freddie's inner workings and motivations resting on the performances and the audience's perceptions. But in *Rocketman*, the director uses the lyrics of the song as another tool in his toolbox to tell the story. It's obvious that he's an Elton John fan and has familiarity with his work.

Rocketman is a psychologically intense and musically magnificent character study of Elton John, using songs he and Bernie Taupin have written as both illustration and explication of what he was going through at particular points in his life. One gets the sense that in some ways, Reg puts on the guise of Elton John reluctantly at times, and living this "dual life" has been difficult for him over the years. Being "on" as Elton—while really being the shy, reserved, quiet songwriter and "regular" person—has tormented him and is one reason for his struggles with drinking and drug abuse. But the real Elton is in a fulfilled, happy place now as he retires from touring to be with his family.

Rocketman was widely reviewed after release, and Elton, Taron, and Bernie were all interviewed for the movie's release. From all the interviews, reviews, and articles about the movie, we learned some fun facts:

- The "I'm Still Standing" video at the end of the movie is the original Elton John video with CGI used to replace Elton John with Taron Egerton in character as Elton.

- Elton spoke out after Russia censored *Rocketman* upon its release in that country. What did they cut out of the movie? Take a guess. The gay sex scene, and the text scene at the end that said Elton and David were married and had two children. The other text scenes that were allowed to remain included Elton being sober for twenty-eight tears, him still being close friends with Bernie and that they've never had an argument, and that he has raised over $400 million for his AIDS charity.

- Taron Egerton sings every note in the movie himself. He sings with his own voice so he doesn't always sound like Elton, but there are moments when the resemblance in their voices is uncanny.

- Elton John and Taron Egerton had worked together prior to *Rocketman*. They were in *Kingsman: The Golden Circle* together.

- Elton John was almost completely hands-off during the production of *Rocketman*, leaving everything except Elton-specific decisions to the movie's producer, his husband David Furnish. He said something like, people don't need the guy they're making a movie about hanging around the set.

- Beatles connection: Giles Martin, son of George Martin, the Beatles legendary music producer, was the music producer of *Rocketman*. He also produced the music for the Beatles *LOVE* show.

THE CRITICS SAY...

Molly Freeman, *Screen Rant*: "*Rocketman* features a stunning, powerful star turn from Taron Egerton as Elton John in a sharp and entertaining jukebox musical-style biopic."

Joe Morgenstern, *The Wall Street Journal*: "Much of the bountiful pleasure of *Rocketman*, a jukebox musical about the genesis, emergence, and turbulent triumph of a self-creation named Elton John, comes from the film's delight in embellishing its subject's embellishments, gilding its legendary lily. The events of his breakthrough years are heightened with fantasy sequences that amount to a swirling, semi-surreal remix of his career and inner life. The colors are stunning, the settings are striking, and the energy is irresistible."

John Nugent, *Empire*: "A sequin-encrusted delight. On paper it reads like a by-the-book biopic; on screen it explodes with the kind of color and energy that only Elton John himself could invoke."

Leah Pickett, *Chicago Reader*: "The story reshuffles reality, especially time and facts, and the film is more enjoyable for it."

James Berardinelli, *ReelViews*: "Although the movie will be rightfully and enthusiastically embraced by the singer's fans, it has something to offer those with no more than a casual recognition and appreciation of the man's music."

Asher Luberto, *Film Inquiry*: "It's soaring yet groundbound, joyous yet joyless, waggish yet wise; an enigma every bit as titillating as Sir Elton John."

Brent Hankins, *The Lamplight:* "Thanks to imaginative musical numbers that aren't always bound by the limits of reality and the irrefutable charisma of its leading man, *Rocketman* manages to break the mold just enough to stand tall above many of the genre's other offerings."

Anne Brodie, *What She Said*: "Dexter Fletcher's supple musical fantasy more akin to a stage play than biopic uses set pieces that flow into one another, tightly and brilliantly episodic, skipping from one eye-popping paragraph to the next."

26 Elton John and Bernie Taupin Songs in *Rocketman*

1. "The Bitch Is Back"
2. "I Want Love"
3. "Saturday Night's Alright (for Fighting)"
4. "Thank You for All Your Loving"
5. "Honky Cat"
6. "Candle in the Wind (Instrumental)"
7. "Border Song"
8. "Daniel"
9. "I Guess That's Why They Call It the Blues"
10. "Sad Songs (Say So Much)"
11. "Rock and Roll Madonna"
12. "Your Song"
13. "Amoreena"
14. "Crocodile Rock"
15. "Tiny Dancer"
16. "Take Me to the Pilot"
17. "Hercules"
18. "Don't Go Breaking My Heart"
19. "Rocket Man"
20. "Bennie and the Jets"
21. "Victim of Love"
22. "Don't Let the Sun Go Down on Me"
23. "Sorry Seems to Be the Hardest Word"
24. "Goodbye Yellow Brick Road"
25. "I'm Still Standing"
26. "(I'm Gonna) Love Me Again"

Rocketman Credits

1. Taron Egerton	Elton John
2. Jamie Bell	Bernie Taupin
3. Richard Madden	John Reid
4. Bryce Dallas Howard	Sheila
5. Gemma Jones	Ivy
6. Steven Mackintosh	Stanley
7. Tom Bennett	Fred
8. Matthew Illesley	Young Reggie
9. Kit Connor	Older Reggie
10. Charlie Rowe	Ray Williams
11. Peter O'Hanlon	Bobby
12. Ross Farrelly	Cyril
13. Evan Walsh	Elton Dean
14. Tate Donovan	Doug Weston
15. Sharmina Harrower	Heather
16. Ophelia Lovibond	Arabella
17. Celinde Schoenmaker	Renate
18. Harriet Walter	Helen Piena
19. Stephen Graham	Dick James
20. Sharon D. Clarke	Counselor
21. Aston McAuley	Dave Godin
22. Jason Pennycooke	Wilson
23. Alexia Khadime	Diana
24. Carl Spencer	Richard
25. Jimmy Vee	Arthur
26. Leon Delroy Williams	Clint
27. David Doyle	Pub Man 1
28. Leigh Francis	Pete
29. Dickon Tolson	Barman
30. Diana Alexandra Pocol	Mary the Receptionist

31. Eddie Mann	Band Member
32. Josh McClorey	New Bluesology Band Member
33. Rachel Muldoon	Kiki Dee
34. Benjamin Mason	Bryan
35. Guillermo Bedward	Geoff
36. Max Mackintosh	Stephen
37. Micah Holmes	LA Transgender Maid
38. Charles Armstrong	Mr. Anderson
39. Barbara Drennan	Mrs. Anderson
40. Jason Sellars	MC / Drag Queen
41. Graham Fletcher-Cook	Maître D'
42. Sian Crisp	Waitress
43. Dale Monie	1st Hanger-On
44. Alex James-Phelps	Young Guy
45. Fabian Sgoluppi	Kid
46. Leon Cooke	Hugh
47. Max Croes	Venus Valentine
48. Stevee Davies	Minion
49. Nia Towle	Sushi Girl
50. Lee Bridgman	Steve
51. Rob Callender	Rory
52. Demetri Goritsas	Carter

Written by	**Lee Hall**
Directed by	**Dexter Fletcher**
Produced by	**Adam Bohling**
Produced by	**David Furnish**
Executive Producer	**Elton John**

8

ROCK OF THE BESTIES

THE BEST OF ELTON AND BERNIE

Best Rocker:
"The Bitch Is Back"
Runner-Up:
"Saturday Night's Alright (for Fighting)"

Best Ballad:
"American Triangle"
Runner-Up:
"Your Song"

Best Instrumental:
"Carla/Etude"
Runner-Up:
"Funeral for a Friend"

Best Lyrics:
"Someone Saved My Life Tonight"
Runner-Up:
"Mona Lisas and Mad Hatters"

Best Album:
Madman Across the Water
Runner-Up:
Peachtree Road

Best Video:
"Blue Wonderful" (Thibaut Duverneix)
Runner-Up:
"Rocket Man" (Majid Adin)

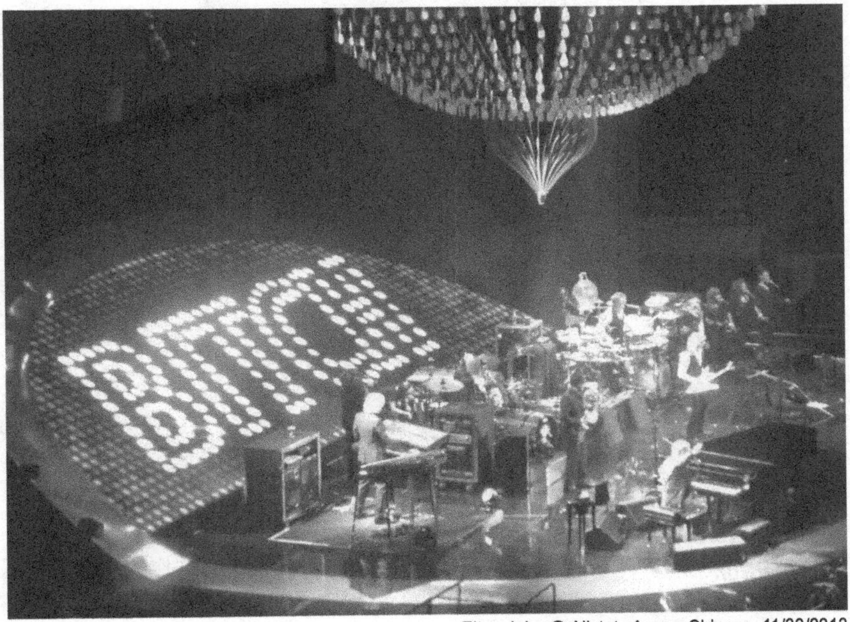

Elton John @ Allstate Arena, Chicago, 11/30/2013

aphrodite-in-nyc via Flickr, 2010

(L. to R.): Sting, Debbie Harry, Lady Gaga, Elton, Shirley Bassey, Bruce Springsteen

Nigel Olsson B. Kim Hagar via Flickr, 2007

PART II:

ESSAYS AND INTERVIEWS

9

THIS ESSAY HAS NO TITLE (JUST WORDS AND A SOUNDTRACK)

BY BEV VINCENT

Bev Vincent, although primarily known for his essays and books about Stephen King, has been a lifelong fan of Elton John's music. More of a brown dirt cowboy than a Captain Fantastic, he grew up in rural eastern Canada before setting out down the yellow brick road for the big cities of Halifax, Nova Scotia, Zurich, Switzerland, and, finally, north Houston, Texas, where he lives with his wife. Vincent is also the author of over ninety short stories. His work has won the Al Blanchard Award and been nominated for the Bram Stoker Award (twice), the Edgar Award, and the ITW Thriller Award. Learn more at bevvincent.com.

THE FIRST LP (long playing vinyl album) I ever purchased was *Elton John's Greatest Hits* (Volume 1, the *only* volume at the time). That statement is not precisely true, but I'll get back to that in a minute.

I grew up in a rural community in the northeastern corner of the Canadian province of New Brunswick. After the two-room schoolhouse near my house closed, I had to take a bus nine miles into town each day.

My next-door neighbor owned several school buses, and the one that took me to high school started its run from his backyard. Technically, I should have waited for another bus to pick me up at the end of its run, but it was more convenient for me to walk next door, especially during the brutal winter months. Instead of standing on the side of the road, I could wait on a warm, idling bus. This also afforded me access to the highly prized back seats, where the older kids carried on a long-running debate about the relative merits of Ford versus Chevrolet.

They also talked about music. One guy kept raving about someone named Elton John. To fit in, I decided I was an Elton John fan, too. The next chance I got (and my opportunities to shop were limited to infrequent trips to the nearest small city, or even rarer journeys to one of the larger cities in southern N.B.), sometime in 1974 or 1975, I bought a copy *of Elton John's Greatest Hits* (for $4.99, as I recall).

That's when I discovered I was already a fan, without realizing it.

You see, the other, unacknowledged records I'd purchased prior to this one were of the K-Tel variety. I don't know how many of you remember those albums. They were compilations of the most popular songs of the moment; however, they were like Reader's Digest Condensed Books (and, wow, how many of you remember *those*?). The songs were edited—entire verses were removed—to cram as many as possible onto a single disk. It wasn't unusual for a K-Tel record to contain nearly two dozen songs.

Fantastic: 22 Original Hits/22 Original Stars, released in 1973, featured the likes of Garry Glitter, Cliff Richard, Rod Stewart, Donny Osmond, Lobo, Maureen McGovern ("There's Got to Be a Morning After") and Vicki Lawrence, along with other names, many lost to history (Who was Focus?).

What stands out most clearly in my mind about this compilation—which contained not one, but two hits by Elton John—is my older brother yelling at me from his room upstairs. Words to this effect: Yes, "Crocodile Rock" is a good song, but not *ten times in a row*!

I'd liked the song so much that, as soon as it ended, I would pick up the tone arm and reposition the needle so I could listen to it again.

And again. And, apparently, again! I can't recall if I made the connection between "Crocodile Rock" and the other Elton John song on side two ("Rocket Man"), but I certainly liked *that* song!

And, lo and behold, there it was on *Elton John's Greatest Hits*. Peer pressure had encouraged me to buy the record and, from that moment on, I became a die-hard Elton John fan.

A fact about me—when I like something a lot, I'm all in. I owned every single Hardy Boys book and, as my tastes evolved, every Agatha Christie, even those written under pen names. So, over the next couple years, I completed my Elton John collection, usually during trips to Moncton, four hours away, where there was a shopping mall with a real record store, not just a few record bins at the back of the "local" K-Mart, twenty miles away.

I remember finding a copy of *Empty Sky*, with its trippy sphinx-inspired cover, and almost buying the album again some time later when I saw the cover with the sketch of Elton John on it, thinking I'd found something different. Then the coup of discovering a copy of the *Friends* soundtrack in what I now know to be a remainder bin—the gaudy pink cover had a huge hole punched in the upper corner and the album was priced to sell at $1.99!

A few of the early albums came without lyric sheets, and I spent long hours trying to transcribe some of the songs from *Tumbleweed Connection*. Years later, I would discover how badly I had misinterpreted the lyrics to "Son of Your Father." Van Bushell, what?

I bought every new record as soon as it came out, even *Victim of Love*, which my friends and I dubbed *Victim of Disco*. I listened to them over and over again. I can still recite the lyrics to even the more obscure tracks.

♫

When I was young, my parents decided I should learn to play the piano, like my older sister had. (For reasons I don't know to this day, my brother was spared this requirement.) Between the ages of five and ten, I got off the bus once a week on my way home from school and spent an hour with the same older lady who had taught my sister to play.

I didn't have any particular aptitude for the instrument, but I learned the basics, at least. After five years, I was allowed to quit. However, when I was sixteen and starting to really discover music for the first time, I wanted to be able to play the songs I was listening to. I found a couple of Elton John songbooks, compilations of all of his songs to that point, including many I'd never heard of—non-album tracks or B-sides like "All Across the Havens" and "It's Me That You Need."

I found a new piano teacher and, for the next eight months, tormented her with EJ songs whenever I could convince her to diverge from the program she'd created for me. I remember when I first played "The Greatest Discovery," she became so immersed in the lyrics (certainly not in my tortured rendering of the song!) that she forgot to turn the page for me. Over the years, I added an impressive pile of Elton John piano books to the huge stack of EJ vinyl.

The only piano I had access to while living in residence at university was in the cafeteria at the women's dorm. I sometimes attracted the interest of co-eds studying in the cafeteria in the evening by playing "Tonight" or "Chloe" or "Funeral for a Friend." So, thanks for that, Elton!

Back then, I never thought I'd get to see him in concert. Big-ticket acts didn't include eastern Canada on their itineraries. There was a concert in Toronto that some of my friends went to in the early '80s, but I couldn't afford the trip.

Then, in 1984, I spent a couple of months in Oxford, England, as a graduate student. Shortly after I arrived, I found out there would be a day-long concert at Wembley Stadium (built in 1923, a building that no longer exists) at which Elton John would be the closing act as part of his *Breaking Hearts* tour. Billed as the "Summer of '84" concert, it was scheduled for the day *after* I was supposed to return to Halifax. I immediately rescheduled my return flight and then went into London to get a ticket to the event, which cost the princely sum of twenty-five or thirty-five pounds (more than seventy-five pounds in today's pounds).

The concert started at noon and ran until about 10:30 pm, with Elton playing for the final two and a half hours. Among the other acts appearing that day: Big Country, Kool & the Gang, Nik Kershaw, Sector 27, and Wang Chung. Alone in a crowd of 72,000 people, it was definitely a day to remember. The souvenir booklet from that concert is among my trophies. A buddy from the lab recorded the simulcast from BBC Radio on cassette and sent a copy to me after I got back to Canada. I played the crap out of that tape. (It was a famous show, released on VHS sometime later. Maybe you've seen pictures—Elton is wearing a tuxedo where the jacket is black on one side and white on the other, while the pants are reversed.)

Over the years, I've had the opportunity to see him several more times: in the Hallenstadion in Zurich for the *Reg Strikes Back* tour, where I was pressed up against the stage by the surging crowd; at Wembley Arena in London; three times at the Woodlands Pavilion a few miles from my house (including two solo shows where he played deep cuts with percussionist Ray Cooper); at the Alamodome with Billy Joel on the Face 2 Face tour; and at the now-defunct Summit, former home to the Houston Rockets, during his tour for *The One*.

I missed out on tickets to his two Houston appearances for his farewell tour last fall; those sold out in mere minutes. I wasn't too devastated. I'd seen him during his prime often enough.

My vinyl collection was subsequently replaced by CDs and, later, by a digital library that now consists of over one thousand EJ songs, including dozens of live performances. I still play his songs on the piano from time to time, and I'm very much looking forward to seeing the biopic *Rocketman*, which, based on the trailer, looks like it captures the essence of an amazing life.

If *my* life ever ends up having a soundtrack, many of the songs would come from the impressive discography of Sir Elton John.

10

CANDLES IN THE WIND

BY KEVIN QUIGLEY

Kevin Quigley is a novelist and nonfiction writer whose first book of music criticism, *The Sound Sent Shivers Down My Back: Inside Blitzen Trapper's Masterpiece FURR*, debuted in 2018. His novels, *I'm On Fire* and *Roller Disco Saturday Night*, were released to widespread acclaim, as were his books on the writer Stephen King, *Chart of Darkness*, *Stephen King Limited*, and more. His first short story collection, *This Terrestrial Hell*, was published by Cemetery Dance, and will soon be followed by a second, *Damage & Dread*. Kevin is a graphic designer in Boston where he lives with his husband Shawn.

I HEARD IT in reverse.

1987: I'm in my dad's living room with my stepmother and we're watching MTV. I'm currently wrangling with her decision to decry the new Springsteen video (it's "Brilliant Disguise," at least a year removed from the flashpoint of Brucemania) as being "boring." I'm not yet the Springsteen fan I would become, but I have a healthy fascination for this new, non-bombastic version of the Boss. Maybe I'm about to say something when everything stops. Elton John arrives on the TV in, for some reason, a Colonial-style wig and a glittering white suit. The song identification pops up in the corner of the screen: Elton John, "Candle in the Wind," from the album *Live in Australia.* He's solo, at a piano in front of a massive audience, and before I can come to terms with his costuming, or the live setting, or the fact that this is, somehow, the first time I've ever seen Elton John in motion, he sings three words: "Goodbye Norma Jean." I'm thunderstruck.

I'd heard Elton John before. Of course I had. Like a lot of kids, my first exposure to music was what my family listened to. That was always a hodgepodge. My grandparents were into oldies, so when I spent the summer with them, my entire musical experience started with the Ronettes and ended with the Beach Boys. Dad was into new stuff, whatever that new stuff was. He's the one who got me into bands like Hole, which is weird if you're a kid used to listening to the Righteous Brothers' "Unchained Melody" eighty times in a row and now you have to figure out what "Doll Parts" means.

Mom was the traditionalist. John Lennon. Billy Joel. And, of course, Elton John. It was her copy of *Elton John's Greatest Hits* I first picked up from the bottom of a box of cassettes with no cases. This was the ten-song version that came out in 1974; Elton's eleventh official release, it was the best-selling album of 1975, the year I was born. Only ten songs, but when I discovered it, twelve years later, it opened up a whole new corner of the world to me. It shocked me that the plaintive, falsetto-chorused "Goodbye Yellow Brick Road" came from the same guy who did the guitar-fronted hardish rock of "Saturday Night's Alright (for Fighting)." (This was a mistake I would repeat when I discovered Queen and realized that "We Will Rock You" and "You're My Best Friend" came from the same band. The fact that bands could have different styles was just starting to occur to me and blew my sixth-grade mind.) There was a key in those songs, some magical key that opened a door to a new universe, under whose stars I would finally understand what "Rocket Man" really meant. I had a feeling that if I could grasp the implications of Elton John's lyrics and why the music moved me so seismically, I could understand something about myself, too.

And, okay, Elton John was *different.* I didn't totally get it then. I was twelve and there was this junior biography of him in my school library. It hit on the basics—the real name, the flamboyant costumes, the songwriting partnership with Bernie Taupin—but mostly stayed on the surface. It also featured a lot of pictures of John on stage, usually at the piano, usually shouting something forcefully into a microphone. Something about that level of passion stirred something inside me, the way the words and the music had done. I had no idea then that I had a crush on the man. I wouldn't figure anything like that out for four more years, when the floodgates opened and so much of my fascination with certain celebrities (often overweight, often balding) made way more sense.

But, at the time, I was either in deep ignorance or deep denial. Soon after seeing the "Candle in the Wind" video, I confessed to my stepmother that he was one of my favorite singers. I didn't dare hint at anything beyond that, maybe because I didn't have the vocabulary for it. She informed me that he was bisexual, and explained that that meant he was into women *and* men. The idea was frankly *insane* to me, so much so that I shut down my crush before it could even form the basis of an idea in my mind. I think, reflecting on this many years later, that I decided I couldn't associate myself intimately with anyone who was openly *outré*. Even if he was a celebrity that everyone liked enough to keep putting in the Top 40 every year. Suburban adolescent homosexual self-loathing: eventually I would quit those days and my redneck ways, but that was not the day.

Let's go back to the now: I recorded the song off the radio—I was still two years away from buying my first cassingle (Michael Damian's "Rock On," and we don't have to talk about it)—so the beginning and end were cut off whenever I made mix tapes. But even this truncated version was powerful, and it grew more potent each time I listened to it. My father had loaned me his ancient over-ear headphones for late-night listening, and there were hours when I would turn off the lights and listen to this song over and over, knowing exactly how long to press the rewind button.

When you fall in love with a song and play it on perpetual repeat, there's a magical time between "I can't listen to this enough" and "I can't listen to this again." Inside that aural gloaming, the song gives more of itself each time. Nuance and inflection that you didn't quite detect on the first few listens eventually become the reasons you're listening again. There are so many standout moments on this track, tiny twists away from the straightforward, that any of them elevate the song, and all of them render this version definitive.

So much of it is the sound itself: huge and booming and round. Before you hear those first stirrings of the audience, you know you're inside a big place. This isn't a studio sound; this is the sound of a man singing in a 13,000-seat arena and filling the whole space with his vocals, even in the quieter moments. At first, he's not belting, but he's emphatic. Even when his lyrics aren't italicized, there's an urgency to the things he's singing. He's lost in this memory of Marilyn Monroe and how her fame was her downfall. Of course, by this point in Elton John's career, he can't help but draw parallels to his own career. Drug abuse. Hiding his true self. Barely-escaped weddings to people he didn't want to be married to. He almost gives himself away in this performance, almost takes off the wig and the mask and allows himself to be confessional instead of reverential: "They crawled out of the woodwork...*and* they whispered into your brain." That small laugh in the *and* says so much, that he understands how the press can turn on you, how the world can turn on you, even as they idolize you. It's the moment in which you realize this isn't Elton John singing about Marilyn Monroe: it's Reginald Dwight singing to Norma Jeane Mortenson. [**Ed. Note**: Marilyn's real name was "Norma Jeane" with an "e" at the end. The sheet music and most published lyrics for "Candle in the Wind" omit the "e" and refer to her as "Norma Jean."] They didn't make Reg change his name, but now he's as locked in as Mortenson had been, chained to a public life that, by its nature, dominates his private.

Some of that is the weight of years, the heft of having experience to back up these sentiments. Elton John typically does not write his own lyrics; those duties tend to fall to his longtime collaborator, Bernie Taupin. John brings himself into it with the music and the way he sings, the way he plays. Now, I'm not going to say that a singer can't inhabit a song they don't write. That would put a lot of careers on notice, from Elvis Presley to Meat Loaf to Britney Spears. But I do think it can take time to completely feel the words, to get to a place where the words feel like a singer's own. That only happens with repetition, living with the song, elevating it, reinventing it. Overlaying the meaning of the song with the life the singer is leading. Elton John had been put on the treadmill, and Elton John had lost himself in drugs and excess. He could have died multiple times. By 1987, the meaning of the song had changed for him. He was singing about himself.

I don't remember how I first heard the original version (although I do remember how I heard the newest version, the one whose lyrics changed to reflect the death of Princess Diana—everywhere, on every radio, all throughout 1997; I'm not really discussing that one here because it's essentially a different song). I know I had the record of *Goodbye Yellow Brick Road*, back when owning records was about to be lame but before it was cool. But for the life of me, I can't ever recall *listening* to this song back then. I listened to the title track. "Bennie and the Jets." "Funeral for a Friend/Love Lies Bleeding," because the local AM radio played it once and Spotify wasn't real yet. Not "Candle." Maybe because I knew I already had the best version so there was no need? I think I used to believe I had room for one version of a song in my head and my life. I was young. I hadn't yet started spending rent money on bootleg CDs, or, even later, spending whole afternoons on *Archive.com*, getting those same types of bootlegs for the price of absolutely nothing. It's kind of a shame, too, because the original version is fantastic.

There are parallel universes out there in which I hear the *Goodbye Yellow Brick Road* version first, and I envy those doppelgängers of me drifting through time, their musical tastes shifting and mutating as the universe of music grew exponentially more complicated and diverse. The original version of "Candle in the Wind" is kind of a beast, and you know it almost immediately. Starting off as the 1987 take does—those simple, sad piano notes—but then: wait! Guitars? Both electric *and* acoustic? And an unexpected drumbeat sneaking in, right where the song hesitates in '87. And we're still only in the first ten seconds?

Then, *bam*, the first chorus, and hiding deep in the mix is this guitar riff that *almost* doesn't belong. Not at first, anyway; we're still getting used to all these other sounds. Then, even though it's the least prominent part of the chorus, it starts to feel more urgent, more necessary. Then Elton, *many* Eltons, come in to back up Elton Prime in this almost spiritual chorus of *aaaaaaah*s and *ooooooh*s—lonely and sighing but very much on key. That double-tracking, hitting on the title and the "when the rain set in": those harmonized voices, those insistent lines, making sure to underscore how important these words are. At this point, that sneaky guitar riff decides it's spent too much time in the background, and forces itself forward. The piano works inside the riff coming out of the chorus, counterpointing, as the drums find a new, faster beat to make sure the other instruments don't get lost. This chorus is *muscular*. It's undeniable.

Then why isn't it as good as the one from *Live in Australia*?

It should be. Technically, it's the more complete song. The layers of sound aren't studio frippery; everything is in there on purpose, everything belongs. That second harmony voice, my God; Elton John backing himself up is like grabbing the listener by the collar and shaking them to pay attention. When we have that third-verse return to the original refrain—"Goodbye Norma Jean"—Elton is no longer approaching quietly. A little bit of that live-version casualness is in him by now, familiarity with this memory he's singing to. He does it in "Daniel," and even in "Crocodile Rock"—when the first verse returns and he wants us to feel as familiar with the memory as he now is. It's a wonderful song. One of Bernie Taupin's best written, and one of Elton John's best performed.

But—and I hate sounding like a broken record—it's not the best version.

And maybe it has something to do with me, and who I was when I first heard it. It's so hard to be subjective about art, especially music. It doesn't exist in a vacuum. You can enjoy "The Bitch Is Back" and "Someone Saved My Life Tonight" without knowing Elton John's real story, but knowing about his life enhances those songs. And knowing about who I was enhances my love of "Candle in the Wind." My own crush on the man presaged who I would become; my rejection of him when I found out that he was able to live a life I was not—yet—echoes through me to this day. Now that I can see him as something more than sexual, more than just *my* Elton John.

There are a lot of Elton John best-of compilations out there. When they include "Candle in the Wind," they don't include either charted version. The version whose lyrics were changed to create a threnody for Princess Diana reigned at the top of the charts for fourteen weeks in 1997; a decade before, the *Live in Australia* version soared to Number 6. But the original version, the one I heard second, is the one on all those best-ofs. Maybe it makes sense, going back to the beginning. Maybe it's even the right way to go, providing the bedrock of a song before exploring how malleable it is, how indestructible. But, if I were compiling those anthologies, I'd make sure the *Live in Australia* version was prominently placed somewhere between "Tiny Dancer" and "Sad Songs (Say So Much)," offering a more complete sound picture of a singer and a man at one of the most crucial moments of his career and life.

11

THE GREATEST BUILD OF ALL TIME?

BY TYSON BLUE

Although he is primarily known for his expertise regarding the work of Stephen King and the various media projects based thereon, **Tyson Blue** is also knowledgeable about other things as well. Among those things is music. A lifelong fan of rock 'n' roll, he is also a founding member and sometime lead singer for the New Hampshire-based rock band The Cataclysmic Domestics, now in their fifty-first year. The composer of more than 150 songs, he now serves as bass drummer for the Rochester Scottish Pipes and Drums, formed one hundred years ago (his wife, Janice, is the band's current Pipe Major). As a songwriter, composer, musician, and producer, he, as they say, knows his shit.

WHEN IT COMES to great rock 'n' roll songs, is there anything better than a good build? You know, where the song starts out simple, with one instrument laying down the basic track, and then as the song goes along, layer after layer joins in, building and building the tempo until the whole thing suddenly explodes into an anthemic musical tsunami that engulfs you in a sea of driving rhythm?

One example of this is the classic opening track to one of the few perfect albums ever made ("perfect" meaning "there are no bad tracks anywhere on the album"), The Who's 1971 album *Who's Next*. That song, "Baba O'Riley" (not "Teenage Wasteland," as some listeners mistakenly call it), may be the greatest rock song of all time. It starts off with a lilting synthesizer riff, then adds a piano track, then Roger Daltrey's searing vocal, and finally, after the first verse, Pete Townshend's powerhouse guitar finally comes in and lifts the whole thing into the stratosphere. That build lasts for one minute, forty-eight seconds.

Also released in 1971 is one of the most classic build songs of all time, Led Zeppelin's "Stairway to Heaven," the fourth song on the band's rune-entitled fourth album. This one starts out slowly and quietly, with a softly-plucked acoustic guitar and recorders accompanying Robert Plant's vocal for the first verse. At the two-minute mark, an electric guitar enters the mix. At the three-minute thirty mark, the tempo begins to gradually increase, and the guitars come to the forefront. Drums come in at the four minute, eighteen-second mark. Finally, at five minutes, thirty-two seconds, Jimmy Page's iconic solo begins, and the tempo continues to slowly build until the final, racing burst of power chords and Plant's trademark vocals kick in (6:44) and bring the song to its climax, fading to Plant's softened, gentle, unaccompanied coda.

Then there's "Thunderstruck," the classic AC/DC anthem which opens *The Razor's Edge*. It starts out with Angus Young's rippling guitar intro with high-hat cymbal accents, followed by the snarling backing vocal. This is followed by the pounding bass drum, followed closely by the chant of "THUN-DER!" on top of it. Then the throbbing bass enters. Brian Johnson's ragged lead vocal comes in on top of all of this, and the build is still not done. Midway through the first verse, accenting power chords enter the mix, and finally, with a crash of drums, one minute and fifty-two seconds into its four minute, fifty-two second running time, the song finally crescendos and takes off with all its parts blended into a truly stunning whole.

But one of the greatest builds in all of rock is one which builds so slowly and deliberately that it takes an entire song to reach its peak. I am referring, of course, to "Funeral for a Friend/Love Lies Bleeding," the song which opens Elton John's classic seventh studio album, widely regarded as his best and most popular, *Goodbye Yellow Brick Road* (1975). You *have* noticed, have you not, that all but one of these tracks open the albums on which they're featured. Long a staple opener for John's live shows as well, "Funeral for a Friend/Love Lies Bleeding" is currently the opener for the second set of shows in his ongoing "Farewell Yellow Brick Road" tour.

"Funeral" (as we'll refer to it here for the sake of brevity), runs for eleven minutes and nine seconds from start to finish, of which "Funeral for a Friend" takes up about five minutes and ten seconds—almost half the total running time. That's longer than all of "Thunderstruck" (four minutes, fifty-two seconds), and ten seconds longer than all of "Baba O'Riley" (five minutes, seven seconds). It's not longer than the build of "Stairway to Heaven" (six minutes, forty-four seconds), but there's *another whole song* afterward.

And with all of this extra time to play with, "Funeral" is a much more ambitious and complex piece of music than the other three examples. Where the other two songs basically start things out simply and gradually build up to the point where they are off and running, this one has a lot more to do, and pulls it off masterfully.

Elton John has stated that the two songs were not written to be a single piece of music, but each started out as a separate piece (John Knowles reference intended). "Funeral" was written when John was thinking about the kind of music he would want played at his funeral, according to the song's Wikipedia entry. No information could be found regarding the origins of "Love Lies Bleeding," although it is apparently the name of a flower. The song, with lyrics by longtime Elton John lyricist Bernie Taupin, is an angry breakup song whose composition is not set down anywhere. They were put together later, since "Funeral" ends and "Love Lies Bleeding" begins with an A chord.

"Funeral" begins quietly, with a haunting, spooky, synthesized wind howling up and down, conjuring up an image of a lonely graveyard at night, with a mournful, rhythmically-tolling bell (also synthesized) adding to the solemn atmosphere (the current live version of the song prefaces it with an impressive indoor thunderstorm). Then, a lilting, processional ARP synthesizer riff begins, a movement which calls to mind (and bears a striking similarity to) Maurice Jarre's emotional music for the funeral scene which opens the main story of David Lean's epic film, *Doctor Zhivago*. In that scene, the young Zhivago attends his mother's funeral in a small town in the Ural Mountains, and the music reflects his emotions.

The synthesized music, performed by the album's engineer, David Hentschel, builds, adds layers, and finally reaches a crescendo, ending with a flourish which incorporates a brief fragment of John's elegy to Marilyn Monroe, "Candle in the Wind," which comes later in the album, serving as a prelude to that song, and adding another funeral element to the song.

In an interview published on the singer's official website, Hentschel explained how the intro was put together. "The working title for the album was *Silent Movies and Talking Pictures*. [The] original idea was to use the 20th Century Fox music overture as the introduction to the album. But he couldn't get clearance to use the music, so (producer) Gus [Dudgeon] said to me, 'Why don't you write an arrangement? And we'll segue it into the song [recorded in France].' I had done some ARP (synth) work on earlier Elton records, like 'Rocket Man' and 'Hercules.'

"The concept was to have it as a kind of overture, but it was down to me to juggle with some of the tunes from the songs [on the album]," Hentschel explained. "It was almost a mathematical exercise as much as anything. Find things that would run together easily melodically, basically, and then make a melody that flows within itself. I know I used some lines from 'Danny Bailey,' 'I've Seen That Movie Too,' 'Candle in the Wind' [other tracks on the *GYBR* album], and one or two others."

Hentschel would write the charts out first, then play them monophonically on the synthesizer with one hand while adjusting the gain with the other, to eliminate the flat sound that resulted from the analog synthesizers of the day and to give a sense of dynamics and movement to the sound.

"The intro was on a separate piece of 16-track tape and we stitched it together [with Elton and the band's recording] in the mixing stage. Because I had written out the arrangement first I could pretty much say, 'Right, we'll do maybe six or seven "string" parts, and then we'll mix those down to a stereo pair.' And we'd build it up that way on the multitrack. I think I had three or four days to do it and write it down, and then when I got to the studio we did it all in about seven or eight hours."

For the full interview, which offers an in-depth look into the production and recording of this landmark album, go to:

https://www.eltonjohn.com/stories/engineerdavidhentscheltalksaboutgoodbyeyellowbrickroad

But I digress—back to the song.

The synthesizer intro fades, to be replaced by a solo piano, playing a slow, stately, melancholy processional, with a quiet woodwind accompaniment, then building to a flourish of guitars, drums, and rippling synthesizers, which builds and builds to a fast, piano-driven rock demo with more synth flourishes, which erupts into a cabaret-sounding, Rockettes-high-kicking plateau, and then takes off into another build, with the tempo getting faster and faster, driven by drummer Nigel Olsson's galloping high-hat and Davey Johnstone's rippling guitar riffs, until finally, the thrashing opening chords of "Love Lies Bleeding" signal the switch to the second song.

Taupin's lyrics use imagery of death and violence to convey the anger the narrator feels over a relationship which has died, meshing perfectly with the searing guitar chords. The narrator is a musician who has sacrificed his band to be with a fan, only to find that "my guitar couldn't hold you," that she felt that "If I don't change the pace/I won't face another day."

"And love lies bleeding in my hands," John sings in the chorus. "[I]t kills me to think of you with another man." Without her, "the roses in the window box/Have tilted to one side/Everything about this house/Was born to grow and die."

The second verse is sung with the same anger, but the lyrics are softer, wondering if "those changes/Have left a scar on you," and compares her to "a bluebird on a telephone wire," saying "I hope you're happy now"—but how is that phrase meant? Is it sincere or sarcastic?

After the second chorus, there is a quiet piano solo, augmented with synthesized flutes, which builds back into the same searing guitar attack which began the song, and, with a final chorus, drives the song through to its conclusion.

Once the song reaches its peak at the end of "Funeral," it never fully winds down. From its quiet beginnings, with wind and bells, through its fiery climax, "Funeral for a Friend/Love Lies Bleeding" is one of the greatest building rock songs ever written. And it is indisputably a high point in Elton John's career.

12

E-L-T-O-N

BY RICHARD CHRISTIAN MATHESON

RC Matheson is a #1 bestselling author and screenwriter/producer for TV and film. He has written, produced, and created television series, films, and mini-series and had scores of episodes and sixteen movies produced, including cult favorite *Three O'Clock High*. His celebrated adaptation of Stephen King's "Battleground" won two Emmys. He has worked with Steven Spielberg, Dean Koontz, Mel Brooks, Roger Corman, Nicholas Pileggi, Stephen King, and many others and *The New York Times* calls him "...a great horror writer." Matheson's dark, psychological stories appear in his acclaimed collections *Scars and Other Distinguishing Marks*, #1 Amazon bestseller *Dystopia*, *Zoopraxis*, and 125 major anthologies, including many "Years Best" volumes. He is the author of the suspense novel, *Created By*, and surreal, Hollywood novella "The Ritual of Illusion." Matheson is a professional studio drummer and studied privately with *Cream*'s Ginger Baker. He has played with Stephen King's Rock Bottom Remainders and The Smithereens' Pat DiNizio. He is the president of Matheson Entertainment.

A MILLION YEARS ago, I played drums in a band that dared to tackle Elton John's "Funeral for a Friend/Love Lies Bleeding"—a majestic song of vast challenge.

Our keyboardist mimicked every cool synth, our bass player plucking a credible throb. I gripped sticks, high-diving into the pocket. After hours of rehearsal, doing it zero justice, we finally nailed what dimly resembled the song; minus its depth and epic feel. We only played it live once, at an LA club, mostly getting lost in the middle, and never tackled another Elton song; undoubtedly our greatest contribution to his music. But whenever I hear that song on *Goodbye Yellow Brick Road*, it transports me; somehow sacred, amid glorious, haunting melody. It is a grand creation.

Music genres are many, new ones cross-breeding as we sleep. There's Blues. Jazz. Rock. Pop. Classical. Reggae. Folk. Opera. Calypso. Country. Acid-jazz. Funk. Punk. Rap. On and on.

And then there's Elton.

Able to gene-splice them all, at what seems bewitching whim, into countless gems, joyous and hurt; ballads that break the world's heart, and rockers that turn up hope to ten. Entertaining as any lead singer that ever pranced, posed, or went Kama Sutra on a Steinway, Elton leaves them all in his bejeweled wake.

On countless, SRO nights, he's a Kabuki storm. Mad-hatter costumes, Jumbotron glasses spelling E-L-T-O-N, Rocket Man boosters fully aflame. Famously, jubilantly, he once waddled onto the stage as Donald Duck, crooning with flirtatious, feathered glee, his webbed mitts a blur of stabbing flourishes. All in a hip night's work.

In interviews, on talk shows, introducing songs at concerts or goofing with the press, his half-subversive, self-effacing silliness and Cheshire charm make fast trouble, slyly getting every joke...nonchalantly dashing off more wicked ones. Like his peerless ivory-tickling, Elton's comic timing slays.

Trained at London's Royal Academy of Music, he was soon to brilliantly detonate. As fame and privilege shot him from dizzying cannon, he partied in the jet stream, hiding deeper hurts with kliegs of charade: coy Pagliacci, diva, cynic. No galaxy could contain him and, however much his world soared, tilted, or randomly freefell, Elton's music was always there to fly into the sun and catch him. When the twenty-four-karat deluge almost drowned his life, he became a twelve-step survivor of heartache and excess...finally finding his way home as a husband and father.

It's said that when the prodigious Bernie Taupin hands over his newest lyrics, like miniature, Faberge rock/pop novels, Elton sits alone at the piano, and tinkers, drifting into a wondrous trance. If the eighty-eight-key genie isn't in the mood, and nothing comes to him, within twenty minutes, Elton moves on; a virtuoso in restless, poetic motion.

By recent count, the collaborators have written 197 songs, recorded thirty-three studio albums, four live albums, three musicals, seven soundtrack albums, and sixteen compilation albums; sold thirty-eight Gold and thirty-one Platinum or Multi-Platinum albums; and, for completists, produced three extended-play albums. A grand total of 250 million records sold. A sublime soundtrack, gift-wrapped for the world. And for every brilliant song, twenty minutes did the trick.

For Sir Elton Hercules John, touched by magic, no bow is deep enough.

13

WHY WE LOVE ELTON JOHN AND WHAT HE STANDS FOR

BY SAMANTHA LEWIS AND SYDNEY LEWIS

The younger generation—Generation Z—weighs in on EJ

Sydney Lewis (left) and her older sister, Samantha Lewis

SAMANTHA AND SYDNEY are the daughters of co-author Michael Lewis. In 2018, Samantha received a BA in musical theater, and in May 2019, received a master's degree in elementary education. Sydney finished her first year majoring in civil engineering (minoring in psychology), sports a 4.0 GPA thus far, and is on the Dean's List. Sam and Syd are both on their way to bright futures and are ready to change the world that we older folks kinda messed up.

Sam and Syd grew up to love classic rock, with their parents exposing them to all kinds of music from the start. We asked them why they appreciate Elton John and his music.

How did you first hear Elton John's music?

Samantha: Both my parents listen to Elton John, and my mom always showed me the costumes he would wear, and I immediately thought he was so cool and that it was so inspiring how he chose to express himself.

Sydney: I have more memories of my dad playing his songs for me on our car rides to softball games and things like that. I always got, though, the sense that my mom may have been more into his whole vibe and nature as an artist. She always emphasized her love for his costumes and glittery glasses. I know her favorite song of his is "Crocodile Rock." [Ed. Note: Your dad's favorite is probably "Bennie and the Jets." –Mike]

What are your favorite Elton John songs and why?

Sydney: My favorite Elton John songs are probably "Don't Go Breaking My Heart" and "I'm Still Standing." I like "Don't Go Breaking My Heart" because of its upbeat tempo and fun attitude that just leaves the listener happier than they were before pressing play. It's honestly a song that I love belting out in my college dorm. I also love "I'm Still Standing" because I feel like it perfectly embodies Elton John's persona and what he stands for in overcoming obstacles and encouraging others to be something, even if society says they shouldn't. It's a song that I believe everyone can relate to and listen to if they need a little boost or are feeling down.

Samantha: My all-time favorite Elton John song is "Your Song." I think it's absolutely beautiful, and I have dedicated it to someone special in my life. "I hope you don't mind that I put down in words, How wonderful life is while you're in the world"—those are some of the most touching lyrics I have ever heard in a song, and I will always carry them with me. So many artists have covered his music, and that just goes to show how many people he has inspired, which I personally think speaks for itself about his impact.

"Rocket Man" and "Bennie and the Jets" are always songs that I blast in my car whenever they come on shuffle. There's just something about them that make me want to dance and sing at the top of my lungs. It's magical, really.

Do you prefer his earlier music, or more recent things *(Lion King etc.)?*

Sydney: I prefer his earlier stuff, the music that really brought him into the music scene and are his staples as an artist. Songs such as "Tiny Dancer," "Rocket Man," and "Your Song" immediately transport the listener back to when they were first released, when he took the music industry and pop culture by storm.

Samantha: I'm a major Disney fan, and *The Lion King* is one of my favorite Disney movies. I think his music in it is so fitting. It really captures the essence of the movie and I love it. However, some of his earlier music is so exotic and wonderful that I have to say his earlier music is my favorite.

Do you like any other music that was originally released before you were born?

Samantha: I grew up listening to "oldies" (as my generation would now call it). While some only know ABBA because of the play and movie *Mamma Mia*, I knew their music before I ever even saw the movie, and I think the originals are irreplaceable. I also love Aerosmith; Steven Tyler's voice is a memory from my childhood and I love the way they incorporate meaningful lyrics into classic rock. Last, and quite positively most of all, I love the Beatles. The fact that there are some people my age who don't even give their unique music a shot, while it inspired so many artists that they listen to today, really hurts me. Music is such a huge part of my life and I wouldn't trade that for the world.

Sydney: We grew up in a Beatles household. We both listened to Beatles music since day one, and I have grown to love and appreciate them on my own over the years.

Is there any other artist from today that you can see having a fifty-year career like EJ?

Sydney: I don't feel any artists will have a fifty-year career like Elton John. I think notable bands from today such as the Jonas Brothers may end up having reunions down the road for an album and tour or two after virtually "ending" their careers in music. If there were to be any artist that would have a fifty-year career, I would think it would be an artist who prides themselves in being different from the mainstream pop artists of today, not abiding by society's standards for what a successful artist must be. Therefore, I could see someone like Lady Gaga—who has adapted her music and work with the times as they happen, including her work in movies—she could end up having a long career. In all honesty, though, it seems that all of today's most popular artists quickly fade in and out of the picture, while artists such as Elton John, Michael Jackson, and Paul McCartney have left an impression on people of all different generations.

Samantha: I picture myself still listening to the music I listen to now in fifty years. I'd love to see where Panic! At the Disco's Brendon Urie's career is in fifty years. He's been writing and making music since he was seventeen years old, which isn't far off from when Elton John started his career. While Alternative music isn't something that many people listen to everyday anymore, Urie knows how to adapt to what's popular now, and does just that, reaching as many audiences as possible. Now you hear his music (new and old) on multiple radio stations, and while his look has changed, his voice and talent certainly has not.

Do you share your love of Elton John with your friends? Do they like it?

Samantha: Most of the people I surround myself with listen to music that is older because we have a greater appreciation for music in general and the impact it has had on society. I haven't met a single person that doesn't like Elton John, and if I did…I'd have some questions for them.

Sydney: I do tend to share my love of EJ with friends who also appreciate his talent and music. Sometimes, though, I find that many of my friends were not gifted with the same exposure to older music as I was, and therefore don't see the same value and greatness in it as I do, as someone who has had a taste of music from all sorts of genres and periods of time.

Are you aware of his life and his charity work?

Sydney: I'm so excited to see the new movie coming out so I can really learn more about what makes Elton John who he is. I learned a bit about his charity work with the Elton John AIDS foundation and with Ryan

White when I had to do research for a presentation. My presentation was inspired by the recent movie highlighting the life of Freddie Mercury, *Bohemian Rhapsody*, but was mainly about the early days of the AIDS epidemic. I could really sense just how strong Ryan and Elton's bond was, and I think this spoke volumes about the things that Elton John stood for and wanted to make a positive impact on.

Samantha: I love what the Elton John AIDS Foundation stands for. Their aim is to create an AIDS-free world for the future and I think it's beautiful. I love the fact that he not only devotes his life to music that has changed the world, but he's also supporting people who need help, and doing it with a huge smile on his face. He is more than just a musician, he's an inspiration.

Do you think people will be listening to his music in fifty years?

Sydney: I think people will be listening to his music so long as people in my generation, Generation Z, don't forget to expose their children to his music and pass it along for generations to come. As one of the artists whose music displays the epitome of "good music," I think Elton John's most popular songs and legacy will live on for centuries to come.

Samantha: I believe that more and more people will discover his music as time goes on. He is a fashion icon, he has inspired so many people that are celebrities today, and he continues to inspire people. While he's on his last tour right now, his career won't stop there. He will continue to live on as a legend, and, long after he's gone, people will still look at him in awe, and listen to the music that started it all.

Sydney: As society has evolved, it seems to be facing more hate and bitterness towards people designated as being different, who oftentimes find it hard to emerge from the silence. Those discriminated against include political figures elected into office that defy the previous norms, as well as groups affiliated with the LGBT+ community. The ones that are seen to be "lesser" are most of the time just trying to express themselves and find a place in society. Music artists and philanthropists who dare to be different while spreading positivity and joy, such as Elton John, cannot be forgotten in times like these. The messages shared in his songs, and shown in his selfless acts towards others, can inspire anyone who decides to listen to them. As someone who already sees how beneficial and healing music can be, I find it to be my duty to share the music with others.

14

AN INTERVIEW WITH DAVID BODOH

FOUNDER AND WEBMASTER OF *Eltonography.com*

I UNDERSTAND DAVID Bodoh.

David's Elton John website *Eltonography.com* is the result of a fan utterly consumed by the work of one of his favorite artists.

Elton may, in fact, be David's all-time favorite singer/songwriter, considering the effort, passion, and time it takes to put together as comprehensive a site as *Eltonography.com* undoubtedly is.

Such devotion does not come cheap; commonly, much of ordinary life is pushed aside to work on such a massive passion project. I went through this when I researched and wrote my *Complete Stephen King Encyclopedia*, which took five years, with one assistant. It ended up being 800,000 words about King and his work.

Thus, my understanding of my friend David.

And now, our talk about *Eltonography.com* and the work of Elton John.

Stephen Spignesi: Your excellent website *Eltonography.com* may be the most comprehensive Elton John site on the web. How did it come into being? How long have you been running it?

David Bodoh: For as long as I can remember, I've been interested in collecting things: baseball cards, *Star Wars* toys, Dave & Buster's prizes. Soon after graduating college with a computer science degree, I saw some real potential with this new technology called the World Wide Web. Once I had built some simple pages for a client, I realized I could fairly easily create my own website that cataloged my current collection focus: Elton John music.

I had already been compiling lyrics and albums in data files on a computer, so it was pretty simple to convert the information to a format that I could share with a wider Elton John fan community.

That website first went public around 1995. There was a positive response from fans all around the world, and some time later I adopted the name *Eltonography.com*, a mashup of "Elton John" and "discography."

SS: How long have you been an Elton fan, and what was your first exposure to his music?

DB: I grew up in the '80s, and pop music had ushered in a new class of artists like Madonna and Prince and Michael Jackson. So my first recollections of Elton John were mainly the few pop music videos he had produced during that era, like "I'm Still Standing" and "Sad Songs."

It was around this time that a friend of mine in high school mentioned she really liked Elton's music, and so I took a more critical look at his catalog, beginning with his old *Greatest Hits* albums. That's when I realized that this Elton John guy actually had a widely successful career that had started a decade earlier.

Of course I recognized all the hit songs, but didn't know they were all by the same person! This epiphany coincided with the release of *Reg Strikes Back*, so all albums prior to then were still very new to me. As I went in pursuit of adding more Elton John albums to my collection, I wouldn't have any context about their original popularity or significance.

There were times I'd be blindly debating my next purchase; which one to take home: *Madman Across the Water* or *Victim of Love*? It was a comical coin-toss in retrospect. It took me several months to piece together the chronology of albums before I could re-assemble the full progression of his recording career.

SS: What is it about Elton as an artist that spurs you to put in as much time as you obviously do to maintain your site?

DB: Clearly an artist as popular as Elton, who's been generating hit music this long, will have a tremendous following of fans around the world—even multiple generations of avid fans who have discovered him at different celebrated points along his career.

I think when I started this extended project that I wanted to provide the same guidance I needed when it was all new to me. I am a researcher, after all; I recognize the inherent value of compiling data and presenting it in a structure that most people can easily absorb. So, once I started getting positive feedback from strangers who appreciated the work I was doing, I knew it was all worth it.

As my hobby of collecting grew, and as I was able to add more details to the website, and as Elton kept producing material, I had something to not just keep me busy, but also be of service to the growing audience of fans who would discover Elton's catalog and its presence on the internet.

Other researchers had published discographies in print, but Elton's frantic pace of outputting new material warranted a dynamic resource that could keep up. That's where I feel my website fits in rather well.

SS: Elton once said he thought his career would last one-and-a-half years and that he would then fade into obscurity. We're fifty years on now. Why do you think he's lasted so long, and outlasted so many other singer/songwriters?

DB: Elton John has a genuine passion for music and musicianship. He's not only making his own music, but he stays on top of current trends, current artists, and current music culture. And he generously uses his celebrity and wealth to support the young artists where he recognizes talent and potential.

I think maybe we would have more longevity in pop music if the industry focused more on the artists than the art. And I think Elton has been able to survive this long because he recognizes the value in performing live, and balancing that above making records or profits. So it goes beyond natural talent; it's survival through adapting to change. Also, we don't just listen to music, we experience it—and the experience of attending concerts is what Elton does a great job at delivering!

SS: And now, the inevitable questions for someone so immersed in Elton's career and artistic output: What is your favorite Elton album? Elton song? Elton musical?

DB: It's really impossible to narrow down an answer here. Elton's catalog crosses so many flavors and styles. The great thing about his music is that I can always play something that suits my current mood.

Many people will say he reached perfection with *Goodbye Yellow Brick Road* or *Captain Fantastic*. But those early albums predate my formative years. So I would say that *Sleeping with the Past* is a solid album I would rate as a favorite. All the songs hold together very well, and to me, the "Elton John voice" is unmistakable throughout.

Certainly any of his Top 40 hit singles would be a favorite on my list, but lately I've really been enjoying "Hey Ahab," the song he did with Leon Russell, as a track that really stands out. Bernie Taupin often injects historical or literary character into his lyrics, and Elton John energetically brings that song to life, both vocally and on piano.

Although the longest-running Broadway musical with Elton's involvement is *The Lion King*, I prefer the music for *Aida*, which won four Tony Awards! There was an *Aida* album issued with various artists performing the Elton John/Tim Rice compositions, but I think that Elton's unreleased demo versions are superior. I recommend fans check with their trading circles for that gem!

SS: What kind of feedback, if any, from Elton or Bernie or their people have you had about the site?

DB: Thanks to my website, I have been very fortunate to make some contact with a few people who work closely with Elton John. I am told the staff at his management office have often turned to *Eltonography.com* for some quick answers. They are certainly grateful for the effort that goes into it.

Around 1998, Colin Bell was Elton John's new manager, and he was looking into pursuing some official online presence for his client. He contacted me to say how much he was impressed with my website, and how he wanted to arrange a meeting to discuss some options. But alas, his tenure was cut short, and we never got beyond a few phone calls.

Not long afterward, *eltonjohn.com* was up and running with other people in charge. Another time, I was actually contacted by Sir Tim Rice himself with a request to make a correction on my website. Apparently there's a discrepancy between the written lyric and the way Elton sings one of the *Lion King* tracks. It was certainly a humbling experience!

SS: Thanks so much, David, for talking to us for *Elton John: Fifty Years On.* We can't recommend your website highly enough for all Elton John fans!

DB: You're welcome! Happy to be a part of the book!

15

THE UNLIKELY FRIENDSHIP OF ELTON JOHN AND EMINEM

BY ANDREW J. RAUSCH

Andrew J. Rausch is a film journalist, author, and celebrity interviewer. He has written more than twenty books about popular culture, including *I Am Hip-Hop: Conversations on the Music and Culture*. He loves music and is equally passionate about the Beatles and the Wu-Tang Clan.

FOR MANY OF rock's elder statesmen, hip-hop has often been dismissed as some sort of musical bastardization. In the genre's earliest days, it was commonplace to hear older musicians complain that it wasn't "real music" or that it was simply people speaking over stolen music. These statements were ignorant half-truths, and ignored the artistry being achieved in this new form. While it's true that not all hip-hop songs contain meaningful artistry (typically the most visible, radio-friendly tripe), this is true of any musical genre. But from the beginning, there were always artists on the cutting edge, creating new sounds and pushing musical boundaries. As such, it was inevitable that artists like

Run-DMC, the Beastie Boys, and Public Enemy would eventually fuse rock and rap. So, while the older rockers mostly disregarded hip-hop as a novelty with little value, hip-hop artists were attempting to bridge the gap. (It's no coincidence that producer Rick Rubin, the mastermind behind most of these projects, later went on to produce some of the most respected rockers in history, including Tom Petty and the Heartbreakers, Metallica, Black Sabbath, and Mick Jagger.)

There is a commonly-held notion that these types of music are radically different, but this is categorically false. The genres have much in common in terms of their brash defiance of tradition, their take-no-bullshit attitude, and their both having originated as forms of black music.

In the end, it wouldn't matter whether rockers acknowledged the new music or not, because their being dismissive did little to slow its growth. Within a few years, hip-hop music and culture expanded from the inner cities, spreading to white suburban living rooms, and eventually to every corner of the globe. Today, hip-hop is the most visible, highest-selling form of contemporary American music. Whether or not one chooses to acknowledge its artistic merits, it cannot be disputed that hip-hop music currently dominates American charts in a way no other music does. Today, the vast majority of pop and R&B music is heavily influenced by and blatantly incorporates the hip-hop sound and aesthetic. Quite simply, hip-hop has become the new rock.

Over the years, a number of rock music's old guard have come to acknowledge and embrace hip-hop. Legendary rockers such as Paul McCartney, the Beach Boys, Aerosmith, and Stephen Stills (among others) have collaborated with these artists. Others, such as Lou Reed, have been quick to acknowledge the artistic contributions artists like A Tribe Called Quest and Kanye West made. They recognized that these young upstarts were displacing the music (and contemporary cultural relevance) of their elders, just as they themselves had done to those who preceded them.

Elton John was one such member of rock royalty who took notice of what these younger artists were doing. John had always been a bold musician who was willing to work within and fuse together different types of music to create new sounds. As such, he recognized the artistic risks being taken and the musical statements being made by the more

Hector Mata via Getty Images

Elton and Eminem

avant-garde artists. John has been extremely vocal about his love for A Tribe Called Quest and their music, pronouncing them the "seminal hip-hop band." But John's appreciation of the group hasn't been limited to lip service; he performed (along with Jack White) on the group's 2016 "Solid Wall of Sound." Additionally, he has allowed his vocals to be sampled on numerous hip-hop songs.

One hip-hop artist John appreciated was a Detroit "honky cat" who recorded under the moniker Eminem. In the rapper, John may have seen similarities to himself. While this comparison may seem absurd on the surface, it's more accurate than you might think. Just as John was a bit of an outsider as an Englishman working in the American rock scene, Eminem was an outsider as a white artist working in a predominantly black music. This is not to say John was the only Brit—there were many—but it's a fair comparison in that Eminem wasn't the only white artist working in black music either. But each of them dominated their respective niche, despite their differences. Like Eminem, John had also experienced significant crossover success with black audiences, having performed on *Soul Train* in 1974, becoming only the second white artist to do so. John's spirited performances of "Philadelphia Freedom" and (most notably) "Bennie and the Jets" were among the program's many highlights. In addition, "Bennie" soared to Number 1 on the R&B chart. Beyond this, John and Eminem share a primary attribute that binds them—an unwillingness to compromise artistically.

But there were other things John appreciated about the younger artist. He applauded Eminem for having achieved rock god touring status, calling him the "first [hip-hop artist] to really go out and conquer big arenas." (This claim is factually incorrect, by the way. Other artists, such as Run-DMC, had preceded him. With all due respect to Eminem, and respect *is* due, the fact that he is frequently recognized for originating things he didn't speaks to his being a white artist receiving more public attention than his black counterparts. This isn't Eminem's fault, but it is reality.) He has also commended Eminem's longevity and passion (saying "if you lose your passion, you're dead"), which are further significant similarities. Also like John, Eminem achieved the rare feat of having multiple albums certified Diamond, meaning they sold more than ten million units.

But to many, Eminem was problematic due to his frequent use of homophobic slurs ("fag," "faggot," and "queer") in his lyrics. While it's true that Eminem used the words primarily for shock value, his repeated use of them, even after being criticized for their hurtful impact, is the least redeeming trait of his music.

So when John, an LGBT icon, chose to perform with him at the 43rd Grammy Awards ceremony, people were stunned and outraged.

According to Eminem, his inviting John to accompany him on stage started as a joke. "We were debating on whether I was going to perform the Grammys or not," he told *MTV News*. "I was like 'The only way I'll perform at the Grammys is with Elton John.' And I was kind of saying it in jest, thinking it would never happen. The idea of it started becoming more, 'Okay, this is a way to flip it around and really f—k people's heads up.'" Eminem also claims that he didn't know John was gay, which seems unlikely. "I didn't know he was gay," he said. "I didn't know anything about his personal life. I didn't really care. But being that he was gay and he had my back, I think it made a statement in itself saying that he understood where I was coming from."

So why did John decide to perform with Eminem? "He was accused of being homophobic by so many people because of his lyrics, which I thought was nonsense," John later told Graham Norton. "And I came out and supported the fact that he isn't." Further, John told *Rolling Stone*, "I always admired Eminem's thinking. That's the reason I wanted to appear on the Grammys with him when I was asked, despite all the nonsense talked about him being homophobic." John doesn't explain why he believes the assertions to be false, but the reasons don't matter. The point is that, right or wrong, John respected Eminem's artistry and defended him based on his beliefs.

The two artists met in person for the first time at a rehearsal at LA's Staples Center on February 21, 2001, where they would perform that night. "When I saw [Eminem] rehearsing, I got chills up my spine," John later said. "I hadn't seen anybody do that kind of thing to me since I saw Mick Jagger in the early days." This is a bold claim, but it serves as a testament to not only John's appreciation of Eminem, but also to his willingness to recognize and embrace new musical trends and artists.

That night, the two men performed Eminem's hit "Stan" at the awards ceremony, with John singing hook, which had originally been sung by Dido (by way of a sample from "Thank You"). "I was the one that took the 'L' out of Dido," John later quipped. Some critics, such as *MTV News*'s David Basham, complained that the duet was boring and uninspired, but the performance ultimately achieved what it was intended to (repair Eminem's problematic image) and it remains one of the most memorable performances (mostly because of its unlikely pairing) in Grammy Awards history. When the song concluded, the two artists embraced and held hands in solidarity. *Entertainment Weekly* referred to it as "the hug heard 'round the world."

The appearance was a brave move for John, whether one believes his stance correct or not. He knew going into this that the union would result in outrage and potentially lose him supporters, but he did it anyway. As a result, John was condemned by the Gay & Lesbian Alliance Against Defamation (GLAAD) and criticized heavily within the LGBT community. Singer Boy George remarked, "It's like me singing with Pol Pot. People call you a fag or whatever occasionally, but it's so much more prevalent now and he [Eminem] has to take some responsibility. He was an arsehole and I think every gay person with a brain cell found it hideously offensive to see Elton performing with him."

We can never truly know whether Eminem initially invited John to perform out of sheer admiration or simply for the positive PR, but it's likely that both of these things are true. That Eminem (as producer) later utilized John (again via sample, this time from "Indian Sunset") on the hook for Tupac Shakur's posthumous single "Ghetto Gospel" three years later can be seen as evidence that Eminem was a genuine fan of John's work. If he hadn't started out a fan, he'd become one.

If the public viewed Elton John and Eminem as unlikely allies and duet partners, the later news that they had become close friends behind closed doors must have been even more shocking. "We've been amazing friends ever since," John told Graham Norton. "He's an amazing guy.... I just adore him."

In 2005, when John formed a civil partnership with his longtime companion David Furnish, the couple received an unusual gift from the rapper. "I got this package from Eminem," John said. "And it shows you how homophobic he isn't. We got two diamond-encrusted cock rings on velvet cushions." John laughed and paused before adding, "And I have to say, they have remained unused." (Whether or not giving "cock rings" to a homosexual couple proves Eminem isn't homophobic is debatable. It could be argued that the gift points to its giver focusing primarily on the sexual aspects of the couple's partnership rather than their love.)

As John's romantic union was soaring to new heights, Eminem's was falling apart. His wife, Kim Mathers, filed for divorce in 2006. Adding to the turmoil in his life, Eminem lost his best friend and D12 bandmate DeShaun "Proof" Holton to a shocking murder the following year. Eminem, who had been to rehab just two years before, started to slide deep into depression and turned again to drugs. He began abusing a number of prescription medications, including Vicodin, Valium, and Ambien. After suffering a methadone overdose and then a drug-related seizure, it became clear that Eminem had to clean up his act. During this time, he reached out to his new friend Elton John, asking for help. In this regard, John became a sort of mentor for his younger colleague.

John had a reputation for counseling other stars, including Robert Downey Jr. and John's songwriting partner Bernie Taupin, who wrote the song "Someone Saved My Life Tonight" after John talked him out of killing himself. John had also attempted to counsel the late singer George Michael, whom he saw struggling, but Michael had rebuffed his efforts, telling him to screw off.

John had firsthand experience with addiction. "He had a substance abuse problem in the past," Eminem said. "So when I first wanted to get sober, I called him, because he's somebody in the business who can relate to the lifestyle and how hectic things can be. He understands the pressure and any other reasons that you wanna come up with for doing drugs."

In 2009, John told Radio 5 Live's Danny Baker that he'd been helping Eminem for the past year-and-a-half and that the rapper was "doing brilliantly." He explained that his own experience had taught him that getting clean often gives a person an erroneous belief that everyone else has also stopped using drugs. "But of course it is just as prevalent as it ever was," he said. "And nowadays pills, such as downers, are even more damaging."

The two musicians met up again publicly for a 2017 *Interview* magazine piece in which John questioned Eminem. The two, longtime friends by this point, opened the interview in a humorous manner that provided a glimpse into what their behind-closed-doors banter might look like:

ELTON JOHN: Hi, Marshall.

EMINEM: How are you doing, cunt?

ELTON JOHN: I'm very well, you old bastard.

In the published conversation, Eminem opened up about his addiction, admitting he'd been high when they'd first met at the rehearsal. "I couldn't tell," said John. "I was mesmerized by you and your performance; it made the hairs on the back of my arms stand up.... I hadn't really been exposed to that kind of rap in live performance before, and it was electrifying." The two musicians then expressed how grateful they were to have started a "lovely friendship."

The rapper told John he'd been clean since they'd first started talking about the situation a decade before. "Your sobriety day is in my diary," said John. "I'm so proud of you. I'm twenty-seven years clean, and when you get clean, you see things in a different way. It makes your life so much more manageable. It seems to have made all the difference—I can tell when I speak to you."

In October 2018, John interviewed Eminem again, this time for his Apple Radio *Rocket Hour* program. He referred to him as "you gorgeous thing," once again showing how close the two friends had become. John complimented Eminem on his most recent album, *Kamikaze*, remarking that it was the "grittiest thing [he'd] done in a while" and saying he was a "big fan of [his] gritty stuff." Despite Eminem making more homophobic remarks on the album, John commended him for deciding to no longer use the word "faggot." It's unclear whether John hadn't actually listened to the music he was praising or, more likely, this was a reference to a private discussion they'd had. Whether or not Eminem will continue using the word remains to be seen.

None of this is to take attention from John and place a spotlight on Eminem, but to look at an important event in both of their careers. The Grammy Awards duet is significant because it highlights John's willingness to view the artistry of younger musicians with an open mind, even if what they're creating likely sounds completely foreign to him. But that's the point, and John recognizes that—creating something that breaks new ground will always be jarring at first. It's no coincidence that Elton John, Paul McCartney, and the Beach Boys—artists who built legendary careers and created masterpieces by taking risks and experimenting with new sounds—are the members of the old guard who have opened themselves up to collaboration with hip-hop artists.

It might be tempting to suggest that John's performance with Eminem is insignificant in an overview of his career, but the opposite is true; it's essential in that it highlights one of the primary attributes of John that make him the unique and groundbreaking trendsetter he's always been: his being an uncompromising artist willing to embrace and venture into (what might seem like) the most radical forms of music.

Beyond all that, this is the tale of two extraordinarily talented, seemingly different human beings who became close friends in the face of trials and adversity. If this isn't as revealing (and defining) a story as there can ever be about Elton John as both a musician and human being, I don't know what is.

16

WE STAN A QUEEN: A GAY DUDE'S PERSPECTIVE INTO THE UNLIKELY FRIENDSHIP BETWEEN ELTON JOHN AND EMINEM

BY KEVIN QUIGLEY

IT STARTS BACK in the early 1990s, when gay culture was finally starting to step out of the shadows and become prominent. Elton John had been out of the closet for a while and had been sober for a few years when Freddie Mercury, lead singer of Queen, passed away from complications due to AIDS. I was sixteen, had only very recently gotten into Queen, *and* come out of the closet myself—two events that didn't seem linked back then, but maybe they were—so these were heady days. Elton was still an outlier in rock 'n' roll—truly, in the world of mainstream pop culture. Being gay wasn't accepted as *regular*, just as *okay*. For a lot of people, it was still a lifestyle rather than a life. To this day, I'm not sure how much Freddie Mercury finally coming out a few days before he died of AIDS helped or hurt the perception of gay people in the eyes of the world at large. He was still a big deal—"Bohemian Rhapsody" appearing both in

Wayne's World and the *Billboard* charts had a lot to do with that—but I definitely remember hearing jokes about him being buried face down so he could see all his friends on the way down to Hell.

It was a transitional time.

The reverence for Mercury—the elevation of him as a pop-culture idol rather than just as a respected front man of a rock band—seemed to come in 1992's *Concert for Freddie*: a huge concert featuring the remainder of Queen and a number of hyper-prominent singers of the day. George Michael (still in the closet himself, bizarrely) had a hit with his cover of "Somebody to Love." Annie Lennox was in raccoon makeup. And Elton John was going to play the first third of "Bohemian Rhapsody" on piano...while the hard-rocking last third was going to be taken by Guns N' Roses front man, Axl Rose.

There was an uproar.

Rose had long been seen by many as homophobic. Metal in itself was fairly homophobic, which was odd in the '80s and '90s, given how often the men dressed and made themselves up to look like women. The first record I ever owned was Poison's first album, *Look What the Cat Dragged In*; I spent a good deal of time trying to convince my dad that there were two guys and two girls in the group, based on the cover that one might confuse with that of the Go-Go's. In 1992, Judas Priest's Rob Hanford wasn't out yet (that would take six years), so when it came to gay representation in metal, it had to be with the man that sang, "Immigrants and faggots/make no sense to me" and went on to complain about them spreading disease. This man? *This* man?

Of course, Elton must have understood something that the outraged didn't. Rose had long stated how much he worshipped Queen, who had a proto-metal side (their "Stone Cold Crazy" would later be covered by Metallica with no real changes), and his desire to lionize Freddie was apparently genuine. At the end of the song, Elton and Axl came out to sing the coda—"nothing really matters"—and put their arms around one another. It was a small moment (in retrospect, it seems unbelievably insignificant), but it sent some shockwaves through the world. I remember articles talking about how it was the end of homophobia. And it *felt* that way to me at the time. Two years later, Axl Rose would induct Elton John into the Rock and Roll Hall of Fame. Things change slowly, but they do change.

And here we come to rap. There's a sad abundance of homophobia and anti-LGBTQ+ lyrics in rap and hip-hop songs. When you're coming from a place where the Beastie Boys wanted to name their first album *Don't Be a Faggot* and Notorious B.I.G. rapped that "two dicks and no bitch" don't mix, there's going to be a huge uphill battle. Eventually, major rappers like Kanye West and Ice-T would call out homophobia as being backwards, and Tyler the Creator and Frank Ocean would declare their bisexuality openly and without (much) rancor, but in 2001, we were nowhere near as enlightened. On Eminem's *Marshall Mathers LP*—nominated for a Grammy for best album that year—Eminem released a torrent of gay slurs, from "faggot" to "lez" to "homosex," and specifically called out trans people in his song "Criminal." He drills down with "hate fags? The answer's yes." Confusingly, he later states, "Come on, relax, guy! I like gay men." Now, look. I liked "Stan." I liked "Stan" a lot. Because I'm a huge fan of how language shifts and transmogrifies, I like that the title of the song has become shorthand for obsessively loving pop culture. But the song also references Eminem's discomfort with meeting a fan who's attracted to him. That doesn't make it homophobic, but combined with "Criminal," the attitude seemed so regressive and backward. By this point in culture, I'd started to think, *Well, dammit, I came out, like, nine years ago. When do we get into a place when homophobia just kind of dies out?*

Then I found out that Elton John was going to perform "Stan" with Eminem on the Grammys, singing the interpolated Dido verses sampled on the record. It was a great performance. A maybe-PR move turned brilliant bit of collaboration. After the song, John got up and embraced Eminem and held his hand—"the hug heard 'round the world," as reported by *Entertainment Weekly.*

It was history repeating itself. It was *the* defining moment in rock history...again. Didn't we already have the hug heard 'round the world with Axl Rose in 1992? Didn't Elton John *already* knock out homophobia by bridging gaps between a homophobic music culture and his elder-statesman gay-okay classic rock? From the point of view of someone who loves music—and even loves Eminem songs ("Lose Yourself" is a stone-cold classic)—this gets *tiring.* In Rausch's essay, you see John making excuses for Eminem's music over and over (even as recently as 2018, when Eminem called Tyler the Creator a faggot on his diss track

"Fall"), because the two have become legitimately close friends. But it's one of those cases where you have to wonder how many chances you give someone before your own credibility is shot.

I'm glad Elton and Eminem are friends; the only way to really break out of stereotypical thinking is to expose yourself to other people and other ways of living. I love that Elton John loves rap; he provided piano and vocals in Kanye West's "All of the Lights," and he didn't have to try to cover up any homophobia while doing it. I guess the question here is: is it enough to tolerate homophobia in the people we admire, and maybe try to gently steer them away from it…or do we, at some point, have to give up?

Elton John has found a way to reconcile his hard-won openness as a gay man with Eminem's public/lyrical persona as a homophobe. As a gay guy living on the outside of Elton John and Eminem's inner lives, I don't know if it's right or it's wrong. I don't have the answers. I just have some songs that I'm uncomfortable with liking, and I have to reconcile that, too.

17

MY FAVORITE ELTON JOHN ALBUM IS....

BY ANTHONY NORTHRUP

Anthony Northrup is a writer, pop culture authority, and webmaster of the popular Stephen King Facebook group, *All Things King*. He lives in North Dakota with his wife Gena.

WHEN I WAS asked to write something about my favorite Elton John album, it was actually easy: it's the 1975 classic album *Captain Fantastic and the Brown Dirt Cowboy*! Not only because of the music, but because of the personal connection I have with the album…my mother.

Growing up with a single parent (my father died a month before I turned four), I had no one to teach me the things a father teaches his son when they're a kid. My mother raised my sister and me the best she could, and although I learned all I needed growing up, there was something more she taught me: the appreciation of great music—all types, from all eras. She once said, "No matter what music you listen to, movies you watch, listen to everything! Watch everything! Then decided what you really enjoy." This has stayed with me my entire life.

When it came to what is now called Classic Rock, she introduced me to some of the most influential artists of our time: Led Zeppelin, David Bowie, the Rolling Stones, the Beatles, Pink Floyd, Rod Stewart, and even Barry White. And, of course, Elton John. I was between four and five years old when we began listening to these amazing artists. This was definitely a bonding time for our little family of three.

In the 1970s, I didn't have many friends; however, music and movies were my constant companions, especially music. We had this monstrosity-sized stereo with a record player, and 8-track player (yes, we're going *that* far back). It came with these *huge* black headphones, and when I wanted to listen to music, I'd plug them in, close my eyes, and drift away. Although I didn't always know the lyrics then, I still knew good music when I heard it.

As I got older, many a Saturday afternoon was spent with headset plugged in, music blasting, looking at the album covers, the photos inside, and reading lyrics. It was the covers that caught my interest most. Fantastic works of art on square pieces of cardboard, some of which folded out to double their size—what could be better than that? As I went through them, I came across the album *Captain Fantastic and the Brown Dirt Cowboy* by Elton John. "Who is Elton John?" I asked myself. I put on the record, and listened.

The album was released on May 19th, 1975, by MCA Records. The music itself was interesting, but what *really* blew me away was the cover, an amazing art treasure. Sheer genius. There was so much going on. Birds, snakes, rabbits, owls, fish, frogs, a man with a top hat, an old gypsy woman, a man carrying a clock on his back, bubbles, glass globes.... There was so much to take in. Then, of course, Captain Fantastic himself, Elton John, in a blue velvet suit, a cape, huge silver platform boots, top hat, and huge signature glasses—an outfit that only he could pull off. To this day, I wish I had that album cover framed and on a wall.

The songs were beautiful and magical. "Bitter Fingers," "Tell Me When the Whistle Blows," "Better Off Dead," "We All Fall in Love Sometimes," but it is "Someone Saved My Life Tonight" that still resonates with me. Even as a kid, I felt something strong about that song. This is possibly Elton's most personal and revealing song of his entire career and his own situation in life at that time. Music makes such an impact on us all. For me, the discovery of this album—and this particular song—was huge.

So this brings me back to the advice my mother gave me way back when. If she hadn't had such an appreciation for music, and a very impressive collection of records, and, of course, those headphones, I never would've happened upon Elton John's *Captain Fantastic and the Brown Dirt Cowboy*, that amazing double-art cover, nor the song, "Someone Saved My Life Tonight," which would make an impact on me again later in life.

So, after some forty-odd years from when I first listened to her advice, and after twenty-five years of not being in touch with her, but recently reconnecting, I want to simply say: *Thank You, Mom*, "Someone Saved My Life Tonight!" You *did* make a difference in my life, in many, many ways.

18

JIM COLE'S ELTON JOHN "DESERT ISLAND" ALBUM

BY JAMES COLE

James Cole is a writer, artist, and screenwriter whose essays have appeared in several of *Elton John: Fifty Years On* author Spignesi's books on the works of Stephen King, and he has been published in *Sci-Fi Universe, Video Watchdog, Newsweek, Cinefantastique, The New York Times* and the *Los Angeles Times.* He also wrote the award-winning short film *The Night Before.* Jim has loved music since his dad gave him his first record player—a portable General Electric "Wildcat"—at age seven. He currently lives on Cape Cod, where he pens weekly film reviews for the *Cape Cod Chronicle* and is writing his memoir.

HOW DOES ONE pick a favorite Elton John album?

I have loved the music of Elton John since I was about seven years old, and Elton is one of my favorite artists of all time (along with the Beatles). Elton has produced an astonishing body of work in the last fifty years, and I consider his best works like children. So how does, how *can* I pick a favorite child?

My earliest experiences with Elton weren't actually on the radio. They were 45s played during lunch in my elementary school cafeteria during first grade: "Goodbye Yellow Brick Road" and "Bennie and the Jets." (Considering the teacher who supervised lunch also allowed Brownsville Station's "Smokin' in the Boy's Room" to be played, you could say my elementary school was progressive.) From second grade onward, I began to notice Elton's songs on the FM stations out of New York City (Dad was vice president of CBS-FM, so my brother, sister, and I rarely ever listened to AM, which frankly sounded awful).

In terms of Elton John's evolution as an artist, I was growing up in a golden era. Between 1971 and 1976, as I aged from five to ten years of age, Elton became a superstar. Among the classics he and his band recorded: "Your Song," "Tiny Dancer," "Rocket Man," "Daniel," "Crocodile Rock," and "Saturday Night's Alright (for Fighting)," as well as singles like "Pinball Wizard," "Philadelphia Freedom," and "Lucy in the Sky with Diamonds" (which featured an uncredited John Lennon playing guitars). If you're reading this book you know them all by heart. As for the albums, I gravitate to Elton's early, "classic" phase: *Elton John, Tumbleweed Connection, Madman Across the Water, Don't Shoot Me I'm Only the Piano Player, Goodbye Yellow Brick Road,* and *Captain Fantastic and the Brown Dirt Cowboy*. I have recently discovered and come to love the albums *Jump Up!* and *Too Low for Zero* from 1982 and 1983 respectively, but the mid- to late-'80s were a hit-and-miss period for the artist. Though I admire *The One* from 1992, it was not until 2001's *Songs from the West Coast* that Elton, reuniting with his lyricist Bernie Taupin, reached a new creative peak.

Of course, Elton's most beloved work is 1973's *Goodbye Yellow Brick Road*. I consider it Elton's own *Sgt. Pepper* (or perhaps, as it's a double-album, his *White Album*). Ironically I never owned any Elton albums as a kid, and did not discover *Yellow Brick Road* until I borrowed it from my seventh grade music class. (The first Elton collection I bought with my own money was *Greatest Hits, Volume II* in eighth grade.) The first time I put needle to vinyl, I was stunned. My horizons weren't just broadened by the seventeen tracks; they were shattered. My favorite album track is "Funeral for a Friend/Love Lies Bleeding." I actually used "Funeral" as the soundtrack to *I Was a Teenage Vampire*, a silent short film I made with my ninth grade drama class.

With that kind of review, you'd think *Goodbye Yellow Brick Road* would be my pick—my favorite Elton album. It's close, along with *Madman Across the Water* (*Yellow Brick Road* and *Madman* rated number one and number two in a 2013 *Rolling Stone* readers' poll). But there is another album from this classic period, one I did not discover until adulthood. (I picked up the CD used while living in Los Angeles.) This particular album has such variety and is so compulsively listenable; every song is a personal gem. As such, I declare *Don't Shoot Me I'm Only the Piano Player* my Elton John Desert Island Disc.

SELECT BIBLIOGRAPHY

Anderson, Kirsten. *Who Is Elton John?* New York: Grosset & Dunlap, 2016.

Bernardin, Claude. *Rocket Man: Elton John From A-Z*. New York: Praeger, 1996.

Black, Susan, ed. *Elton John: In His Own Words*. London: Omnibus Press, 1995.

Buckley, David. *Elton: The Biography*. Chicago, Illinois: Chicago Review Press, 2007.

Cassata, M. A. *The Elton John Scrapbook*. Citadel, 2017.

Doyle, Tom. *Captain Fantastic: Elton John's Stellar Trip Through the '70s*. New York: Ballantine Books, 2017.

Norman, Philip. *Elton John: The Biography*. New York: Harmony Books, 1991.

Rosenthal, Elizabeth J. *His Song: The Musical Journey of Elton John*. New York: Billboard Books, 2001.

Scott, Ken and Bobby Owsinski. *Abbey Road to Ziggy Stardust: Off the Record with the Beatles, Bowie, Elton & So Much More*. Chicago, Illinois: Alfred Music Publishing, 2013.

Tatham, Dick and Tony Jasper. *Elton John*. London: Octopus Books, 1976.

ABOUT THE AUTHORS

STEPHEN SPIGNESI is a writer and retired Practitioner-in-Residence from the University of New Haven where he taught composition and literature for ten years. He writes extensively about popular culture and is considered an authority on Stephen King, the Beatles, Elton John, Robin Williams, Woody Allen, *The Sopranos*, *The Andy Griffith Show*, *ER*, and other pop culture subjects and TV shows. His other areas of interest and expertise include American history, the US presidents and Founding Founders, the *Titanic*, true crime, and the paranormal. Spignesi was christened "the world's leading authority on Stephen King" by *Entertainment Weekly* magazine and taught the courses, "The New Gothic Horror of Stephen King" and "The Legacy of the *Titanic*" at the University of New Haven. He appears in the *A&E Biography* of Stephen King and the ITV documentary *Autopsy: Robin Williams*. His first novel, *Dialogues* (Random House), was hailed as a "reinvention of the psychological thriller." He lives in New Haven, Connecticut, with his cat Chloe.

MICHAEL LEWIS is a lifelong marketing and communications professional. After toiling first in marketing and promotions positions, by happenstance, he stumbled into the publishing world, and for the last twenty-plus years he has been an acquisitions editor. He has acquired and edited more than five hundred books, and wrote thirteen of his own (with this book being number fourteen). Among the books he's edited have been perhaps a dozen(?) books by Stephen Spignesi (maybe one day we'll count them up). Mike's own books include *A Guy Walks Into a Bar* and *Random Commuter Observations*. With Lee Pfeiffer, he wrote his first book, *The Films of Harrison Ford*, as well as *The Films of Tom Hanks*, and with Steve Spignesi he wrote *The 100 Best Beatles Songs* and *Outdated Advertising*, and more to come. Mike teaches an adult school class on how to get a book published, coaches high school students how to improve their writing, and has a growing freelance editing business as Mike the Editor (check out his site!). He is frequently an assisting minister and usher at his church, works part-time in a funeral home, and knows how to create balloon sculptures (but not during funerals). Mike lives with his wife, Amy, and daughters Samantha and Sydney in Westwood, New Jersey.

ACKNOWLEDGMENTS

Stephen

I'd like to thank, with love, **Valerie Barnes, John White, Janet Daniw, Tom D'Agostino, Nick Fradiani Sr., Kris Webster**, and **Lee Mandato** for their help and support during the writing of *Elton John: Fifty Years On*.

I would also like to thank my Permuted Press editors, the inestimable **Maddie Sturgeon** and **Michael Wilson**, H.B. Steadham, Devon Brown, and all my friends at Permuted Press for their kindness and help.

Also, boundless gratitude goes to the contributors to this book, Elton fans all, for their insights, and wonderful essays and interviews: **Bev Vincent, Tyson Blue, Samantha Lewis, Sydney Lewis, Anthony Northrup, Andrew Rausch, Kevin Quigley, James Cole, Richard Christian Matheson**, and **David Bodoh**.

And, finally, special thanks to my co-author **Mike Lewis**, a mega-fine collaborator whose contributions and insights made this book better than I could have done on my own.

Michael

I'd like to thank my family—**Amy, Samantha, and Sydney**—for putting up with me as I worked on this book. I keep promising this and one day I'll actually do it: When I'm buried in the next one, I promise to be less of a horrible person. Forgive me. I love you forever.

Thank you to **Marilyn Allen**—you're more than my literary agent. You're a cheerleader, partner, and a believer in me, and I can't thank you enough for your support, encouragement, job advice, and positive vibes for all these years.

And, finally, special thanks to my co-author, **Steve Spignesi**, who wrote this great book with minimal contributions from me (and I'm almost embarrassed to see my name on the cover as prominent as yours). My partnership with you began twenty-plus years ago and I can't imagine how my personal or professional life would have been without you in it. You've helped me through a tough time. May we continue to challenge each other and produce many more creative projects in the future.

THE ELTON JOHN AIDS FOUNDATION

http://newyork.ejaf.org/

Elton John AIDS Foundation
584 Broadway, Suite 906
New York, NY 10012

+1.212.219.0670

info@ejaf.org